D0187679

About Island Press

Island Press, a nonprofit organization, publishes, markets, and distributes the most advanced thinking on the conservation of our natural resources—books about soil, land, water, forests, wildlife, and hazardous and toxic wastes. These books are practical tools used by public officials, business and industry leaders, natural resource managers, and concerned citizens working to solve both local and global resource problems.

Founded in 1978, Island Press reorganized in 1984 to meet the increasing demand for substantive books on all resource-related issues. Island Press publishes and distributes under its own imprint and offers these services to other nonprofit organizations.

Support for Island Press is provided by The Geraldine R. Dodge Foundation, The Energy Foundation, The Charles Engelhard Foundation, The Ford Foundation, Glen Eagles Foundation, The George Gund Foundation, William and Flora Hewlett Foundation, The James Irvine Foundation, The John D. and Catherine T. MacArthur Foundation, The Andrew W. Mellon Foundation, The Joyce Mertz-Gilmore Foundation, The New-Land Foundation, The Pew Charitable Trusts, The Rockefeller Brothers Fund, The Tides Foundation, and individual donors.

About the Natural Resources Law Center

The Natural Resources Law Center was established at the University of Colorado School of Law in 1982. Its primary goal is to promote the wise use of natural resources through improved understanding of natural resource issues. The Center pursues this goal through three areas: research, public education, and visitors.

The Natural Resources Law Center has sponsored over twenty educational programs dealing with water issues, including its annual water conference, which draws participants from across the country. The Center has published numerous books, research papers, and articles on water resources, including *Controlling Water Use: The Unfinished Business of Water Quality Protection* (1991); *Instream Flow Protection in the West* (1989); *Water and the American West: Essays in Honor of Raphael J. Moses* (1988); *Tradition, Innovation and Conflict: Perspectives on Colorado Water Law* (1987); and *Special Water Districts: Challenge for the Future* (1984).

The Natural Resources Law Center's professional staff includes Lawrence J. MacDonnell (Director), Sarah F. Bates (Assistant Director), and Teresa A. Rice (Senior Staff Attorney). Inquiries may be directed to Campus Box 401, University of Colorado School of Law, Boulder, Colorado 80309-0401; tel. (303) 492-1286.

Searching Out the Headwaters

Searching
Out
the
HEADWATERS

Change and Rediscovery in Western Water Policy

Sarah F. Bates

David H. Getches

Lawrence J. MacDonnell

Charles F. Wilkinson

Natural Resources Law Center

University of Colorado School of Law

ISLAND PRESS

Washington, D.C. ❑ Covelo, California

Copyright © 1993 by Natural Resources Law Center, University of
Colorado School of Law

All rights reserved. No part of this book may be reproduced in any
form or by any means without permission in writing from the publisher: Island Press, Suite 300, 1718 Connecticut Avenue, NW,
Washington, D.C. 20009.

Maps and illustrations by Ann-Marie Kuczun

Permissions to quote from copyrighted material appear on pages
231–232.

Library of Congress Cataloging-in-Publication Data
Searching out the headwaters : change and rediscovery in western
    water policy / Sarah F. Bates . . . [et al.].
        p.   cm.
    Includes bibliographical references and index.
    ISBN 1-55963-217-8 — ISBN 1-55963-218-6 (pbk.).
      1. Water-supply—Government policy—West (U.S.)—Congresses.
    2. Environmental policy—West (U.S.)—Congresses.   I. Bates, Sarah
    F.
    HD1695.A17S4   1993
    333.91′00973—dc20   93-4637
                                                                                    CIP

Printed on recycled, acid-free paper

♻

Manufactured in the United States of America
10   9   8   7   6   5   4   3   2   1

Contents

Preface

The legal and policy framework governing western water resources has been a focus for research and education by the Natural Resources Law Center since its inception ten years ago. Water is in many ways the heart and soul of the West. It has been the source of great conflict, but it is also the glue that binds the region into a living system. The study of western water policy is first and foremost the study of the West itself—its history, its geography, its peoples and communities, its possibilities.

This is a book aimed at the growing number of people concerned about the way water resources are used in the West. Ultimately, its concern is water policy, but much of the text addresses a broad consideration of the water resource itself and the changing western landscape of which water is such a critical part. This book seeks to set out a way to think about western water issues and about the kind of water policy we want, rather than to offer detailed proposals for reform. In fact, many reforms are under way, and the economic and demographic changes at work in the West demand that this process continue and grow. One purpose of this book is to articulate the reasons for this reform movement—a purpose that led us on a search for a principled foundation for making water policy: a water ethic rooted in basic values of our society.

A generous grant from The Ford Foundation in 1988 made it possible for the Center to embark on an ambitious effort to draw together our thinking about western water and to search out the expertise of others with experience in this area. Initially we envisioned a traditional policy analysis, analyzing and critiquing familiar issues of western water law and offering recommended changes. In the fall of 1988 we brought together our "advisory group," expecting to get a blessing for our proposed work plan. Instead, we came out of the meeting with a whole new vision of our project in which the advisory group became a *working* group and the focus broadened from water law to water and the American West.

The project became a collaborative, highly interactive exercise, anchored by our core group and enriched by outside participation. The work of the project grew and developed out of the discussions in our workshops and the interactions of group members over a more than three-year period. We convened six workshops during this period, at which we discussed a series of topics ranging from values of water to constitutional protection of water rights to Indian water issues. We commissioned leading thinkers to prepare discussion papers that served as the focus of the workshops. We are grateful for the fine work of the discussion paper authors: Reid Peyton Chambers, John E. Echohawk, John A. Folk-Williams, Helen M. Ingram, Arthur Maass, Cy. R. Oggins, Holmes Rolston III, Joseph L. Sax, Theodore M. Schad, Steven J. Shupe, Gary D. Weatherford, and Charles F. Wilkinson. The Center published the papers as part of a special Western Water Policy Project Discussion Paper Series (listed at back of book). We invited others to participate in workshops to which they could add particular knowledge and breadth of view (participants listed at back of book). Several of our working group members prepared papers and led their discussion at a workshop; others led discussions of particular topics without a formal paper.

In May 1992 we convened our group a final time to comment on the first draft of this book. Once again, the group lived up to its name. By the end of the daylong session, we had completely reorganized and redefined our approach. In the truest sense, this book is the product of the thoughts and efforts of many people. The members of our working group—F. Lee Brown, James E. Butcher, Michael Clinton, Harrison C. Dunning, John E. Echohawk, Kenneth D. Frederick, Helen M. Ingram, Ed Marston, Steven J. Shupe, John E. Thorson, Gilbert F. White, and Zach Willey—amount to co-authors.

We are deeply grateful to all of those who opened our eyes to new perspectives—our colleagues on the working group, the workshop participants, and the dozens of authors whose work we studied and drew upon. We would especially like to acknowledge Jim Butcher, then with The Ford Foundation, who saw the possibilities of this project, and Walt Coward, who has supported its completion. We want to acknowledge the valuable assistance of a number of University of Colorado School of Law students who provided research help along the way. They forced us to challenge and question our own approaches and ideas, and we pressed one another.

We also thank The Ford Foundation for the opportunity to put together, and participate in, this extraordinary process. This is a dynamic time in western water policy, and the subject needs, and deserves, the kind of vision that we have tried to pursue.

SFB, DHG, LJM, CFW
May 1993
Boulder, Colorado

Searching Out the Headwaters

Chapter One

The West's Gordian Knot

Water is H$_2$O, hydrogen two parts, oxygen one, but there is also a
third thing, that makes it water and nobody knows what that is.

D. H. LAWRENCE : "The Third Thing"

WATER has been at the front
edge of initiatives to create new settlements and economies ever
since Americans took control of the arid landscape of the American
West in the 1840s. The great rush that drew settlers west and that
made the United States a force in the world's economy was built on
the gold country streams that carried the precious metal, supplied
the domestic needs of the mining camps, and drove the powerful hydraulic hoses that blew lode deposits out of the hillsides. A generation later, water was the essential ingredient in fulfilling the Jeffer-
sonian ideal of allowing farmers and ranchers to settle new lands,
lands where crops grew only if the settlers put water on the fields by
means of irrigation. Still later, elaborate plumbing systems transported water over great distances, often across natural divides, en-
abling growth of industry and development of housing subdivisions
in booming metropolitan areas. Today, water feeds the rivers, lakes,
and landscapes that attract millions of tourists and recreationists to
the region.

Yet, while there is agreement about water's critical role, water policy has become the Gordian knot of the American West, a system so
tangled that it can never be untied. The subject of water policy and
law is daunting, almost forbidding. The ancient, intricate, and
seemingly solid structure of water policy, like King Gordius' tangled
knot of old, is surrounded by an aura of unapproachability. Deci-

3

sions governing the public's waters involve little public participation. Laypeople perceive the subject as too complicated and hypertechnical and are intimidated by the confused web of engineering jargon and legalese—cubic feet per second, transmountain diversions, hydroelectric power grids, and senior and junior water rights, for example. The whole structure is so complex, delicate, and interrelated, and the stakes so high, that reform seems risky.

Leave it to the experts. Don't try to untie the knot, let alone slice through it.

The root difficulty with preserving the status quo is that western water is governed by one of the most outmoded collection of rules found anywhere in American public policy. The society that created the current system well over a century ago saw the rivers of the American West through a particular lens: Water was a commodity that needed to be removed from the river channel and "put to use." Water left wild and flowing in the channel was "wasted." Extravagant government expenditures to impound and transport water were justified in the name of "conservation."

This single-minded focus on the extraction of water at any cost was overwhelmingly successful in achieving the objectives of official nineteenth-century policy: to encourage American citizens to settle the broad, dry, and inhospitable western lands. The federal and state governments made western water development—dams, reservoirs, transmountain tunnels, pipelines, and canals—a first-line priority and laid out a sprawling program of subsidies that led to engineering triumph after engineering triumph. The human effort and ingenuity were extraordinary, and the benefits were many, whether measured by solid farm and ranch communities, construction jobs, or the museums and symphonies of the region's urban centers.

Today's westerners expect some of the same things from the rivers of the West—farms, ranches, mines, and shining urban centers— but they also expect much more, for the region has become a very different place. The end of World War II marked the beginning of an era every bit as important as the California gold rush. The postwar population in the West boomed from 19 million to 51 million.

This influx of newcomers, along with larger national and global economic and environmental trends, has created a new context. Today, the public treasuries are stretched thin. People increasingly appreciate the great stresses facing all of our natural resources, water included; they see that long-term sustainability is in jeopardy.

There are other new perceptions. Westerners now view water as more than a commodity. They see western rivers and lakes, like the mountains, forests, and wide-open spaces, as public assets of inestimable value. By and large, today's populace came west, not to wrestle an existence out of a harsh land, but to capture the privilege of living, working, and raising their families in a blessed place. To do that requires some water development, but it does not require the radical posture that water policy adopted and has held since the middle nineteenth century.

The western water regime has caused serious, deeply embedded problems. The most pressing problems—for example, vanishing Pacific salmon in Washington, overtapped groundwater in Arizona—may vary, and the severity may differ, but all western states share the essential commonality of aridity and scarcity when it comes to water. That is logical and inevitable, for water policy in every western state traces to the same era and the same attitudes.

While there is no definitive, formal, West-wide inventory of the region's mounting water problems, some current vignettes may help suggest the magnitude of the difficulty. To be sure, there are success stories, and we will recount many of them in this book. In our judgment, however, the necessary starting point is to understand the depth of the chasm between western water policy and what the modern West demands of it. The following episodes, like many others that we will describe in the pages to come, represent the West's challenges:

• The National Marine Fisheries Service, warning that 100 stocks of salmon and steelhead have become extinct and that most of the remaining runs are in danger, has put the chinook salmon and four other runs on the threatened species list for most of the rivers of Washington, Oregon, and Idaho. In 1991 the American Fisheries

Society expressed concern for the survival of 214 native naturally spawning salmon and steelhead stocks in California, Oregon, Washington, and Idaho.

• In the early 1980s thousands of birds were poisoned in the Kesterson National Wildlife Refuge by irrigation drainage waters tainted with toxic levels of selenium leached from the waterlogged fields of California's Central Valley Project, a federally financed water supply project that has encouraged large expansion of irrigated agriculture in the San Joaquin Valley.

• The future of the Pyramid Lake Band of Paiute Indians is in jeopardy because it depends on the fate of Pyramid Lake and its fishery. Beginning in the early twentieth century, a federally subsidized dam and canal system began diverting more than half of the water from the Truckee River in Nevada to another watershed to grow alfalfa. Congress has approved a last-ditch attempt to resuscitate the Truckee River system, recognizing that insufficient water remains in the Truckee to stabilize Pyramid Lake, which has no other source and has already dropped 70 feet and lost one-fourth of its surface area. The cui-ui, a fish species unique to the Truckee River–Pyramid Lake system, is on the federal threatened species list, and the Lahontan cutthroat trout survives only through a hatchery program.

• Beaches deep in the Grand Canyon—sand deposited perhaps a millennium ago—are being scoured away by bursts of water released from Glen Canyon Dam to generate cheap electric power during the hours of the day when it is most in demand in southwestern cities. With the sand goes the habitat of plants, animals, and fish, as well as recreational opportunities for thousands of people.

• In 1961 an international incident erupted when Colorado River water delivered to Mexico under a treaty became too salty to irrigate crops after being used north of the border. In response, the United States has spent a billion dollars on salinity control measures, half of that sum for a desalination plant to clean up water spoiled by irrigation and return it to the river. These measures were intended to avoid any reduction in irrigation in the United States, but the Bureau of Reclamation estimates additional palliatives will be needed in less than a decade.

• Stretches of Montana's blue-ribbon Gallatin River are drained dry each summer by irrigation in spite of the area's heavy economic dependence on recreation from West Yellowstone to Bozeman.

• According to the U.S. Geological Survey, ancient Ogallala Aquifer, underlying eight states (Wyoming, Colorado, South Dakota, Nebraska, Kansas, Oklahoma, Texas, and New Mexico), is in dire jeopardy. The nation's largest deposit of groundwater could be depleted, its stores beyond the economic reach of most pumpers, in only sixty years.

• A 1992 Wyoming state court ruling prevents the tribes of the Wind River Reservation from dedicating the reservation's water rights (though recognized in 1988 as being the oldest and largest in the watershed) to maintain and restore natural streamflows. This means that trout populations managed by the tribal wildlife department cannot be rehabilitated to meet the growing demands for recreation on the eastern side of the Wind River Range. Meanwhile, nearby non-Indian irrigators extract Wind River water and, like growers across the West, pour it on their fields in profligate amounts, using outmoded flood irrigation methods that are wasteful and inefficient by any modern standard.

• Metropolitan Denver has obtained water rights on rivers in western Colorado without making any payment to the state or federal governments, and has transported the water under the Continental Divide for urban use, away from communities on the Western Slope. Half of all the water in the Denver area, as in other cities in the West, is used for lawns and other exotic landscaping.

These and similar episodes throughout the West are explained by the narrow perspective of traditional western water law. Water policy shuts out large segments of the population and, with them, a set of ideals for how water should be used. Rigid patterns of water allocation that made sense generations ago now create divisiveness, bad economic results, and destruction of aquifers, rivers, lakes, and wildlife. The outmoded way of governing water fails to respond to the whole community.

Thinking of a "community" evokes an image, usually of a geographic community, a collection of people living in proximity to one another. Community in this sense is critical to water policy, for water is essential for the close-knit, prosperous, and lasting communities that westerners are determined to create. Yet western water policy has developed only the most rudimentary means for addressing the varied and changing needs of geographic communities.

But there are other types of communities—communities composed of people, wherever located, with shared interests in an issue or a resource. Water, more than any other resource, has encouraged the formation of many diverse kinds of communities of interest. Water communities have included groups of rural irrigators, real estate interests, and boaters and anglers, for example. Sometimes a single individual identifies with several different communities. Many of these communities—some well established and some still emerging—express increasing dissatisfaction with how water decisions are made.

In modern water policy decisions it is important to recognize the breadth of communities of interest. The demands of the Seattle and Portland metropolitan areas for low-cost power from hydroelectric dams affect commercial fishers and their customers from Alaska to British Columbia to Northern California; Indian tribes with treaty-guaranteed fishing rights on nearly every river system in the Pacific Northwest; sportsfishers (and the economies that have grown up around them) from the coast of Alaska to the interior of Idaho; irrigators and electric rate-payers in Oregon, Washington, Idaho, Montana, and Canada; and people the world over who visit, or plan to visit, the wondrous rivers of the Northwest.

The same is true in other metropolitan areas. Because Denver's reach extends far beyond its political boundaries, the city's desire for water for urban growth affects competitors for water development from Nebraska to Southern California to the state of Sonora in Mexico. Also affected are citizens of the United States and the world who treasure the in-river values from the Rocky Mountain snowmelt that carves and enlivens the deep redrock canyons of Colorado, Utah, and Arizona, all of which are impacted by Denver's water use. The sweep of the communities of interest of Seattle, Portland, and Denver is matched or exceeded by that of Los Angeles, Las Vegas, and Phoenix. The range is substantial, too, for western cities such as Tucson, Albuquerque, Las Vegas, Reno, Boise, Colorado Springs, and Salt Lake City.

Just as the geographic reach of communities of interest has broadened, so too the membership within water communities has expanded far beyond the small number of interest groups that structured western water policy in the last century. The Clark Fork and Milk River in Montana, the Big Horn and North Platte in Wyoming, the Sevier and Duchesne in Utah, the Umatilla and Deschutes in Oregon, the Pecos and Chama in New Mexico, and other western watersheds all implicate more diverse communities than ever before. Today's community of interest is likely to include—in place of the old miner-farmer-rancher-industrial coalition that made western water policy—citizens determined to reduce government expenses; Indian tribes; residents opposed to continued rapid growth in their geographic communities; environmentalists; citizens who want western rivers, lakes, and aquifers managed to guarantee sustainability for their children and grandchildren; recreationists of all stripes; businesspeople whose livelihoods depend on the West's emerging recreation economy; and those who simply believe, fervently, that western rivers should be allowed to retain the incomparable, eternal qualities that provide so much inspiration, reflection, and fulfillment.

All of these and other identifiable interests need to be represented in modern water policy, and in most watersheds nearly all of them are already clamoring for recognition. They will be heard, one way or another.

In light of this groundswell of concern and interest, it is not surprising that reform efforts have begun to emerge in the states and at the regional and federal levels. These efforts are important and show a determination to increase public participation, to add measures for environmental protection, and to face up to economic realities. Most western water proceedings now take public values into account in some way.

But these responses are incomplete, still in their infancy. The changes affect only some newly granted rights and rarely touch thousands of water rights that grew up under the traditional system. The initiatives have yet to set serious standards for water conservation. For example, instream flow programs, while promising, have had little impact on most rivers. The reform effort still has not come to grips with the critical issue of sustainability, scarcely acknowledging that many aquifers are declining and that heavy extractive uses draw down many rivers, or dry them up completely, so that they hardly can be considered rivers. Many economic issues remain unresolved. In short, despite beginning reforms, western water policy fails to require or encourage efficient, equitable, and ecological uses of water.

We have structured this book by, first, tracing the evolution of the uses of western water, exploring the special qualities of the waters of the West, describing the changing West, and identifying the many contemporary communities of interest and the varied ways in which they view and care about water. The first five chapters, in other words, are not about "policy" or "law" but are about water and its relationship to people. Then, in the final three chapters, we describe our vision of how decision making might be opened up in order to accommodate the views and needs of the whole community. Our approach is in no way Platonic. Rather, it suggests a realistic process of phasing out the aberrations of western water policy, preserving the useful contributions, and returning to first principles. It is a matter of searching out the truest headwaters.

Chapter 2, "Water in a Changing West," discusses the diverse uses people have for water—the values that people have seen for water at different times and places. This chapter reflects the view that we must all gain a much deeper understanding of the history of the relationships of society to western water. The common perception that the value of western water is illuminated by the California gold rush plus later eras involving farmers, ranchers, and urban development, as we described at the beginning of this chapter, is only part of the story. While those eras will always remain relevant, the full history of water use in the West is much richer and more complicated: As we suggest in the title of this book, reform includes both change (developing new ideas consistent with recent trends) and rediscovery (revitalizing traditional values and approaches recognized before the discovery of gold). There is a great deal to learn from the dignity and length of the Native American experience, including the spirituality Indian people have always seen in water and the care and skill with which they have carried out their subsistence farming and fishing operations. Other uses, including the use of rivers as transportation corridors, preceded the extractive uses that dominate water policy. Today, westerners expect far more from their rivers, including the sense of spirituality that is still part and parcel of moving, natural water. When viewed objectively, history tells us that the gold-rush–irrigation–industrial-development view of water, a view that has a stranglehold on the current legal structure, was the dominant perspective for a very short time, for just a few generations of the hundreds of generations whose lives have been tied to the waters of the West.

In a somewhat similar vein, chapter 3, "Voices," is a series of excerpts from the rich, colorful literature that reflects the diversity of values people see in water.

Chapters 4 and 5 depict the current situation. "The West Today" examines present water uses and the demographics of the region, showing, among other things, the dramatic changes that have taken place since the ground rules for western water were established. "River Basin Stories" explores the sagas of water development in the West's largest river systems: the Columbia, the Rio Grande, the Sacramento, the Colorado, and the Missouri. These compelling stories show, in graphic terms, how the West's vibrant rivers have lost much of their life, largely through water projects—dams and diversions—but also through timber harvesting, irrigation, domestic grazing, industrial development, and other land-use practices that have fundamentally altered watercourses through deposits of soil, agricultural chemicals, and other pollutants.

Chapter 6 is entitled "Losing Sight of the Headwaters." It examines the central precepts that have driven western water policy for so long. A few ideas were conceived to meet immediate needs; those ideas became entrenched and eclipsed the original premise for water law, that water should be used for public benefit. Those few ideas for achieving a narrow set of goals so firmly charted the course of water law and practice that they essentially describe a resulting "water policy": water is a free good, available without charge to water developers; rivers are open for capture, first in time, first in right; and water, once diverted, becomes a permanent property right. These ideas might properly have some place in a sensible modern water policy, though they are far more appropriate to a society whose goals were aimed specifically at rapid expansion and development of the region. Western water policy, as we know it, is extreme in that it accepts all these early ideas, essentially without consideration of changing western needs and values, and gives short shrift to other ideas.

Chapter 7, "The Journey to Rediscovery," examines some of the threads of thinking and on-the-ground practices, some new and some ancient, that have begun to emerge. While these promising developments have not yet dislodged the dominant ideas, they have begun to qualify them. They point the way toward the future by showing the creative ways in which science, economics, and law can be used by water communities to create a dynamic new approach to western water.

The final chapter, "Change and Rediscovery in Western Water," articulates the foundation for a water policy to meet the needs of the modern West and its future. The answer lies in a return to some of the most fundamental and deeply rooted values of our culture. The foundation for a new water policy is a water ethic that calls on principles of conservation, equity, and ecology—guiding ideas that are widely shared, though rarely applied to water use. This water ethic can be implemented by several approaches involving market economics, regulation, the broad-based use of scientific knowledge, and open and full public participation to fulfill the objectives of water communities. The best water policy should rise up from the people and the waters they care for; we hope our approach is true to both.

Throughout these chapters we have attempted to communicate the essential ideas of water in language that is understandable to all. We believe it is wrong that many people feel excluded from the realm of water issues because they do not understand the technical terms used by lawyers, scientists, and others. Yet any discussion of western water requires some use of the language peculiar to the subject. Thus, we have provided, on pages 203–205, an appendix entitled "The Language of Water."

The thick and sturdy knot that comprises western water policy, unlike the Gordian knot of old, will never be cut through by a single stroke. The cords are too many—there are policies of seventeen states, and most watercourses have their own traditions and practices—and they have been pulled tight over a great many years. Yet, strand by strand, with many people and much patience, the knot can be undone. A growing number of westerners are determined to unravel the accumulation of rules and practices, sort them out, dispose of some, keep others, and create some new ones.

This is an endeavor in which people who care about the West and its future can, and must, participate. The issues are complex but not nearly as difficult as some beneficiaries of the existing system would have us believe. By understanding the waters of the West, their people, and their history, concerned citizens can comprehend the current situation, and its seriousness, and help create straightforward approaches toward reform. It is a worthy and urgent task.

Chapter Two

Water in a Changing West

Restless water, worrying the land, has left its marks. Supporting vegetation and wildlife, it has inevitably governed the distribution of human beings. It was deeply important to the aborigines, to explorers and to those who followed—the fur traders, settlers, miners, railroad-builders and stockmen. Water was a prime influence in establishing centers of population. Rival users battled for it, courts awarded rights to its use, legislatures apportioned it and almost always it has been in short supply.

SAMUEL G. HOUGHTON : *A Trace of Desert Waters*

WATER, or its absence, has always been a defining factor in the western part of the United States. The vast openness that marks much of the American West is a product of its aridity. Mountain ranges that interrupt the openness are the primary source of the water that creates and feeds most of the region's streams and rivers. Deserts lie in these mountains' rain shadows. Flowing water has shaped much of the western landscape—whether by gully-washing torrents over the course of a few hours or by slow, persistent, canyon-carving rivers over millennia. Rich green ribbons of riparian vegetation provide habitat for animals living near permanent water sources.

Because water is essential to life, because it supports plants and animals that in turn support others, because it enhances and enriches life, natural systems develop in relation to water. For these same reasons, water is at the center of human communities.

At an earlier time, this basic link between water and community was perhaps more obvious. Directly or indirectly, water made it possible for human communities to develop—through the fisheries it

14

sustains, the wildlife habitat it nourishes, the edible vegetation it
supports, the navigational network it provides, the energy it generates, and more. Where water is relatively scarce, its centrality is more
apparent.

Many thousands of years ago, human societies began to develop in
the West. Some of the people remained close to the Pacific Coast,
harvesting and thriving on the abundant fish in the coastal rivers.
Others followed the woolly mammoth and other wildlife onto the
plains. As the climate warmed and the glaciers retreated, the mammoth became extinct. Some of the nomadic hunters pursued bison,
elk, deer, and antelope. Others began to cultivate the plants whose
fruits and seeds they had collected for food.

The Plains and Pacific Coast Indians ranged over large expanses
of land in their search for plants, animals, and shelter to meet their
needs, and adopted seasonal homes to take advantage of the natural
bounty of different areas during different times of the year. Their
movements were directed by natural events such as annual salmon
spawning runs, periodic bison migrations, or seasonal abundance of
nuts or grains. In some areas, Indian communities established more
permanent settlements. Some dug irrigation channels and flood
check dams to capture water for their crops; some established vi
lages where water and other resources were plentiful. These ear
water users viewed the resource with reverence; water was the lif ·
blood of their communities.

Later, Anglo-European explorers, trappers, miners, and settlers
moved into the West, seeking the region's copious natural resources.
Converting those resources to wealth, in turn, required control of
the region's water. In many places the security of a water supply was
the critical factor in determining whether settlement would succeed.
Spanish missionaries promoted the community-based *acequia* system that brought water through small earthen ditches to farms in
the Southwest, and Mormons built towns around collectively controlled water supplies in the Great Basin. Miners required water for
their sluice boxes, their hydraulic mining devices, and their camps.
Homesteaders—lured by the promise of productive agriculture but
stopped short by the fact that few crops would grow on rainfall alone
west of the 100th meridian—influenced federal lawmakers to create

whole new government agencies and subsidy programs to build water projects to "reclaim" those arid lands. Cities sought water for their growing populations and for industry. In the twentieth century, communities of water users expanded to include boaters, recreational anglers, ecologists, and others who value water in new and different ways.

The emergence of varied uses of water paints a historical picture of the West in transition, in constant change and adaptation. Westerners learned to move, to adopt new lifestyles, and to manipulate the land and water to fit their needs. They formed new communities—alliances and organizations—in their efforts to survive and prosper. These associations were not static: just as human needs for water have changed over time, so, too, have western communities.

WATER AS A SOURCE OF SUSTENANCE

> As for men . . . what were they but a way that water has of going about beyond the reach of rivers? . . . I was three-fourths water, rising and subsiding according to the hollow knocking in my veins: a minute pulse like the eternal pulse that lifts Himalayas and which, in the following systole, will carry them away.
>
> LOREN EISELEY : *The Immense Journey*

The original, most essential use of water is for drinking—for humans like any other creature. The amount of water needed to sustain an individual is not large; the average person takes in fluids and foods containing about two quarts of water per day. Water also supports human sustenance by meeting the basic human needs for nourishment by providing habitat for animals and fish and moisture for plants.

Fishing and Food-Gathering Communities

> Theirs was a way of life rooted in the nature of the plants and animals of the land and in the small social groups which spent their entire lives together within the same circle of friends, a thinly populated world full of uncertainty, unpredictable food, and potential starvation.
>
> MARTHA C. KNACK AND OMER C. STEWART :
> *As Long As the River Shall Run*

Water was surely the source of sustenance in the ancient Pacific Northwest, where the Columbia River supported huge populations of anadromous fish (fish such as salmon that are hatched in fresh water, migrate to the sea to grow to maturity, and then return to their home streams to spawn). For one coastal tribe, the Makah, the same word was used for "food" as for "fish."

At least eleven thousand years ago Indian people up and down the Pacific Coast lived off the seemingly limitless runs of salmon. Skillful Indian fishermen used all manner of nets, traps, weirs, and spears to remove the giant fish from the streams. The Indian take during aboriginal times was much greater than commonly realized. The fifty thousand Indian people who lived throughout the Columbia River basin harvested approximately 18 million pounds of salmon annually—about 360 pounds per person. (Today, the total take by all fishers from the depleted Columbia River salmon runs ranges between 6 and 10 million pounds yearly.) The people living in those early fishing communities consumed this rich source of protein on the spot, dried it or pounded it into pemmican for later personal use, or used it as a medium of barter with other tribes and non-Indian explorers and settlers.

Natural streamflows made it possible for a group of the Northern Paiute to live on the shores of Pyramid Lake on the western edge of the Great Basin. In the early spring the Indians used lines, nets, harpoons, and spears to harvest the Lahontan cutthroat trout and the Pyramid Lake cui-ui (a large sucker), which migrated from Pyramid Lake up the Truckee River to spawn. The spawning fish were so abundant in the Truckee River that explorer John C. Frémont, passing through in 1844, named it the Salmon Trout River. Beyond supporting fish, the Truckee provided sustenance by nourishing vegetation and attracting waterfowl. The Pyramid Lake Paiute harvested the wild seeds and rice grass that ripened shortly after the spring rains irrigated the desert. In the fall, migrating waterfowl, pausing for food and rest in the area's lush wetlands, supplied food for these Indians. Throughout the winter the people subsisted on piñon nuts and other foods collected during the year.

Southwest of Pyramid Lake, other bands of Paiutes lived in what is now called the Owens Valley. They developed land-use patterns that minimized conflict—cultivating and gathering seeds and tubers in designated, band-owned territories, for example. Similarly, families owned territories in the mountains for collecting pine nuts. Like the Paiutes, many communities whose well-being depended on hunting and food gathering developed sophisticated social organizations, rules for sharing resources, and institutions to foster trade and communication.

Ancient Irrigators

> It was no accident that civilization had its origin in rainless districts, in Egypt and Peru, rather than on the banks of the Amazon and Mississippi. In rainy districts, agriculture left the primitive man as it found him, an isolated being, depending more on the favor of the season than on sustained efforts for his support. On the other hand, where irrigation was necessary, he must make provision for the future, subordinate himself to the requirements of system and order, and hence to form laws. Above all, he learned the value of co-operation to a common end.
>
> ELWOOD MEAD : *The Ownership of Water*

North American agriculture emerged in what is now the American Southwest between 3500 and 2500 B.C., with the cultivation of maize, squashes, pumpkins, gourds, and beans to be used by entire communities and perhaps traded to others. By about 1000 B.C., the Indian people that the Navajo later called "Anasazi," or ancient ones, were growing a variety of vegetables with water diverted from nearby streams. Their settlements in today's Four Corners region (Utah, Colorado, Arizona, and New Mexico) included such familiar irrigation components as check dams, canals, and headgates. At Chaco Canyon, a complex array of irrigation works supported a population of about ten thousand people. This cooperative water development was an efficient division of labor, facilitating farming while allowing other individuals to spend considerable time creating baskets and pottery, weaving cloth, and carving distinctive rock art into the canyon walls.

Water development for irrigation became a pattern throughout the Southwest. The engineering feats of the Hohokam—who constructed elaborate canals in what is now Arizona's Salt River valley— rival that of modern aqueducts. Hohokam canals were built with a perfectly calibrated drop of 2.5 meters per mile, just steep enough to flush silt through the channel, but not too steep to make it difficult to turn water into lateral canals and fields. The Hohokam built an irrigation system containing more than 125 miles of canals, some of which were 30 feet wide, 10 feet deep, and up to 15 miles long. Numerous other Indian societies in the areas now known as California, Arizona, New Mexico, and Texas used irrigation as a primary means of food production in an arid environment.

Sometime in the thirteenth century both the Anasazi and the Hohokam abandoned their farming communities. (In the Pima language, the word *hohokam* apparently means "finished" or "gone.") Historian Donald Worster has speculated that the Hohokam overextended their irrigation beyond the capacity of the land, leading to increased concentrations of salts in the soil, which poisoned their crops. The Anasazi's migration may have been driven by drought, and possibly soil erosion, that made irrigated agriculture difficult. As food became scarce, it appears that village groups began raiding others' food stores; their hard-to-reach cliff houses may have been a form of defense during this period.

The Pueblo Indians, whose settlements began to flourish in the middle Rio Grande Valley about the same time that the Anasazi moved out of their communities to the north, built reservoirs to capture rainwater and constructed irrigation ditches to bring water to their crops of maize, squash, beans, melons, cotton, and chilis. Pueblo residents built different types of reservoirs depending on their needs and proximity to water. Those living on top of mesas, for example, filled natural depressions in the stone by rolling snowballs into them. Pueblos lacking such natural amenities built small reservoirs near groups of houses. And, in the Zuni Pueblo, women carried water from streams to their fields in jars on top of their heads.

To the south and west of the Pueblos, the Tohono O'odham of the central Sonoran Desert also exerted control over natural waterflows. They planted crops along floodplains and blocked arroyos with brush dams to channel rainwater onto their fields. The Tohono O'odham still live in the northern reach of the Sonoran Desert, and a few still practice the floodwater irrigation practices of their predecessors. When heavy summer rains come, they hold floodwaters and nourishing sediments in catchment basins. As these waters seep into the soil, the farmers plant fast-germinating seeds, which they are able to harvest before the soil dries out completely. Their crops require no diversions from streams, no pumping of groundwater, and almost no structures. As ethnobiologist Gary Nabhan has pointed out, the Tohono O'odham's cultivation of drought-tolerant crops, their understanding of the roles that insects and weeds play in crop management, and their proven ability to sustain food production for centuries without destroying the desert soils provide priceless lessons for today's agricultural researchers.

The Owens Valley Paiutes, generally described as hunters and gatherers, also developed irrigated agriculture. They constructed diversion structures in the valley's creeks, as well as regularly spaced ditches lateral to the creeks, each about 40 inches wide, and temporary dams to regulate water flow. They elected or appointed a head irrigator, who enjoyed high status. For the Owens Valley Paiutes, author John Walton concluded, "agriculture was tightly integrated with the broader patterns of settlement" in the valley.

Even in those early eras of human development, the western environment began to show the impact of manipulation. "Irrigation farming, even in its crudest form, set in motion ecological chain reactions," wrote Michael Meyer. He gave these examples of change: "Plants were introduced into habitats where they could not have sustained themselves previously. Terracing changed the natural flow of streams, and man-made water diversions modified the natural vegetation, changed the organic matter in the soil, and began to alter the migratory patterns of birds and animals." These changes were significant in particular areas, yet overall the region suffered little impact from early inhabitants. Some researchers speculate that the early irrigators moved between homeplaces frequently enough to allow cultivated lands to recover to their natural conditions. Having a large enough land base and farflung populations helped mitigate the effects of human manipulation.

Missions and Acequias: Spanish Exploration and Settlement

The *acequias* of northern New Mexico were both a technological and orga-
nizational device. Technologically, irrigation was necessary to supplement
rainfall, and so the colonists established their communities in the river
valleys. The ditches that brought the streamflow to the fields commonly
began at a diversion two to four miles upstream from points of use. By
gravity water flows in the *acequias* along the foothills and then into the
fields below. Organizationally, the acequias originated as associations of all
persons served by the ditch and had an elected official or officials to supervise irrigation affairs. Members of the *acequia* contributed labor for repair
of ditches and gates.

F. LEE BROWN AND HELEN M. INGRAM:
Water and Poverty in the Southwest

The sixteenth century brought a new set of immigrants to the West:
the Spanish explorers and settlers. Some came in search of gold;
others followed to bring the teachings of Christianity to the Native
Americans. One of the early Spanish expeditions was led by Francisco Vásquez de Coronado. He embarked from Mexico in 1540
with an army of 250 cavalrymen, 200 foot soldiers, 1,000 Indians,
pack trains, cattle, sheep, goats, and pigs. Seeking the fabled Seven
Cities of Cíbola, he found instead the Pueblo villages. He was finally
forced to turn back southward when his band came up against the
chasm of the Grand Canyon. Other expeditions followed, and Juan
de Oñate established the first permanent Spanish settlements north
of Mexico in 1598 in present-day New Mexico.

Bringing their own traditions of irrigation to a new home, the new
Spanish settlers transported water from rivers to crops through
hand-dug ditches (they called these ditches *acequias*). The first ditch
was constructed by Indian laborers under the direction of their new
Spanish landlords on the Rio Grande near today's San Juan, New
Mexico. In the next two centuries Spanish settlers would construct
164 acequias. The Spanish brought new crops to the region: wheat,
barley, oats, citrus fruits, apples, apricots, pears, grapes, chickpeas,
carrots, radishes, and onions. These food crops marked a departure
from the drought-resistant crops that the Pueblos had developed
(corn, squash, and beans, for example); none of the new crops could
survive without considerable water.

The Spaniards also brought new ideas of property ownership, social structure, and man's relation to nature—as well as more powerful weapons of warfare than the Indians had ever seen. "For the first time Indians were instructed by example in what must have seemed a string of absurdities," Michael Meyer observed. "Man was not a part of nature but was somehow set apart from it to use it. His goal was not to adapt peacefully to his habitat but to dominate and change it. Water was suddenly a source of private wealth, of capital, of rent, of income, and most importantly, of human power over one's fellow man."

Despite these differences, the Spanish brought a strong sense of community to their water organizations, not terribly different from those of the Paiute, Pueblo, and other Indian societies. Within the community of the acequia, water belonged to all, and all water users shared in the maintenance of the ditch. In the book *Mayordomo*, Stanley Crawford described an acequia in northern New Mexico by recounting his year as ditch manager (*mayordomo*). In times of good supply, he explained, farmers along the ditch are free to use as much water as they want. In periods of shortage, though, water use is rotated among acequia members. The mayordomo becomes "the pump, the heart that moves the vital fluid down the artery to the little plots of land in each of the cells, the *parciantes*."

The growth of agricultural uses of water (and the increasingly complex social organizations to administer its use) signaled the development of new valuable uses for water beyond human sustenance. Water became a tool for other human endeavors—organized settlement movements, large-scale farming, industry, navigation, and urban development. The use of water for sustenance paled relative to other uses since the early twentieth century. Fishing is in serious decline; the Columbia River produces fewer fish today than it did fifty years ago. Diversions of water for non-Indian settlers beginning in the early 1900s nearly dried up the Truckee River, and the Pyramid Lake Band of Paiute Indians found their traditional lifestyle severely threatened by the disregard of the most basic function of water: sustenance.

WATER AS A SOURCE OF SPIRITUAL AND COMMUNITY IDENTITY

> There has been a lot said about the sacredness of our land, which is our
> body; and the values of our culture, which is our soul; but water is the
> blood of our tribes, and if its life-giving flow is stopped or it is polluted, all
> else will die and the many thousands of years of our communal existence
> will come to an end.
>
> FRANK TENORIO, GOVERNOR OF THE SAN FELIPE PUEBLO:
> in *Indian Water Policy in a Changing Environment*

From the beginning, people have viewed water as possessing spiritual and community values that transcend any specific uses. In the West, control over water enriches and empowers communities. This was evident in the pervasive influence of and reverence for water and for the bounty made possible by water in Indian societies.

Pacific Coast Indians used the salmon not only for food, but also as the focal point for their ceremonies and their culture. All of society was organized around pursuing, preparing, and trading fish. The roles of men, women, and children were defined by the central importance of the fish of Northwest rivers. Each spring when the chinook salmon returned from the sea on their long journey to their spawning grounds, the Columbia River tribes gathered for the first salmon ceremony. The first fish caught were roasted over a fire, and then served equally among all tribal members gathered in a longhouse. Music accompanied the ceremony, a religious leader said a prayer and thanked the salmon and the Creator, and the participants took drinks of water to acknowledge it as a source of life. Some Northwest tribes continue this tradition today.

The Pueblos of the Southwest are remarkable for their longevity, especially considering the scarcity of water in that area. Pueblo villages were situated in places with some perennial water supply to provide for the direct needs of the Indians. The Pueblo Indians trace their origins to water, as here explained by a father to a son in Frank Waters' *The Man Who Killed the Deer*:

> You will be taught the whole history of our people, of our tribe. How they
> had their last arising from the deep turquoise lake of life at the center of

the world, the blue lake in whose depths gleams a tiny star, our Dawn
Lake. How they emerged from a great cave whose lips dripped with water
to congeal into perpetual flakes of ice white as eagle-down. You will understand, then, son, why those of our clan are called the Deep Water
people: why our kiva, this kiva, is called the eagle-down kiva; the meaning
of our masks, our dances, our songs. You will see this cave. You will see
this lake—our Dawn Lake.

Nancy Wood described the Taos Pueblo's annual ceremony celebrating this sacred source of life:

> Every August since time immemorial, the entire tribe, except for the in-
> firm or aged, walks forty miles round trip to Blue Lake, there to immerse
> themselves in the deepest, most secret of all their Indian devotions. This
> is a time of intense spiritual regeneration, when old feuds are momen-
> tarily forgotten, and a cord of communality ties them to the mysterious
> lake of their origins. For three days, the Taos rejoice together and at the
> end of this time, the people emerge cleansed.

The long struggle of the people of Taos Pueblo to regain control
of Blue Lake reflects the religious value that water may have to
tribes. Located at 11,000 feet on the flank of Wheeler Peak, this lake
is the site of an annual religious ceremony of major importance to
the Taos. In the early 1900s this lake was included in a national forest, denying the Pueblo's exclusive right to the sacred place. After
many years of protest, Congress enacted a bill returning the lake
and 45,000 acres of land to the Taos in 1970.

Water as a community good was historically paramount in Hispanic communities, where the acequia system not only was a means
to agriculture, but also became a principal community institution,
creating benefits and obligations that bonded citizens. Lee Brown
and Helen Ingram, in their book *Water and Poverty in the Southwest*, described how the acequia system promoted the community values of
fairness, participation and local control, opportunity, and stewardship: "The staying power of the *acequia* system in northern New
Mexico lies to a large extent in local autonomy in management, according to local customs and traditions. Individuals are bound to the
community through their participation in water matters." Under
Spanish law, the community held the right to use water, and water

was tied to the community. Even today, acequia associations in the Southwest provide the focus of rural Hispanic communities.

The idea of the community value of water was part and parcel of the early United States irrigation movement. In his influential 1878 *Report on the Lands of the Arid Region*, John Wesley Powell argued that irrigation ought to be implemented by a "colony" system, so that the residents of those communities would gain from the larger opportunities held out by the control of water: "That the inhabitants of these districts may have the benefits of the local social organizations of civilization—as schools, churches, etc., and the benefits of cooperation in the construction of roads, bridges, and other local improvements, it is essential that the residences should be grouped to the greatest possible extent."

Mormon irrigators who moved into the intermountain West in the middle of the nineteenth century placed great emphasis on the community model of water development. They planned towns around shared water sources, and local people worked cooperatively to develop water. In the book *Mormon Settlement in Arizona*, James H. McClintock explained:

> There was need for the sustaining power of Celestial Grace upon the average desert homestead, where the fervent sun lighted an expanse of dry and unpromising land. The task of reclamation in the earlier days would have been beyond the ability and resources of any colonists not welded into some sort of mutual organization. This welding had been accomplished among the Mormons even before the wagon trains started southward. Thereafter, all that was needed was industry, as directed by American intelligence.

The Union Colony in Colorado was another settlement that placed high community value on water. Conceived as a self-sufficient "complete community," it sought participants throughout the eastern United States. As a promotional circular explained, "The colony digs the ditches, and each member of the colony is liable to an assessment for keeping the same in order." The colony, founded in 1869, spent about $350 per member to construct irrigation ditches. Looking back in 1890, the Union Colony's founder disclaimed credit for the successful irrigation system. "It was the farmers themselves who took hold of the work and carried it on in a most admirable manner," N. C. Meeker said. "I only claim as founder of the colony, to have provided for a system of co-opera-tion, within limited bounds, by which these things became possible."

Arthur Maass wrote of the agricultural colonies established in California's Central Valley between 1880 and 1910. Unlike the Union Colony, which was driven by Horace Greeley's utopian ideal, the Central Valley colonies owed their existence to profit-motivated developers who acquired large blocks of land, built irrigation canals, subdivided the land into small farms, built community facilities, and recruited colonists from throughout the world. The area around present-day Fresno drew colonies of Swedes, Danes, Finns, German Mennonites, Armenians, Syrians, and significant numbers of colo-nists from the Portuguese Azores. When the developers withdrew, these homogeneous groups assumed responsibility for operating the water facilities and thus organized lateral and ditch associations that bound them formally as well as socially.

In recent years, community values for water have evolved beyond cooperative efforts to develop water supplies. For example, in the early 1990s people living in Colorado's San Luis Valley joined in op-position to a private company's proposal to pump groundwater from their basin for export to distant cities. Diverse and unlikely al-lies found a community bond. Anglo and Hispanic farmers, local business people, and artists formed a united front in opposition to the proposal. They expressed their new sense of community by forming a group called Citizens for San Luis Valley Water and by voting to impose a tax on themselves to help pay the costs of oppos-ing the project they believed would draw off the water that holds their valley together. This new community illustrates well how inter-ests in western water overlap and change with time.

WATER AS A MEANS OF NAVIGATION

> We are three-quarters of a mile in the depths of the earth, and the great
> river shrinks into insignificance as it dashes its angry waves against the
> walls and cliffs that rise to the world above; the waves are but puny ripples,
> and we but pigmies, running up and down the sands or lost among the
> boulders.
>   We have an unknown distance yet to run, an unknown river to explore.
>
> JOHN WESLEY POWELL : *The Exploration of*
> *the Colorado River and its Canyons*

Navigation played an important role in Manifest Destiny. In 1803, the young United States, seeking land in which to expand and prosper, acquired much of today's western lands from France in the Louisiana Purchase. Although the Pacific Northwest and the Southwest did not become part of the United States until the cessions by England in 1846 and Mexico in 1848, the Louisiana Purchase marked the United States' great leap westward and set the tone for the remainder of the century. Shortly thereafter, President Jefferson sent explorers Meriwether Lewis and William Clark to chart and assess the new territory—especially the waterways that might provide the means for transcontinental navigation and commerce. The western landscape was still enough of a mystery that one of the explorers' goals was to locate the legendary passage connecting the Great Lakes and the Pacific Ocean. Numerous expeditions in Canada had failed to locate the Northwest Passage.

Starting near St. Louis with three boats—a 55-foot keelboat with sails and two smaller open boats with oars—the explorers sailed, pulled, and finally carried their boats to the headwaters of the Missouri River. They then crossed the Continental Divide at Lemhi Pass. As they descended the Columbia River, they found that the Indian mode of travel, dugout canoes, worked better than their original boats. Closer to the Pacific Ocean they observed that the Indians' canoes grew larger, with prominent keels; that was a clue that they were nearing the sea. Along the way, the pair anchored the United States' claim to the territory by designating names for the watercourses they encountered. The following excerpt is from Meriwether Lewis' journal entry of July 28, 1805:

I dispatched two men early this morning up the S.E. fork to examine the
river; and permitted sundry others to hunt in the neighborhood of this
place. Both Capt. C. and myself corrisponded in opinion with rispect to
the impropriety of calling either of these streams the Missouri and accordingly agreed to name them after the President of the United States
and the Secretaries of the treasury and state having previously named
one river in honour of the Secretaries of War and Navy. In pursuance of
this resolution we called the S.W. fork, that which we meant to ascend,
Jefferson's River in honor of that illustrious personage Thomas Jefferson. The Middle Fork we called Madison's River in honor of James Madison, and the S.E. Fork we called Gallitin's River in honor of Albert Gallitin. . . . The beds of all these streams are formed of smooth pebble and
gravel, and their waters perfectly transparent; in short they are three no-
ble streams.

Historian Bernard DeVoto wrote that Lewis and Clark's careful
accounts of the land, waterways, wildlife, and people they encountered on their journey were largely responsible for the influx of settlers soon to follow: "It satisfied desire and it created desire: the desire of the westering nation." After Lewis and Clark had passed
through and designated familiar names to western landscapes, a
large part of North America seemed less of a mystery, and people
were more willing to move there.

A new wave of adventurers responded to William Henry Ashley's
1822 advertisement in the *Missouri Gazette and Public Advertiser* "to ascend the river Missouri to its source, there to be employed for one,
two or three years." For a generation, mountain men who trapped
beaver and hunted the abundant game used rivers and streams all
across the West as a road system for their canoes, bullboats, and
other contraptions. Later, timber companies made regular use of
western rivers for log floats. Even rivers as erratic as the Colorado
transported goods and passengers. Today, commercial transport remains significant on the Columbia, the Sacramento, and the Missouri up to Sioux City.

As commercial boating grew more important, the U.S. Army
Corps of Engineers emerged as the principal agent for making navigation possible on the nation's rivers. The Corps was created to assist the military during the Revolutionary War, but it grew during
the expansion of river transportation in the nineteenth century.
Mark Twain, writing in 1896, observed in awe that "the military engineers of the [Corps] have taken upon their shoulders the job of

making the Mississippi over again—a job transcended in size by only
the original job of creating it." And, as more recently recounted by
Marc Reisner in *Cadillac Desert*, the agency's activities are varied indeed: "The Corps dams rivers, deepens rivers, straightens rivers,
ripraps rivers, builds bridges across rivers, builds huge navigation
locks and dams, builds groins on rivers and beaches, builds hatch-
eries, builds breakwaters, builds piers, and repairs beach erosion. . . ." The Corps has drawn commerce far up the Missouri River
by holding back floodwaters and releasing them to deepen flows
where and when the river flattens out. Structures to stop the water
have inundated farmland in South Dakota and North Dakota, while
"incidentally" creating new reservoirs and opportunities for water-
based recreation. With nearly two hundred million recreation
visitor-days annually at all of its facilities (second only to the U.S.
Forest Service for total recreation use of federally controlled lands
and waters), the Corps now finds itself managing people as well as
floodwaters.

Many different communities of water users emerged as navigation expanded. Trappers, gathering for a rendezvous, steamship
operators organizing for channel improvements, and farmers living
in the floodplains of unpredictable rivers—all of these groups
shared concerns for western water. In recent years, the communities
of people who enjoy and profit from recreational uses of the Corps'
reservoirs are demanding protection against draining their waters
to produce the flows needed to support navigation downstream.
Just as with others who have shared the bounties of great rivers,
emerging recreation-oriented communities are helping to redefine
the valuable uses of the West's water.

WATER AS AN INSTRUMENT
OF LARGE-SCALE IRRIGATION

> It is the proper destiny of every considerable stream in the west to become
> an irrigating ditch. It would seem the streams are willing.
>
> MARY AUSTIN : *Stories from the Country of Lost Borders*

From its original use to enhance sustenance and its subsequent role
as a source of community identity, irrigated agriculture grew into
something much larger—and, ultimately, much different. Early

farmers used water modestly to secure family food needs and community farm plots. That pattern continued with the acequia associations of the Hispanic farmers of the Southwest. Although organized around similar community-oriented purposes, the Mormon irrigators of the 1800s developed a new pattern of water use with more ambitious irrigation enterprises. The vision of a "reclaimed desert" also underlay the 1902 Reclamation Act that built dozens of new dams and water delivery projects in the first half of this century. Water became more than a source of sustenance: it was the key to unlocking the region's prosperity.

The Mormon Settlers

> Frank's father was one of the Mormon colonists sent by Brigham Young to settle and put under cultivation the arid Big Horn Basin. The twenty thousand acres they claimed were barren and waterless. To remedy this problem they dug a canal thirty-seven miles long, twenty-seven feet across, and sixteen feet deep by hand. The project took four years to complete. Along the way a huge boulder gave the canal diggers trouble; it couldn't be moved. As a last resort the Mormon men held hands around the rock and prayed. The next morning the boulder rolled out of the way.
>
> GRETEL EHRLICH : *The Solace of Open Spaces*

On July 23, 1847, an advance party from Brigham Young's Latter-day Saints arrived in the Salt Lake Basin. On the very day of their arrival they began construction of a dam and diversion ditch to bring water from City Creek to irrigate their newly cultivated land. Their early diversion structures were crude—often little more than brush and stones piled in a stream to force water into their hand-dug channels. Working methodically and cooperatively, however, the Mormons soon built extensive networks of irrigation ditches in the farmlands around their community centers. "They took the bee and its hive as a symbol of their industry," wrote Donald Worster, "but a more appropriate one would have been the beaver, for control over water became the ecological basis for their society."

Indeed, settlement on any significant scale would have been difficult without the organization and control of the Mormon Church. The church required a great deal of its members: tithing, community service, and submission to strict rules of conduct. In return, however, members enjoyed ready access to public assistance and well-funded public works. The church provided the core of this new community, and water was one of the important threads that bound community members. Irrigated agriculture thus became more than a strategy for survival; it was also a tool for a great social experiment.

As recounted by Samuel Houghton in the book *A Trace of Desert Waters*, the Mormon irrigating empire grew rapidly throughout the Great Basin:

> Within two years the Latter-day Saints spread 100 miles from Salt Lake City, down along the Wasatch to the Sevier and San Pete Valleys. Then within another two years they reached out as far as western Nevada and California. By the early 1860s they were almost everywhere in the Great Basin. Most important to the emigrant trains were the settlers of this faith who, residing beside the routes west, catered to the basic needs of these transients, while the latter in turn provided an economic blessing to the pioneers themselves.

By 1850 the arid region now within the state of Utah had a population of 11,380, living on a land base of 16,333 irrigated acres, growing 44,000 bushels of potatoes, 4,800 tons of hay, and 107,700 bushels of wheat. These figures multiplied many times in the next forty years; the potato crop alone would grow more than one thousandfold. Until surpassed by California around the turn of the century, Utah reigned as the largest western irrigator, and almost all of that irrigation was originally directly tied to the collective efforts of the Mormon Church.

Westward Expansion: Homesteaders and the "Closing" of the Western Frontier

> It may be anticipated that all the lands redeemed by irrigation in the Arid Region will be highly cultivated and abundantly productive, and agriculture will be but slightly subject to the vicissitudes of scant and excessive rainfall.
>
> JOHN WESLEY POWELL: *Report on the Lands of the Arid Region of the United States*

The year 1890 marked the "closing" of the American frontier, according to historian Frederick Jackson Turner. He based his conclusion on the 1890 census, which revealed that the western population had reached a density of at least two persons per square mile; thus, he declared, "there can hardly be said to be a frontier line." Other

scholars have viewed the frontier as a dynamic concept and have rejected Turner's absolute statement, but, nevertheless, the year 1890
has long been viewed as a milestone in the United States' settlement
of the American West.

While the first outsiders were drawn by furs, precious metals, and
rangelands to graze cattle, this wave of migration was motivated by
farming. Although early visitors dismissed much of the Great Plains
as little more than desert (they assumed that the absence of trees indicated barren soil), later surveys revealed rich, loamy soils and
nourishing native grasses. Congress provided incentives to settlement of the "unoccupied" lands through such laws as the Homestead Act of 1862 and the Desert Land Act of 1877. The government
provided vast tracts of lands to railroads, hoping to recruit their assistance in luring settlers. The railroads, in turn, sang the praises of
the prairie soils and dismissed the difficulties of farming in areas
with low rainfall. These glowing reports lured thousands of people
to the West.

Not surprisingly, the initial growth was in the same states that had
enjoyed gold and silver strikes around the middle of the century.
Frustrated miners decided to settle down and farm instead of pursuing their claims. By 1890, California had surpassed Utah's early
lead for the most irrigated acreage in the nation and had the largest
number of adults earning a living from agriculture. In the same
year, Colorado reported the second highest number of farmers and
a slightly higher percentage of the state population engaged in agriculture. Western irrigation would grow through the next decade
from a total of 3.5 million acres of irrigated lands in 1890 to over 7
million acres at the turn of the century.

Yet this was not simply a period of unmitigated growth and booming agriculture. Farming was nearly impossible without supplemental water, and few of the settlers had the financial resources to develop irrigation supplies. In much of the region, rivers run through
deep canyons and are difficult to reach. The periods of highest flow
do not match the times of greatest need for irrigation water. Thus
many of the settlers failed because they did not have enough water
for their crops.

Sometimes there was not even enough water available for drinking and bathing. Remembering her pioneer days in Montana around the turn of the century, Pearl Price Robertson remarked in an essay in the anthology *The Last Best Place* that "the greatest single hardship was the scarcity of water." She recalled that other settlers had tried to dig deep wells—some going 90 feet down—but found nothing but dust. Her husband had to bring water to the farm from town in a barrel for their home use, and they had to search many miles for a source of water for their horses. Trying to grow crops on rainfall alone proved a failure; even when the rains came, young crops fell prey to grasshoppers. Eventually the Robertsons gave up in their quest "to battle the elements and to tame the desert."

Much of the West was transformed from grassland to cattle range and then to farmland during the nineteenth century. At the same time, several features of the western lands defied large-scale taming by American settlers. For one thing, the western climate—generally classified as arid or semi-arid throughout the interior West—prohibits growing most crops without irrigation. John Wesley Powell, the Colorado River explorer and first chief of the United States Geological Survey, recognized what western aridity meant for agriculture. Irrigation, he observed, was necessary for cultivation of the soils in most areas west of the 100th meridian. But he also pointed out that sources of water that could supply those lands were limited; most areas of the West were suitable only for pasturage. He was right: especially in the Great Plains, livestock grazing has historically supported human settlement to a much greater degree than farming. The earliest western settlers dealt with this reality by cultivating the bottomlands easily irrigated from streams and rivers. But most of the irrigable lands were to be found far above the deeply carved rivers.

Ambitious American settlers could not do much about the region's low rainfall. They first tried to defy it, thinking that cultivation would change the climate for the better. Josiah Gregg's book, *Commerce on the Prairies*, proposed a theoretical basis for this idea: "The extreme cultivation of the earth might contribute to the multiplication of showers, as it certainly does to fountains." The incredibly optimistic theory—later shortened simply to "rain follows the plow"—attracted many believers to the West's parched soils. During the drought of the 1880s it became clear to those settlers that Gregg's theory did not work. John Wesley Powell's 1879 *Report on the Lands of the Arid Region of the United States* underscored the fact that climatic conditions in the American West required different agricultural practices than those common to Europe and the eastern United States. Thus, the settlers turned their efforts to controlling the West's unpredictable rivers. They built dams to hold the heavy spring flows for later use and constructed ditches and flumes to move the water far from the watercourses to their fields.

The irrigation communities coalesced and took cooperative action to bring water to their crops. States assisted these efforts by authorizing the creation of irrigation districts, quasi-governmental entities with authority to tax, to enter into contracts, and to carry out other tasks necessary to provide irrigation water to the lands within their boundaries. Utah enacted an irrigation district law in 1865, which provided for the formation of such districts upon the request of a majority of the residents in an area and authorized the assessment of taxes, upon approval of the voters, to pay for the construction of irrigation facilities. But the genesis of the kind of irrigation district that took root across the western states rests squarely with the Wright Act, adopted in California in 1887.

The Wright Act reflected two decades of debate in California concerning the best institutional means to promote irrigation in that state. The Act was aimed at solving a number of problems: inadequate financial resources available to individual farmers to build expensive water diversion, storage, and delivery systems; conflicts between private water suppliers (who had substantial control of the water resources) and water users; inability to require participation in the costs of irrigation improvements by all who might benefit; and the need of project builders to raise initial large amounts of money that could be paid back over some extended time period. The Wright Act allowed districts to levy an "assessment" against *all* property in the district determined to benefit, directly or indirectly, from the irrigation facilities. In addition, districts were authorized to issue bonds, and district property was exempted from state and local taxes.

As formulated under the Wright Act, the irrigation district represented a locally based, quasi-governmental approach to the development and use of water resources. Other western states followed California's lead and authorized similar districts. Yet, even with the advantages offered by this approach, irrigation developers in the West struggled with problems of planning, management, and, especially, financing.

Dams and Promises: The Heyday of Federal Reclamation

> I have no fear that America will grow too big. A hundred years hence these United States will be an empire, and such as the world never before saw, and such as will exist nowhere else upon the globe. In my opinion the richest portion of it, and a section fully as populous as the East, will be in the region beyond the Mississippi. All through that region, much of which is now arid and not populated, will be a population as dense as the Aztecs ever had in their palmiest days in Mexico and Central America. Irrigation is the magic wand which is to bring about these great changes.
>
> JOHN W. NOBLE, SECRETARY OF THE INTERIOR:
> quoted in *The Independent* (1893)

Around the turn of the century many promoters of western development reached the conclusion that a more ambitious approach to irrigation was needed. One visible proponent was William Smythe, who extolled the benefits of irrigation and the "blessing of aridity" in such publications as *The Conquest of Arid America*. Historian Patricia Nelson Limerick explained Smythe's zeal for irrigation as follows: "He was extremely religious, a believer in the existence of a 'Universal Purpose' and in his own qualifications to act as the Purpose's spokesman in matters related to western North America. . . . It was Smythe's faith that the arid regions of the American West would be both the location and cause of the nation's redemption." Smythe and others concluded that a national "reclamation" program would provide the necessary funds and technical assistance to make irrigation possible throughout the West. Congress responded with the 1902 Reclamation Act, which established a fund of money to be used to construct irrigation facilities that the Secretary of the Interior found to be "practicable."

The physical legacy of the reclamation program is indeed impressive. To date, the Bureau of Reclamation has built more than six hundred storage and diversion dams in seventeen western states with the capacity to store 134 million acre-feet of water. Annual water deliveries from these facilities average about 30 million acre-feet and provide water to about 20 percent of the lands irrigated in the West as well as to cities, industries, and other users. The water is diverted and delivered through more than 15,000 miles of canals, 1,500 miles of pipelines, and 37,000 miles of laterals.

There is another side to this reclamation experience, of course, a side that has become painfully clear. False promises were created by the availability of this water, which, even with subsidies ranging up to 90 percent of the actual costs involved, many farmers could not afford. The plight of irrigator-farmers across the West unable to stay in agriculture is one legacy. The ongoing struggles to limit the benefits of federal subsidies enjoyed by corporate-run farms is another. The late Paul Taylor, professor of economics at the University of California at Berkeley, devoted much of his considerable energies to reminding the federal government that the reclamation program was intended to serve family farms. Marc Reisner has written about another aspect of this legacy of water development: the massive loss of wetlands, impaired wildlife habitat, devastated fisheries, and endangered plant and animal species.

In short, the reclamation law was one of the most influential pieces of legislation for the American West.

WATER AS AN ENGINE FOR INDUSTRY

> For countless centuries the stream had been dropping flakes and chunks of the precious mineral into sand bars, into crevices in the banks, and into "pot holes" in the beds of the rivers. Every stone along a river's course had provided an obstacle behind which fragments might lodge. Water had been the primary agent in storing up this accumulation of wealth, and water was to be the miner's chief weapon in his attack upon it.
>
> RODMAN PAUL:
> *California Gold: The Beginning of Mining in the Far West*

On January 24, 1848, James Marshall discovered gold in a tailrace at Sutter's Mill on the American River in California. This discovery set loose a search for placer deposits (gold washed into gravel over the course of many years) in all of the streambeds of the Sierra Nevada and, eventually, for valuable hardrock minerals in every western state. The lure of instant wealth drew thousands of fortune seekers westward. California's population more than tripled between 1850 and 1860. Gold miners moved whole rivers to reach buried gold and filled the remaining rivers with the debris of washed-out hillsides. A silver strike in Nevada a few years later brought hordes to that state, as well; its population grew by more than 500 percent between 1860 and 1870. During the same decade, Colorado grew by nearly 500 percent, and gold in the Dakota Territory brought a population boom of over 800 percent in the decade between 1870 and 1880. Precious metals drew thousands to the United States' new lands.

Mining techniques evolved from the use of a pan and water to "wash" the lighter, less valuable materials away from the heavier gold particles, to the use of the sluice box, which could handle larger volumes of material and separated the coarser, less valuable material from the finer, heavier gold-bearing material. While a miner could pan for gold in just about any water body, the sluice box required a continuous, reliable stream of water. The miners built ditches and flumes to bring water from rivers to their claims.

Construction of ditches and flumes, especially when built to move water over extended distances, was expensive and difficult work. In some cases miners collaborated to construct those facilities, issuing stock to represent ownership and to raise funds. Private investors also constructed ditches and profited by selling water to miners. The development of hydraulic mining—blasting hillsides, using hoses with powerful streams of water to break loose the gold-bearing rock—greatly multiplied the demand for water, spurring the ditch-building efforts of private companies.

Water—whether for pans, sluices, or hydraulic hoses—was the engine for this social and economic movement. Water was critical to lode as well as placer mining. As some mining camps were located dozens of miles from any reliable watercourse, it was necessary to bring in water through the elaborate, serpentine canal systems that yet today weave their way along the geographic contours of the gold country.

This use of water to produce or process commodities was important in other industries as well. Factories in growing cities required substantial amounts of water. The irrigated sugar beet industry, for example, which emerged in 1870, required water to convey beets through water flumes to processing plants, to wash the beets, and to extract sugar from them. By 1959, the sugar beet industry required 180 million gallons of water daily to process 17 million tons of sugar beets. Steel manufacturing and wood processing plants also required substantial amounts of water for their operations.

One of the largest industries that developed around water use was hydroelectric power generation. Hydroelectric generation boomed at the turn of the century, and then World War II's demands for quick production of airplanes and ammunition enlarged the nation's demand for cheap power. The Columbia River dams—including the enormous Grand Coulee—were constructed to boost the Pacific Northwest's defense industry. Today, one-third of the United States' aluminum production comes from the Columbia Basin, where smelters depend on inexpensive electric power. Consumers in the Pacific Northwest purchased hydroelectric power at about half the national average cost; with little incentive to conserve energy, houses in that cool, damp region were constructed with little or no insulation. (Electric costs jumped dramatically when those homeowners were asked to bail out the utilities that had run into financial problems building nuclear power plants in the early 1980s.) In 1988 the U.S. Energy Information Administration reported that the West produces over half of all the hydroelectric power in the nation. Electricity produced in the Pacific Northwest is exported to far corners of the region, linking people in Seattle, Salt Lake City, and Los Angeles through a huge grid of shared electric power.

Water also figured in the plans of energy companies whose coal mines, oil rigs, and refineries were spreading across the western landscape in the late 1970s and early 1980s. In 1987 the Intermountain Power Plant (IPP), a large coal-burning electric-generating facility, was constructed near Delta, Utah, a location selected largely because water was available for the plant's cooling systems. The IPP purchased stock in local mutual water companies (the privately held counterparts to irrigation districts), thus transferring water from agriculture to industrial uses. The 15,000 acre-feet used by the cooling systems each year previously irrigated about 9,600 acres of land. When the IPP was proposed, Utah officials expected much of the electricity generated to be used in-state, primarily by the MX missile system. When that defense project was canceled, the IPP was scaled back, and cables were extended 490 miles westward to sell electric power to Southern California. Today Californians buy 95 percent of the project's electricity. Thus, the availability of water governed the siting of a plant that now links Utah with Southern California.

In addition to cooling processes, the western coal industry also requires water for transportation. One of the most efficient methods for transporting coal from western mines to distant power plants is through "slurries"—pipelines in which pulverized coal is suspended in water. The Black Mesa coal slurry pipeline, which began operation in 1970, is a good example of the process. It extends 273 miles, from the Kayenta Mine in northern Arizona to the Mohave Generating Station in southern Nevada. The pipeline uses about 4,000 acre-feet of water to carry 4.5 million tons of coal per year. On a much larger scale, in 1982 Energy Transportation Systems, Inc. (ETSI) proposed a coal slurry pipeline to carry coal from Wyoming's Powder River basin to power stations as far south as Texas and Louisiana. The ETSI pipeline would have required about 50,000 acre-feet of South Dakota water annually from the 23-million-acre-foot Oahe Reservoir on the Missouri River. This large diversion was opposed by the states downstream from the Oahe Reservoir, and they secured a 1988 United States Supreme Court decision that declared the government's contract for the project to be unlawful.

In Colorado a new industry known as oil shale was anticipated in the 1970s, premised on the assumption that the expensive extraction process would pay off if oil prices continued to rise. Exxon predicted in 1980 that Colorado's Piceance Basin would produce as much as eight million barrels of oil per day from oil shale within ten years. The federal government cooperated by providing subsidies through its newly created Synthetic Fuels Corporation. Developers expected a huge demand for water for mining and crushing ore, controlling dust at the mining sites, surface retorting (heating), upgrading shale oil by cleaning out heavy sludges, disposing of the spent shale, and revegetating the mining site. It takes three to four times greater volumes of water than shale to produce one barrel of oil. Nearly all the water diverted for use in oil shale production is consumed through evaporation; almost none is available to be re-claimed and returned to nearby streams. Speculation on large-scale production of oil shale touched off a frenzy of schemes to develop and import massive quantities of water from as far away as the Missouri River and the Great Lakes.

Land speculation followed closely on the heels of water schemes. The sleepy towns in this region were not prepared for the enormous influx of new workers flocking to the oil fields and coal mines. For a time, towns such as Rock Springs and Evanston, in Wyoming, were filled with highly paid workers living in tents, pickup trucks, and trailers. William Kittredge observed this boom in his essay "Over-thrust Dreams: 1981" in the book *Owning it All*:

> The rewards of petroleum figured large in imaginations around Evans-ton—airline tickets to romantic places and new hay balers for the ranch-ers, easy sex and pure, clean drugs and booze, and the dancing beguile-ments of rock-and-roll for the roughnecks. And they led people into wistful thinking. Maybe, just this one time—so the reasoning went—we can drill and grade this desert a little bit more to death, and then we will quit. Then we will be home, to live out our lives in harmony with the dic-tates of our secret hearts, at peace with the blossoming earth.

Water was thus an important ingredient for industrial develop-ment in the western United States. Its use linked distant parts of the country, as is perhaps most graphically illustrated by the ETSI pipe-line, which would have used South Dakota water to move Wyoming coal across one-third of the nation to Louisiana and Texas. More-over, the availability of water determined the location of some in-dustrial facilities. When western populations boomed in response to energy growth, water was often the commodity in greatest demand.

WATER AS FUEL FOR URBAN DEVELOPMENT

> Dreams have always shaped cities, and cities have always inspired dreams, and traditionally water has quickened them both.
>
> IVAN ILLICH : "H$_2$O and the Waters of Forgetfulness"

Although water's primary human use as a source of sustenance re-quires comparatively insignificant quantities, people in cities have more elaborate uses for water (flushing toilets, washing clothes and dishes, and watering landscapes), which collectively put major demands and impacts on the West's water. These other uses far exceed human consumptive requirements and make urban use the most rapidly expanding demand for taking water out of rivers and aquifers. Western cities commonly consume well over half of all developed water for lawns and landscaping.

By the turn of the twentieth century, the demand for domestic water supplies for urban development created a new force in western water policy. Furthermore, western cities set out to use water for landscaping and lawns typical of very different climates, and low-cost water made attractive real estate development possible. This urban use of water was fundamentally different from traditional domestic use, because it was driven by a new set of forces—real estate developers and other entrepreneurs who convinced city councils to secure major supplies of water to allow extensive future development. Water thus became a component in real estate speculation and development as never before.

Initially, urban areas tended to develop in locations with locally available water resources. In the West, those resources typically were limited. As local water supplies became fully utilized, cities reached out to distant sources. Around the turn of the century, Los Angeles bought land and water rights in the remote Owens Valley and built a 250-mile pipeline to bring in that water. Anticipating an even greater future thirst, Los Angeles next lobbied for the construction of Hoover Dam and built an aqueduct to the Colorado River. Around the same time, San Francisco was filling Hetch Hetchy Reservoir and building a pipeline that guaranteed delivery of clear Sierra Nevada mountain water to the city 134 miles away.

Perhaps inspired by the efforts of Los Angeles and San Francisco, in 1913 the city of Denver took steps toward importing water from the west side of the Continental Divide. The city formed a partnership with the Denver and Salt Lake Railroad, agreeing to build a set of 6.2-mile tunnels through the Rocky Mountains that would transport water and provide a throughway for railroad tracks. Construction of the Moffat Tunnel began with a 10-foot-diameter "pioneer" bore to serve as a conduit for power, light, and compressed air to supply the builders of the larger railroad tunnel. When the main tunnel was completed in 1927, the pioneer bore was converted to an aqueduct for water diverted from the Fraser River, a tributary of the Colorado River on the West Slope of the Rocky Mountains. Today, with the construction of several additional tunnels allowing diversions from additional West Slope rivers, the Denver Water Department imports 56 percent of the water in its system from the Colorado River basin.

Substantial urban demands for water developed after irrigation uses had claimed most of the reliable flows of surface water. Where urban expansion consumed formerly irrigated land, the water to support growth was simply shifted out of agriculture. Yet, as we have described, large cities like Los Angeles, San Francisco, and Denver also had the financial resources to construct complex water storage and delivery systems to bring water over long distances. Those projects linked people in distant parts of the region and thus created new communities of interest.

WATER AS AN INTEGRAL PART OF THE NATURAL AND HUMAN ENVIRONMENT

> Barring love and war, few enterprises are undertaken with such abandon, or by such diverse individuals, or with so paradoxical a mixture of appetite and altruism, as that group of avocations known as outdoor recreation.
>
> ALDO LEOPOLD : "Conservation Esthetic," in *A Sand County Almanac*

Ecosystems develop in direct relation to the availability of water—a fact illustrated by the classification of life zones according to the precipitation they receive and their elevation. Rivers develop their own special ecosystems, as do other areas where water is regularly available. In the arid West, riparian areas tend to contain especially rich and diverse ecosystems. And, of course, a river's fishery is directly affected by streamflows.

Out-of-stream water use in the West has had major consequences for the natural environment. Entire streams have been diverted from their beds for use in other watersheds. Dams have permanently changed the natural patterns of streamflows, capturing the peak flows that determined channel shape and riparian vegetation, while, in some locations, releasing chilled water from deep in the reservoirs in patterns that allow the creation of new cold-water fisheries. Dams have obstructed natural fish migration patterns in many streams and changed other characteristics of rivers critical to the native fisheries. Dramatic declines in the salmon population in the Pacific Northwest and in the squawfish population in the Colorado River are directly attributable to the effect of dams. Large wetland areas such as Tulare Lake in the Central Valley of California were drained to allow agricultural uses. The water that created those areas has been diverted to other uses. Consumption of water in out-of-stream uses has depleted natural flows—sometimes completely. Wallace Stegner wrote, "Dams do literally kill rivers, which means they kill not only living water and natural scenery but a whole congeries of values associated with them."

Human appreciation for water's role in the environment may arise from ecological understanding, a sense of aesthetics, or a desire to enjoy the benefits of water in recreational pursuits. Sometimes these different paths toward appreciation conflict with one another, such as when a group of boaters trample on streamside vegetation and pollute the water they came to enjoy. But more often the people who develop recreational interests also gain a deeper understanding of the environment. Sometimes this knowledge leads to activism, or at least support for protective laws and policies: Members of Trout Unlimited spend weekends restoring natural waterways damaged by construction or other causes; local Audubon Society volunteers gather annually throughout the country to count migratory birds, a task that would be far beyond the capacity of the state and federal wildlife agencies that need the information; waterfowl hunters donate money to Ducks Unlimited to help purchase and preserve wetlands.

Public appreciation for the importance of maintaining rivers intact first emerged many years ago, but the environmental movement has gained its greatest momentum in the last three decades. Environmentalists have come a long way from their fight to save Hetch Hetchy Valley from San Francisco's water development scheme in the early 1900s, but that early battle remains a touchstone in the history of conservation in the United States. John Muir, the leader of the fledgling mountaineering group, Sierra Club, rallied public sup-

port in opposition to the dam that would impede the Upper Tuol-
umne River and permanently flood the Hetch Hetchy Valley in Yosemite National Park. "Dam Hetch Hetchy!" Muir exclaimed in
outrage, "As well dam for water-tanks the people's cathedrals and
churches, for no holier temple has ever been consecrated by the
heart of man." This public sentiment, however, ran headlong into
the late-nineteenth-century conservation philosophy that empha-
sized making the fullest possible use of all natural resources. According to the conservation school led by Gifford Pinchot (the first
leader of the U.S. Forest Service), a reservoir site that could provide
a major water supply for San Francisco—even one located in a national park—should be used for that purpose. That great battle
came down squarely on the side of water for urban purposes. Damming a river in a national park gained Congressional approval in
1913, largely on the presumption that the highest value of water is
for human use—in that case, an assured water supply for San Francisco estimated to provide all needs until at least the next century.

Shortly after World War II, there was a tremendous expansion of
outdoor recreation, most of it in the West and much of it centered
around lakes and rivers. In an essay titled "The Rediscovery of
America: 1946," Wallace Stegner wrote of Americans' rush to the
highways once wartime restrictions were lifted, estimating that at
least a third of the country embarked on driving, camping, and boating vacations in the summer of 1946. Waxing enthusiastic about all
the natural wonders he intended to visit, and eschewing the conve-
niences of modern highways and motels for bumpy back roads and
primitive campsites, Stegner concluded that "we shall meet most of
America on the road."

The rush outdoors began a radical shift in public opinion toward
the environment. In their passion for recreation, Americans developed a keen interest in the big open spaces of Utah, the craggy
mountains of California, and the deep canyons of Arizona. Hikers
and rafters began to purchase outdoor equipment, which until then
had been the domain of hunters and anglers. Manufacturers, in
turn, developed new products—boots and packs, fabrics and fin-
ishes—making the outdoors all the more inviting and convenient
for recreationists. And, as Americans sought out trails and back

roads to explore, they grew more interested in protecting those areas from development. The environmental movement, although it would not be full-fledged until the 1970s, gained momentum during the post-war boom years.

Consider the fate of the Bureau of Reclamation's proposal to build a dam at Echo Park, where the Yampa River joins the Green River at the Utah-Colorado border. The dam was part of the Colorado River Storage Project drawn up in the 1940s, an effort to make more water available to states in the Upper Colorado River basin. It was to provide water for irrigation on Colorado's Western Slope, but would inundate a canyon containing fossilized dinosaur bones. President Woodrow Wilson had designated 80 acres of the canyon as Dinosaur National Monument in 1915, and President Franklin Roosevelt had expanded it to 210,000 acres in 1938. Located in a remote corner of the Colorado Plateau, the monument had never been much of a tourist attraction. Dam proponents were certain that the National Park Service would raise little fuss over the project.

In fact, the Park Service objected rather mildly to the Echo Park dam. But, for the first time since John Muir's unsuccessful fight to save Hetch Hetchy (and, no doubt, still stinging from that defeat thirty-five years before), environmental groups rose in vocal opposition to the dam. They rallied the emerging ranks of hikers and rafters, decrying the threatened inundation of a national park. Led by Sierra Club President David Brower, a coalition of environmental organizations printed books and pamphlets, ran advertisements, and spoke to congressional committees, always arguing that the integrity of a national park was more important than additional irrigation water. They gained support from writer Bernard DeVoto, whose articles in the *Saturday Evening Post* and *Reader's Digest* appealed to the public's emerging environmental conscience. Letters poured in to Congress, nearly all opposing the dam. In March 1956, the dam was scrapped. Echo Park was saved, and the American environmental movement had found its voice.

In the 1960s the nation learned from Rachel Carson's *Silent Spring* about the links between its use of chemical pesticides and the near-extinction of many bird species. In 1970 the public exercised its growing environmental spirit in the first celebration of Earth Day, and newly formed or reinvigorated conservation groups converged on Washington to bring the environment to the front of the legislative agenda. Congress was moved by the emerging fervor to enact a slew of protective statutes, ranging from the National Environmental Policy Act to the Clean Water Act and Endangered Species Act. This new overlay of federal legislation changed the way federal agencies make decisions about western lands and water resources. It also signaled the new political might of environmentalists, including westerners, rapidly trying to catch up with the power of livestock ranchers, grazers, miners, and other more conventional western interests.

A tradition of appreciating water for wildlife habitat and recreation is deeply rooted in our history and is promoted, not just by federal laws and national organizations, but by countless city, county, and state parks and riverfront greenways. The value of water for wildlife was early reflected in international negotiations, including the Migratory Bird Act of 1920. Ambitious wildlife, regulatory, and licensing systems have long governed fishing and hunting for waterfowl in every state. Protection of wildlife habitat also has specific roots in the national wildlife refuges, many of which are wetlands areas needed for waterfowl breeding or migration. And flat-water recreation has long been recognized as one of the major justifications for building federal dams, while whitewater recreation has surged in popularity—awakening a major source of resistance to the construction of dams.

Protection of natural waterways has also gained support from ecologists, who recognize (and are developing a deeper understanding of) the importance of biological diversity. Many years ago the great naturalist and writer Aldo Leopold eloquently explained the concept in his essay "The Round River": "If the land mechanism as a whole is good, then every part is good, whether we understand it or not. If the biota, in the course of aeons, has built something we like but do not understand, then who but a fool would discard seemingly useless parts? To keep every cog and wheel is the first precaution of intelligent tinkering."

The availability of water often defines natural communities and thus influences the number of species that can survive in a given area. In the arid Southwest, for example, 80 percent of all verte-brates depend on riparian areas for at least half of their life cycles, and riparian areas provide habitat for more species of birds than all other western rangeland vegetation types combined. Obviously, the flowing water in western streams provides critical habitat for native fish, but increasingly biologists are realizing the importance of streamside vegetation in holding down water temperatures, provid-ing protective cover, and maintaining streambank stability—all of which are necessary for fish survival. Moreover, public attitudes to-ward water have become more protective as people accept the need for balance between human development and the natural world—an attitude often expressed as "sustainability." Water itself, not just the uses to which it can be put, is seen as valuable.

Recreation and environmental protection have become more valuable (and valued) as the resources upon which they rely have de-clined or disappeared. The Sierra Club did not become a potent po-litical force until people realized that their favorite backcountry areas were about to be developed. Congress did not enact strict en-vironmental laws until ecologists pointed out that eagles were head-ing for extinction because of pesticide contamination. Environmen-tal and recreational uses of water have maintained a sort of siege mentality from the start, gaining ground sporadically through law-suits, legislation, or volunteer campaigns aimed at the latest insult. Activists are typically motivated by a perception that they are cling-ing to the last vestiges of the resource. This has not allowed for a long-range strategy of protecting the capacity of resources—at the least, water—to sustain the natural and human environment.

Many valuable uses of water have emerged as human settlements have grown and developed in the West. In this arid land, westerners have relied upon water to quench thirst, to feed and clothe, to cleanse, to manufacture, to restore and recreate, to transport, to in-spire and beautify, to extract, to etch and carve, and to shelter and propagate life. These uses have competed with each other from the start, and certain uses have come to dominate and preempt others. For example, water's use as a tool of navigation has, in some in-stances, trumped recreational values for water; water sought by growing cities has sometimes come at the expense of rural communities or the environment. There has never been (and perhaps could not have been) a consensus that agriculture is more important than fish, or industry more important than agriculture, yet competition among uses has forced sacrifices. Today, the region's diverse communities of interest are challenged to consider all valuable uses of water together.

Author Norman Maclean could have been referring to the history of the West when he wrote that "all things merge into one, and a river runs through it." Water—the search for it, efforts to control it, and evolving appreciation for a variety of its uses—links many disparate historical periods. There is a paradox in the way the region's communities relate to water: although it ties them together in the most fundamental way, disputes over water have distanced them from one another in bitter, divisive battles. Westerners are challenged to learn from the lessons of change in western history and to build upon them in designing a sustainable future that respects and balances the multiple values derived from water.

Chapter Three

Voices

Water touches everyone in the West. Thus, we present here the voices—drawn from literature, poetry, and song—of people whose lives have been shaped in different ways by water. In these voices we find anger, hope, and deep love for the West and its water—in short, all the different emotions that people express for the resource upon which their very lives depend.

MARY AUSTIN

From *Stories from the Country of Lost Borders*

It is difficult to come into intimate relations with appropriated waters; like very busy people they have no time to reveal themselves. One needs to have known an irrigating ditch when it was a brook, and to have lived by it, to mark the morning and evening tone of its crooning, rising and falling to the excess of snow water; to have watched far across the valley, south to the Eclipse and north to the Twisted Dyke, the shining wall of the village water gate; to see still blue herons stalking the little glinting weirs across the field.

. . . You get that sense of brooding from the confined and sober floods, not all at once but by degrees, as one might become aware of a middle-aged and serious neighbor who has had that in his life to make him so. It is the repose of the completely accepted instinct.

WILLIAM DEBUYS AND ALEX HARRIS

From *River of Traps*

These hand-carved fields, worked by shovel, ax, and bar, don't want the water.

Only the man does.

Take away the man, and the grass thickens in the ditch, the leaves catch, the silt settles out. Soon the water pools and leaks away.

Take away the man digging year by year, and all the ditches, large and small, swell with the surplus of the field's own growth. The ditch banks flatten under the weight of the hooves. The water spills out, useless.

Say good-bye then to the moist green sod. The broomstraw will take its place. Say good-bye to the mewing phoebe. The insect whine will retreat to the river.

Say good-bye also to the shy green snakes that the hawks love, and the splash from the hooves of the antic mare.

The field lives by the water but does not want it. The man lives by the field and makes it drink. He hears the suck of the sod as he deepens the ditch and the thwack of his shovel beating new clods into place.

"There now," he thinks. "That will hold a while." And he looks down the ditch at two hundred yards of clods undug.

He rests, and his fingers curl in a circle that fits the shaft of his shovel. He gazes upstream toward yesterday's ditch, and the ditches of days gone by—in this field, and that one, and the other through the trees. Fields and ditches that were made by hand.

Take away the man, and you take away the ditch.

Take away the ditch, and you take away the water.

Take away the water, and you take away the man.

You leave only the sound of the water.

STANLEY CRAWFORD

From *Mayordomo*

Spanish water law was set into place in a time before deep wells, massive diversion and storage dams, and before the flows of streams and rivers could be accurately measured, and of course before the various intrastate and regional and international water compacts were created in the southwestern United States. In the face of these developments, traditional water-use arrangements, which still hold over unadjudicated portions of stream systems in New Mexico, appear conservative and even reactionary, an obstacle to economic progress and development. So in fact they are.

Through adjudication of water rights a share of a variable amount of water entering an *acequia's* headgate is, in effect, replaced by a fixed share measured in acre feet of a much larger and less variable whole that consists of an entire regional stream system; a certain rigidity is created at the local level in the interests of quantification and flexibility at the regional level. The traditional arrangement is myopic: it looks at a short stretch of river and whatever water happens to be there at the time it divides up among the *acequias* and, within the *acequias*, among *parciantes*, and each *parciante's* share, his *pión*, varies roughly according to how much water is in the river at that particular point and time. Adjudication and the various regulatory steps that precede or follow it also create a new hierarchy of water users, replacing an oral tradition, in which uses are constantly under negotiation, with one based on a system of documentary evidence.

Each way no doubt has its virtues; sometimes, no doubt, the effects of adjudication and the establishment of water rights and priority dates for irrigation are equitable and fair, and no doubt often they are not. But the main effect of adjudication is that once the process is completed, then a water right becomes a commodity that can be rented or leased or sold anywhere within the state of New Mexico, subject to the approval of the Office of the State Engineer. Upon adjudication, a water right enters a vastly larger market that has nothing to do with the land it was once attached to, or with *acequias*, their commissions, or the community of which it once formed part. This might not be objectionable if the sale of a water right were not, in effect, also the sale, or rather dispersal, of part of an *acequia*, a part of a community at the same time. Without water rights a *parciante* ceases to be one, and a ditch loses thus a member, a taxpayer, a *pión*, a potential worker, a potential officeholder. The *pión* is each *parciante's* share in a corporation that consists of his community, giving him a vote in the conduct of his community's affairs, qualifying him for office within his community, offering him a measure of easily accessible public responsibility that may be becoming increasingly unusual in public life in the United States.

With its interminable court hearings, the adjudicating process can

sweep through a community and undermine traditional arrangements that have stood in place for hundreds of years, in order to
convert what has been held in common to that which can be owned
privately. The bias and intention of water-rights adjudication is obvious: to serve the regional water market and facilitate the transfer
of water rights from rural, water-rich but economically dormant
areas to the expanding metropolitan areas of the arid south. If
northern New Mexico succumbs to the pressure to convert water
from the uses of subsistence agriculture to municipal-industrial uses
for the cities of Santa Fe, Albuquerque, and Las Cruces, something
irreplaceable of a political and cultural nature will be seriously endangered. There are few other civic institutions left in this country
in which members have as much control over an important aspect of
their lives; relatively autonomous, in theory democratic, the thousand *acequias* of New Mexico form a cultural web of almost micro-
scopic strands and filaments that have held a culture and a landscape
in place for hundreds of years.

What is remarkable is how well the *acequia* tradition has been kept
alive deep within a larger Hispanic colonial tradition of government
that has often favored absolutism over more participatory arrangements. And as the costly and socially disruptive process of adjudication is carried out throughout the north, often pitting traditional
Pueblo and Hispanic communities against each other, one may fairly
ask whether it is more important for water to feed material values
than social or civic ones. Perhaps our logic has got turned upside
down: in the north we should be saying that water is essential for
keeping our communities together, and such is its main use now—as
the substance around which a most remarkable tradition of self-
governance adheres. To this, even agricultural use may be secondary.

FRANK WATERS

From *People of the Valley*

Maria rolled a cigarette. "Water District?" she asked slowly. "Is there
not water in all districts?"

"It is like this, Madre. Allow me to explain fully. This valley is one water district of many in these parts. It is a judicial district. It is a County. Do you see? When one regards water, it is as a water district. When one regards justice and law, it is as a judicial district. When one regards government, it is as a County. And none of these districts, of which there are many of each, may be different and thus interfere with the others. Thus we are the United States! Now do you understand? We are no longer merely the valley."

"No, amigo," said Maria puffing deliberately. "It is you who are dumbfounded with words. We are still the valley. Water is our problem; our fights over a stream's flow have always been the fiercest; too much of it has killed us also. We have our Masters of the Ditch. Hence also our need for justice, for government. But with all of these, and more, Señor, we are still the valley. The mountains enclose us, the earth feeds us. It is a thing of itself. Do not talk of a district on paper!"

THEODORE M. SCHAD

From *The Changing Scene in the American West:
Water Policy Implications*

Fifty years ago . . . a young man left his home in Maryland, loaded his personal effects into his car, and set out on what to him was a great adventure. He was going "out West" to take a position as a junior engineer with the U.S. Bureau of Reclamation.

As a civil engineering student during the 1930s it had thrilled him to read of the construction of big dams in the West: Hoover Dam on the Colorado, Grand Coulee on the Columbia, and Shasta on the Sacramento. . . . On his maps he had traced the route of the Central Valley Project in California, amazed to think of water being moved as far as from Baltimore to Boston. He was familiar with only one large body of water, the Chesapeake Bay, and one large river, the Susquehanna. He had traversed the 15 miles of the canal linking the Chesapeake with the Delaware, a seemingly endless distance that taxed the power of the "one-lunger" engine that powered his brother's sailboat. He had explored the reaches of the reservoirs of the

Baltimore City water supply, Loch Raven and Prettyboy, which to a small boy had seemed immense. All puny indeed, compared to what was being done to control water in the West.

And now he was going to be a part of this great effort—a participant in the taming of the West. As he drove west, up the broad valley of the Platte River . . . a sense of history overwhelmed him. He was less than a hundred years behind the pioneers of the Oregon Trail. He could think of them circling the wagons as they camped for the night, to ward off potential attacks by bands of marauding Indians. He was heading for the Rocky Mountains, explored by the fur traders, the mountain men, the miners who had discovered gold. A sense of anticipation arose in him as he recalled the books he had read that made all this seem so very real to him.

Driving up the long hill as the highway climbed up from the Platte Valley to the high plains west of Ogallala—a hill such as he had never seen before, he was filled with wonder at the immensity of the scene around him and he began to search the horizon to spot the crest of the Rockies when it first came into sight. Which it did while he was still over a hundred miles out on the plains. And as he thought of the exploits of Frémont, Long, and Pike, he felt he was following in their footsteps, helping to achieve the fruits of the Manifest Destiny that had led us to wrest this magnificent domain from the Indians as we expanded the country from the Atlantic to the Pacific in less than a century. . . .

It was a heady experience for a young engineer, to design a spillway, and watch the construction and operation of a model one hundredth the size of the prototype; making adjustments in the gates and the stilling basin to smooth the water flow; checking the measured flow of the water against the calculations. An engineer could be happy spending a life-time working in the evolving field of spillway design, and many of the members of the staff were doing just that, specializing in one phase of technical design of dams and appurtenant works. But the young engineer wanted more than that. He wanted to know how the whole picture fit together, how the decisions were made, who was in charge.

He knew there was a Commissioner of Reclamation in Washington, from the reports he had read when he was in college. But nobody in the design sections in Denver seemed to know who he was or what he did. Old Deb in Project Planning seemed to have the best grasp of the overall program. He and his staff located the projects and found the dam sites. Randy Riter, as chief of the Hydrology section, provided the flood hydrographs, and Glen Sloan was even then driving up and down the Missouri River basin looking for projects to be included in an overall plan for water resources in that basin, giving rise to the term, "windshield survey." . . .

After subjecting him to lectures on the duty of water and subjugation of the land, Old Deb agreed to send the young engineer out to the Pacific Northwest to investigate projects in the Crooked River basin in Oregon. A whole new chapter began there. This was the real West, with coyotes howling at night from the rim-rock above the canyon—sage brush desert country, cattle country—with the size of the ranches measured in sections, rather than acres. But there were not many people except on the irrigation projects and in the small towns that served them.

Walking over the ridge that separated the Ochoco Irrigation District from an unirrigated valley to the south, seeing the difference between the green farms of the irrigation project on one side of the ridge and the sage brush desert on the other side, it suddenly came to the young engineer that the fervor for irrigation was like a religion. People could *live* in a valley with irrigation; without it, just cattle, and only 32 head per section of land.

Irrigated farms with houses and barns and tractors and electric lights and children playing and all the things we think of as civilization, contrasted with the desert, a severe landscape, broiling hot in the daytime, cold and inhospitable at night. Yes, the fervor to make the desert bloom was a religion, with roots in the Bible itself. This was the vision of Brigham Young, as he said "This is the place" when he entered the great Salt Lake Valley. This was the motivating force that energized the Bureau of Reclamation.

WOODY GUTHRIE

From "Roll, Columbia, Roll"

There's a great and peaceful river in a land that's fair to see,
where the Douglas fir tree whispers to the snow-capped mountain
    breeze.
The cliffs are solid granite and the valley's always green,
this is just as close to heaven as my trav'lin feet have been.

Roll Columbia won't you roll, roll, roll.
Roll Columbia won't you roll, roll, roll.

Stand upon her timbered mountain, look across her silver strand,
See the crops and orchards springing to the touch of nature's hand.
And it's further up the river where your eye will meet the skies
Where you'll see the steel and concrete of the big Grand Coulee rise.

Roll Columbia won't you roll, roll, roll.
Roll Columbia won't you roll, roll, roll.

There at Priest and Cascade rapids men have labored day and night,
Matched their strength against the river in its wild and reckless
    flight.
Boats and rafts were beat to splinters but it left men dreams to
    dream
Of that day when they would conquer the wild and wasted stream.

Roll Columbia won't you roll, roll, roll.
Roll Columbia won't you roll, roll, roll.

Uncle Sam took up the challenge in the year of '33
For the farmers and the workers and for all humanity.
Now river you can ramble where the sun sets in the sea,
But while you're rambling river you can do some work for me.

Roll Columbia won't you roll, roll, roll.
Roll Columbia won't you roll, roll, roll.

Now there's full a million horses charged with Coulee's 'lectric
    power
Day and night they'll run the factory and they never will get tired.
Well a coal mine gets dug out and an oil well it runs dry,
But Uncle Sam will find his power where the river meets the sky.

Roll Columbia won't you roll, roll, roll.
Roll Columbia won't you roll, roll, roll.

WILLIAM KITTREDGE

From *Owning It All*

Warner Valley was largely swampland when my grandfather bought
the MC Ranch with no downpayment in 1936, right at the heart of
the Great Depression. The outside work was done mostly by men
and horses and mules, and our ranch valley was filled with life. In
1937 my father bought his first track-layer, a secondhand RD6 Cat-
erpillar he used to build a 17-mile diversion canal to carry the spring
floodwater around the east side of the valley, and we were on our way
to draining all swamps. The next year he bought an RD7 and a John
Deere 36 combine which cut an 18-foot swath, and we were deeper
into the dream of power over nature and men, which I had begun to
inhabit while playing those long-ago games of war.

The peat ground left by the decaying remnants of ancient tule
beds was diked into huge undulating grainfields—Houston Swamp
with 750 irrigated acres, Dodson Lake with 800—a final total of almost 8,000 acres under cultivation, and for reasons of what seemed
like common sense and efficiency, the work became industrialized.
Our artistry worked toward a model whose central image was the
machine.

The natural patterns of drainage were squared into dragline
ditches, the tules and the aftermath of the oat and barley crops were
burned—along with a little more of the combustible peat soil every

year. We flood-irrigated when the water came in spring, drained in late March, and planted in a 24-hour-a-day frenzy which began around April 25 and ended—with luck—by the 10th of May, just as leaves on the Lombardy poplar were breaking from their buds. We summered our cattle on more than a million acres of Taylor Grazing Land across the high lava rock and sagebrush desert out east of the valley, miles of territory where we owned most of what water there was, and it was ours. We owned it all, or so we felt. The government was as distant as news on the radio.

The most intricate part of my job was called "balancing water," a night and day process of opening and closing pipes and redwood headgates and running the 18-inch drainage pumps. That system was the finest plaything I ever had.

And despite the mud and endless hours, the work remained play for a long time, the making of a thing both functional and elegant. We were doing God's labor and creating a good place on earth, living the pastoral yeoman dream—that's how our mythology defined it, although nobody would ever have thought to talk about work in that way.

And then it all went dead, over years, but swiftly.

You can imagine our surprise and despair, our sense of having been profoundly cheated. It took us a long while to realize some unnameable thing was wrong, and then we blamed it on ourselves, our inability to manage enough. But the fault wasn't ours, beyond the fact that we all had been educated to believe in a grand bad factory-land notion as our prime model of excellence.

We felt enormously betrayed. For so many years, through endless efforts, we had proceeded in good faith, and it turned out we had wrecked all we had not left untouched. The beloved migratory rafts of waterbirds, the green-headed mallards and the redheads and canvasbacks, the cinnamon teal and the great Canadian honkers, were mostly gone along with their swampland habitat. The hunting, in so many ways, was no longer what it had been.

We wanted to build a reservoir, and litigation started. Our laws were being used against us, by people who wanted a share of what we thought of as our water. We could not endure the boredom of our mechanical work, and couldn't hire anyone who cared enough to do it right. We baited the coyotes with 1080, and rodents destroyed our alfalfa; we sprayed weeds and insects with 2-4-D Ethyl and Malathion, and Parathion for clover mite, and we shortened our own lives.

In quite an actual way we had come to victory in the artistry of our playground warfare against all that was naturally alive in our native home. We had reinvented our valley according to the most persuasive ideal given us by our culture, and we ended with a landscape organized like a machine for growing crops and fattening cattle, a machine that creaked a little louder each year, a dreamland gone wrong.

TIM PALMER

From *The Snake River*

His grandfather raised potatoes, his father raised potatoes, and now Ken Mulberry raises potatoes. And other crops. "We have 400 acres here and 330 down the river. About half are in grains—red wheat for milling, barley, and other cow feed. Then there's the feedlot with 2,000 head of cattle, and the potato packing plant. We ship out a million bags a year to eastern markets." Each bag weighs 100 pounds.

Mulberry stood about six feet tall, strong in build, fair-haired under his ball cap, friendly and ready to share information. His farm lay just above the rim of the Snake River canyon near Twin Falls. Jenny Mulberry tended to five children, all blonde. "Another on the way," she said as she poured a row of orange juices. "Would you like a glass?"

"The family roots are up in the Idaho Falls area," Ken said. "It's colder up there, and the farming economy is depressed. It was time to make a move. Dad and I financed this operation, and it blossomed real fast." What I saw struck me as something that has gone beyond good farming and entered the early realms of agricultural empire. Ken Mulberry came here only seven years ago, when he was twenty-six.

"Let me show you the farm. I have some time now. I got some sleep last night." He slept nine hours for the last three nights, altogether. "We'll stay busy the rest of the season."

We left the wood-sided ranch house, crossed the dirt yard where landscaping was in process, stepped into the pickup, and rode down a lane to a ditch. "This is out of the Twin Falls Main Canal. Our water rights were established when the canal system was built in 1910. On a dry year, if anyone has to cut back, they cut out the users with the junior water rights. Down here, you hardly ever have to worry about managing your water. I watch it real close anyway, but you don't have to." We walked toward the ditch. . . .

"The land erosion is terrible. Some fields, you'll notice, are kind of white at the top. It's hardpan—the topsoil washes off and leaves minerals. White soils produce hardly anything. A lot of fields won't grow 50 percent of what they did. Excess lime is the main problem." We drove up the road. "This farmer's one of the best farmers in the country. You can't see any color change on his fields. See, no white at the top."

Ken pulled over and we walked onto a whitish field he has just begun to farm, a part of Mulberry's chronic expansion program. "Look at this." He crumbled a handful of soil. "Crusted. We'll haul manure up here from the feedlot. With sprinklers, we can avoid this problem altogether because sprinklers save soil. We also cut back on erosion by using a chisel plow and ripper instead of the old moldboard plow. The new method leaves the fiber in the top 4 inches—it leaves the soil profile the same instead of turning it upside down. I'll tell you, farmers today are changing the whole way we do things."

We stopped at an overhead sprinkler—a pipe mounted on wheels powered by a motor. Water sprays downward as the pipe progresses slowly across the field. Evaporation consumes less water than in the old lines that sprayed the water upward. "By going to sprinklers and larger fields, we use one-third the water we used in furrow irrigation." . . .

Ken drove to the top of a furrowed field. "There are new things coming out of the research center at Kimberly, like this gated pipe." At the top of the field, perpendicular to the rows of crops, I didn't see a leaking, open, muddy ditch, but a large plastic pipe. At regular intervals, holes had been cut one-inch square. A roped device traveled down the inside of the pipe and opened and closed the holes—miniheadgates—to allow a precise amount of water to leave the pipe and flow down the furrow. "It saves soil, saves water, saves labor, and makes the field look nice. It's efficient." Wastewater that might flow to the bottom corner of the field was pumped back to the top. "That also carries the suspended soil back to the top, right where it ought to be.

"These guys have enough water rights to irrigate constantly, but that doesn't make sense. If you save water, you save oil and have efficient production." Ken looked at me and shrugged his shoulders, as if his statement was obvious to everyone.

"I think farmers are more open-minded now, and once you're open-minded you start asking questions. People used to tell us things were safe, like chemicals. Farmers doubt that now. I've gotten sick from chemicals. I think chemicals are in their prime now, and we'll see less of them in the future. They're developing biological controls, and I wish they could develop them faster.

"I used to say, 'Damn the conservationists,' but now I see the need to compromise. If we're going to have an organized society, we need some power plants and some irrigation, but some land should never have been put into production. Now they have this CRP program [Conservation Reserve Program]. I call it CPR [cardiopulmonary resuscitation]. It's giving farmers who are going out of business a chance to start something else."

"Isn't that just another subsidy?"

"Yes. I'd like to see an end to the subsidies; let the most efficient farmers win." Ken drove back toward the house.

"You're interested in the river, so I'll tell you, farmers are using less water, and marginal land is going out of production, so there's going to be more water in the river. Yet you won't see farmers giving up their water rights. That'd be like taking away their guns." Mulberry laughed. "You take away water rights and they'll go get their guns. Water rights were the basis of the settlement of this country. Even if farmers aren't using their water, they want to keep their

rights so they won't go short in a dry year. That doesn't mean that agriculture and the river can't coexist. We definitely need minimum
flows for fish. I hate to see the rivers get stagnant."

. . . A religious zeal can be seen in irrigation and farming—the
righteousness of the founding of the West, of the pioneers settling a
hostile land, of people maintaining homes and communities. Today,
there is another religious view—a reverence for life, a reverence
held by people who want to protect and restore the river and the
land. Belonging to the Shoshone and Bannock and their ancestors
long before history, this belief is older than that of any white settler.
Belonging to a people concerned about the river, this view is also
younger—a product of Idaho's conservation movement, of modern
pioneers, and of the emerging, broader-based economy here and
throughout the West.

EDWARD ABBEY

From *Desert Solitaire*

"This would be good country," a tourist says to me, "if only you had
some water."
He's from Cleveland, Ohio.

"If we had water here," I reply, "this country would not be what it
is. It would be like Ohio, wet and humid and hydrological, all covered with cabbage farms and golf courses. Instead of this lovely barren desert we would have only another blooming garden state, like
New Jersey. You see what I mean?"

"If you had more water more people could live here."

"Yes sir. And where then would people go when they wanted to see
something besides people?"

"I see what you mean. Still, I wouldn't want to live here. So dry and
desolate. Nice for pictures but my God I'm glad I don't have to live
here."

"I'm glad too, sir. We're in perfect agreement. You wouldn't want
to live here, and I wouldn't want to live in Cleveland. We're both satisfied with the arrangement as it is. Why change it?"

"Agreed."

We shake hands and the tourist from Ohio goes away pleased, as I am pleased, each of us thinking he has taught the other something new.

WALLACE STEGNER

From "A Geography of Hope," in *A Society to Match the Scenery*

Aridity has been a difficult fact for Americans to accept, and an even more difficult one to adapt to. For nearly the first half of the nineteenth century we avoided the dry country that Pike and Long had called the Great American Desert; but by the 1840s and 1850s we were pushing our agriculture onto the dry plains and trying to mythologize aridity out of existence by such hopeful delusions as that rain follows the plow, that settlement improves the climate. When that myth brought on much human misery and failure as well as much environmental damage, we tried to engineer aridity out of existence by damming and redirecting the rivers. (Most of the results of that plumbing job are still to come, but they are coming.) Or, as a plumbing variation, we robbed Peter to pay Paul: We stole the Owens Valley's water to make the subdivision of the San Fernando Valley richly profitable; we conducted water through the Rockies from the Western Slope to permit the urban sprawl of Denver.

Human ingenuity has been manipulating Western water for nearly a century, but all our ingenuity has not increased the amount of water or solved any of the secondary problems that lack of water creates. In 1878, a hundred and twelve years ago, John Wesley Powell in his *Report of the Lands of the Arid Region* warned that there was water enough in the West to supply only about a fifth of the land. Being a man of his time, though considerably ahead of it in many ways, he was thinking in agricultural terms, and the new survey and homestead laws that he proposed would have eased the difficulty of Western settlement. Congress, dominated by boosters and local patriots, ignored his proposals, and settlement went ahead by tradition, habit, mythology and greed instead of by observation and forethought.

Not even yet has it sunk into some heads that the supply of water is finite. We have water only from the time when it falls as rain or snow until it has flowed past us, above ground or below, to its final ocean or underground reservoir. We can hold it back and redirect it, but we cannot add one drop to its total supply. In fact, the evaporation rate in really dry country being as much as ten feet a year, we may lose almost as much of it by ponding it as we save by slowing it down.

Moreover, in the West, "using" generally means "using up." What we put to municipal or industrial use is not coming back into the rivers to be available for irrigation—or if it does, it comes back poisoned. What is used in irrigation largely evaporates, and any percentage that finds its way back into the rivers is increasingly laden with salts, fertilizers, and pesticides from the fields. And no matter what use you find for the water from a river, every acre-foot you take out leaves a lessened instream flow to sustain trout, salmon, herons, ducks, rafters, picnickers, skinny-dippers, or whoever else might find it useful. In Colorado, as in some other Western states, you can literally dry up a stream if you have prior rights for some so-called "beneficial" purpose.

Aridity means more than inadequate rainfall. It means inadequate streams, lakes, and springs. It means underground water that replenishes itself more slowly than elsewhere. In some places the underground water is fossil water, irreplaceable within any human time frame. And surface and subsurface water are not two problems, but one.

Confronted by the facts of chronic shortage, the decreasing feasibility of more dams, and the oversubscription of rivers such as the Colorado, the boosters sometimes speak of "augmentation" and suggest ever-greater engineering projects, roughly comparable to the canals of Mars, to bring water down to the dry country from the Columbia or the Yukon, or tow it down as icebergs from Glacier Bay to let San Diegans flush their driveways and keep their lawns verdant.

Pipe dreams, arrogant pipe dreams. Why should we expect a desert to blossom? It has, or had until we began to tinker with it, its own intricately interdependent plant and animal species, including the creosote-ring clones that are the oldest living things on earth. The idea of making deserts blossom is something we inherited from Isaiah. It is an idea especially dear to the Mormons, and it has had remarkable short-term successes. But it is open to all sorts of questions when we look very far into the future. For financial and political reasons, more than for technical ones, there are limits to how freely we can move water from one watershed to another. There are ecological and (I would say) moral reasons why we shouldn't. As a Crow Indian friend of mine said about the coal in his country, "God put it there; that's a good place for it." Lots of things have learned to depend on the West's water in the places where it naturally occurs. It would become us to leave them their living space, because if we don't, we are taking chances with our own.

ALDO LEOPOLD

From "Song of the Gavilan," in *Sand County Almanac*

The song of a river ordinarily means the tune that waters play on rock, root, and rapid. . . .

This song of the waters is audible to every ear, but there is other music in these hills, by no means audible to all. To hear even a few notes of it you must first live here for a long time, and you must know the speech of hills and rivers. Then on a still night, when the campfire is low and the Pleiades have climbed over rimrocks, sit quietly and listen for a wolf to howl, and think hard of everything you have seen and tried to understand. Then you may hear it—a vast pulsing harmony—its score inscribed on a thousand hills, its notes the lives and deaths of plants and animals, its rhythms spanning the seconds and the centuries.

The life of every river sings its own song, but in most the song is long since marred by the discords of misuse. Overgrazing first mars the plants and then the soil. Rifle, trap, and poison next deplete the larger birds and mammals; then comes a park or forest with roads and tourists. Parks are made to bring the music to the many, but by the time many are attuned to hear it there is little left but noise. . . .

There are men charged with the duty of examining the construction of the plants, animals, and soils which are the instruments of the great orchestra. These men are called professors. Each selects one instrument and spends his life taking it apart and describing its strings and sounding boards. This process of dismemberment is called research. . . .

A professor may pluck the strings of his own instrument, but never that of another, and if he listens for music he must never admit it to his fellows or his students. For all are restrained by an iron-bound taboo which decrees that the construction of instruments is the domain of science, while the detection of harmony is the domain of poets. . . .

Science contributes moral as well as material blessings to the world. Its great moral contribution is objectivity, or the scientific point of view. This means doubting everything except facts; it means hewing to the facts, let the chips fall where they may. One of the facts hewn to by science is that every river needs more people, and all people need more inventions, and hence more science; the good life depends on the indefinite extension of this chain of logic. That the good life on any river may likewise depend on the perception of its music, and the preservation of some music to perceive, is a form of doubt not yet entertained by science.

WALLACE STEGNER

From *The Sound of Mountain Water*

By such a river it is impossible to believe that one will ever be tired or old. Every sense applauds it. Taste it, feel its chill on the teeth: it is purity absolute. Watch its racing current, its steady renewal of force: it is transient and eternal. And listen again to its sounds: get far enough away so that the noise of falling tons of water does not stun the ears, and hear how much is going on underneath—a whole symphony of smaller sounds, hiss and splash and gurgle, the small talk of side channels, the whisper of blown and scattered spray gathering itself and beginning to flow again, secret and irresistible, among the wet rocks.

RICK BASS

From *Valley of the Crows*

Dave Blackburn lives with his wife and two young daughters and young son above the rocky bank of Montana's little-known Kootenai River. Dave's a logger, but is studying to take an outfitter's exam this October, so that he can take clients down the river to fish, rather than cutting trees. Dave has remodeled a large turn-of-the-century cabin and barn on the north bank of the Kootenai, so close to the river that he can flip a stone in, side-armed, from his back porch. There is a small fence around the yard for his children to play in, and flowers of all colors grow around the borders.

Ospreys, goldeneye ducks, hummingbirds, mallards, mergansers, and an endangered species, the amazing Harlequin duck, are the birds I saw the day I floated the river with Dave. . . .

The nearest town to Dave is Libby, population 2,600, and the mayor and City Council and Chamber of Commerce of that town want to build a dam on the Kootenai, a dam that would put Dave's and his family's house beneath roughly fifty feet of water. . . . the mayor of Libby thinks the energy produced from a dam could be sold to California.

Dave's an expert fly fisherman, and he casts his tiny flies at points distant with unbelievable accuracy, sometimes looking back over his shoulder and talking at the same time.

The water's so clear as we drift along that we can see the trout beneath us, sometimes. Depending on what part of the story Dave's telling me, his casts are either fast or furious—like lashes, as he talks about the town's mayor—or soft and floating. When he talks about the Kootenai's natural values, and his family, he waves his fly rod back and forth like the tiniest, most subtle orchestrations of an overture, and his voice is soft; but when he gets into the politics of earthscraping and concrete-pouring, his voice is still soft, but the rod goes mad, there's a whipping sound, all around my ears—though the fly still continues to land gently on the water.

Letting my wet fly drift along the bottom . . . I catch the first trout, a flashing, leaping bolt of silver that amazes me with its strength.

The fly is so tiny and the leader-line ("tippet") is so light, and my rod's bending so much, that I'm afraid the whole outfit is going to break, and I'm hesitant to fight the fish, I feel as if I might do something wrong. But Dave's howling, he's laughing, moving around the boat to see it and shouting every time it jumps, and then I'm shouting, and the fish dives, darts behind rocks, and there's that wonderful moment when I don't know if I'm going to get it or not—that brief moment when the fish dives, making full use of the river and its currents, is stronger—but then the fish grows tired, I'm bigger than it is, stronger of course, and it has to show me its beauty; it succumbs.

Dave slips the net under it, a two-pound rainbow—I take quick pictures—and then he wets his hands, takes the hook daintily out of the fish's fierce mouth, and lowers it back into the river, holds it there for a moment as it regains its bearings, and then he releases it. The fish darts away, but the river is changed, for me.

I like the river better, now.

Dave spots another, smaller trout rising . . . and whispers to me, "Watch this," and begins casting to a spot where he says he can see fish rising, though I can see nothing, and am still living in my memory, of how my fish leapt so high and so many times, of how a thing was—and then Dave's rod is bent, the line is stretched taut and cutting the water, and I'm beginning to panic, thinking of someone in California turning on a lamp at dusk, or a hair dryer; and of Dave's lovely old turn-of-the-century homestead, submerged, beneath fifty feet of water—and of the whole river disappearing, an entire stretch, and the geese that nest along it, and the wide gravel sandbars, the fast hurry of the current: all of these things being gone.

BRUCE BROWN

From *Mountain in the Clouds*

The wild salmon . . . are Quartz Nose, Two Gills on Back, Three Jumps, Lightning Following One After Another; *tsá tsap, tyee* and the finest of them all, the blueback "Quinnat"; the salmon of "100 pounds or more in weight" that the Spanish explorer Manuel Quimper found at Neah Bay in 1792 and the 102-pound salmon that Ernie Brannon caught on the Elwha 140 years later. They are the early Chinook that people remember used to "knock the boat up out of the water" when they floated over them on the glides of the upper Calawa, and the near-record 31-pound steelhead that was caught on the Bogachiel within the last ten years; the sound of violent splashing off a lonely bridge at night, and the bleached carcass lying on the edge of a gravel bar where a seagull pecks the eye out.

Gifted with the ability to move from one medium to another and then return again to exactly the place where their lives began, the wild fish of the genera *Oncorhynchus* and *Salmo* have played a crucial role in the development of the general ecology of the Pacific Coast of North America. In a region that has been reworked by waves of glaciers for the last million years and which otherwise counts leaching rains as its predominant meteorological phenomenon, the wild salmon serve as nature's principal means of returning nutrients from the sea to the land. Through their passionate, seemingly perverse death, they give life not only to their own progeny, but also to a host of predators and other dependent species. They are, in short, an engine of general enrichment, and an important element in the long-range stability of the Pacific Coast ecosystem. . . .

During the course of my three year's wandering around the Olympic Peninsula, I saw wild salmon of every Pacific species, as well as the two anadromous trout, the steelhead and sea-run cutthroat. Many were beautiful fish, and occasionally the massed display was stunning (as on the humpy glide of the Graywolf River), but nowhere did I find the old glory, or the life it supported. To see relatively unsullied salmon runs and a yeomanry of subsistence salmon fisherman today, one must travel to Alaska, the Northwest Territories and British Columbia. . . .

JEFF RENNICKE

From "The Dolores River," in *River Days*

The canyons echo with history. First came the hoofbeats of Butch Cassidy and his Wild Bunch, who robbed the San Miguel Valley Bank in Telluride on June 24, 1889, to the tune of $10,500, then used the maze of the river's canyons to mask their getaway. Next came the ring of picks and shovels as a string of mining booms—silver, carnotite, vanadium and a list of other mispronounceable minerals—sparked dreams of riches. But every boom was met with a bust and the dreams did not pan out. More than a hundred miles of the Dolores' course have been studied and recommended for inclusion in the National Wild and Scenic Rivers System, but just as with its dreams of mining glory, the protection has not yet come. Now the river flows alone.

Alone except for the paddlers. We push off into the current early, surprisingly easy for a party as big as ours—four rafts and several kayaks—considering how late we stayed up watching the starlight between the branches of the pines. Sunlight replaces starlight as we float through the upper part of the Dolores Canyon known as Ponderosa Gorge. It is a strangely beautiful mix of desert canyons and pine trees that soften the edges of the cliffs.

The river is flowing strong, about 4,000 cubic feet per second; the pace of the river is straight and fast. Canyon walls flip faster than the guidebook pages. The rapids begin where the river's course grows indecisive. At Glade Canyon the river loops like a paper clip, first northeast, then swinging southwest, then northeast again, picking up speed. In the upper stretches the river drops at twice the rate of the lower canyons, making the low gradient figures deceiving. Here, the Dolores runs hard—Glade Rapid, Molar, Canine. . . .

With the big drop at Snaggletooth behind us and a long Class III rapid below known as Mile Long, the river comes out of the high land of ponderosa pines, losing its mountain touches. Here it flows into a harsher place where the shadows are sharper and the light is as clear as broken glass. The river changes too, opening onto a wide flat at Slickrock where there is a small store with ice cream, water for 10 Cents a Gallon and a *Return of the Mutants* comic book that will supplement our river library nicely. While we haul the heavy water jugs back to the river, a trio of ravens is circling the canyon downstream, so high they look like windblown ashes.

Just below the ravens the river drops back into a canyon—Little Glen Canyon—named after the place now drowned by the water of Lake Powell behind the Glen Canyon Dam. The irony is poetic: one canyon drowned by a dam, another that could be dried up. Drifting on the quietwater, I can hear someone up ahead talking about the high-quality trout fishery that will be created in the tailwaters of the McPhee Dam. And it's true: the Dolores could become one of the best float-fishing trips in the Southwest. River otter are being introduced. The changes coming with the closing of the dam upstream will not be as drastic as the drowning of Glen Canyon when that dam closed on the Colorado River. But the place will be different somehow and we can feel it as we drift through the five miles of Little Glen Canyon. . . .

Mesa Canyon is on my mind as the boats drift the last miles of the trip. One of the stories around the campfire last night told of a 4-by-6-foot wooden flume strung 400 feet above the river in the canyon. It was the scheme of the owners of the Lone Tree Placer Mine to construct it. The cliff walls were loaded with gold, or so the engineers thought. The water needed to sluice the gold, however, was 400 feet below in the river. So, a string of workers, perched along a wooden platform suspended from the sheer cliff face, set thousands of brackets one by one to secure the flume.

It was an epic construction job requiring 1.8 million board-feet of lumber and almost costing the life of one of the workers who slipped from the platform and plunged into the river. It was completed in 1891 and, just as the engineers planned, the water flowed. But the gold didn't. The gold flecks were too fine to be sluiced profitably. The chief engineer of the project committed suicide, and the flume was left to rot on the walls of Mesa Canyon. Sections of the flume are still visible today, rotting slowly in the dry desert air, a monument to greed and to the hard way the dreams sometimes die. . . .

Alone, drifting with a boat around the bend, I think about this trip. We came to celebrate a river. But it is too early to say what will happen to the Dolores River when the gates of the McPhee Dam close. Other rivers have survived their dams—the Gunnison River in the Gorge, the Green River through Lodore, the Colorado River in the Grand Canyon. But this is different, more personal. We never knew those rivers before the dams; those are memories that belong to other times. We've run the Dolores and seen it in its prime springtime form. We know Spring Canyon Rapid, Molar, Canine, Snaggletooth and the way the water curls against the walls of Slickrock Canyon at sunset. This loss will be our loss, something we will carry in our own eyes the rest of our lives.

Maybe they are right, those who say the river, with its clear water, trout fishing, river otters and longer rafting season, will be a better place to raft. Maybe, but it will not be the same. It will never be the same.

A tug of current twists my oar and I look up to see the other rafts already far downstream picking up the hikers. I do know that somewhere there have to be rivers that flow free, if only to remind us of what has been lost. I pull hard on the oars to catch up. A canyon wren calls from somewhere in the cliffs, a song that flows like water then slowly fades to silence.

Chapter Four

The West Today

The westerner is less a person than a continuing adaptation. The West is less a place than a process. And the western landscape that has taken us a century and three quarters to learn about, and partially adapt our farming, our social institutions, our laws, and our aesthetic perceptions to, has now become our most valuable natural resource, as subject to raid and ruin as the more concrete resources that have suffered from our rapacity.

WALLACE STEGNER : *Where the Bluebird Sings to the Lemonade Springs*

Western landscapes and western settlements bear little resemblance to the places known by those who arrived just over a century ago; they bear even less resemblance to the homes of the Indian inhabitants who arrived thousands of years earlier. Where bison and elk once roamed across vast grasslands, interstate highways now snake through expansive green fields of crops irrigated with water from sometimes distant rivers and deep wells. The old trading posts and dusty towns have been transformed into bustling cities and sprawling suburbs, hardly distinguishable from those in the humid East.

Today, most westerners live in metropolitan areas rather than on farms. Many of the growing western cities' residents have moved there from eastern states, drawn by the proximity of open space and the sense of opportunity that remains strong. Other urban immigrants have come from rural areas, seeking more reliable sources of income as agriculture becomes a corporate enterprise and family farms become scarce. The very economic base upon which the region operates is in continual flux, but follows a trend of expansion.

Westerners' priorities for, and views toward, natural resources have evolved. While westerners have always hunted and fished and cherished their great land, traditionally they necessarily looked first and foremost to the lands and waters as a way of making a living. Today, fewer individuals depend upon farming, mining, and running livestock for their livelihoods, and urban westerners have become far more interested in fishing, hiking, and visiting natural areas. The western public lands now host over one billion recreational visitors every year. Most westerners describe themselves as favoring strong environmental controls and have questioned proposed dams and energy developments. In western communities such as Bend, Oregon, and Dubois, Wyoming, urbanites are purchasing vacation or retirement homes and are becoming involved in local land-use, forestry, and grazing issues. In short, the new westerners are exerting strong pressures for change in how water and other resources are managed. For their part, westerners who have lived in the region for many years (or even generations) are changing, too. Ranches in Colorado, Wyoming, and Montana are opening their operations to urban guests who want to experience a week or two of ranch living; others have developed profitable backcountry guiding and outfitting businesses. The "new westerner" thus includes both newcomers and those who have changed in response to new conditions.

In addition to the growing cities, vibrant communities have blossomed on Indian lands—reservation and other trust lands that cover 56.6 million acres in the lower 48, approximately 70 percent of which are in the West. Tribes have initiated their own approaches to managing natural resources by joining traditional values with new economic realities, with impressive results. For example, the Confederated Tribes of the Warm Springs Reservation in north-central Oregon own a dam on the Deschutes River, operate a fish hatchery, administer a progressive system of range management, and have, like many tribes, formed their own water management agency. And the Zuni Indian Reservation in west-central New Mexico has embarked on an ambitious sustainable development plan that incorporates cultural values and community input with scientific land management principles. The people helping to articulate and implement these cultural and community values are themselves main contributors to the "new West."

THE NEW WESTERNER

> The shaping of a people by the land they inhabit takes time, and in America it has taken longer, simply because we have never been quite sure that we were here to stay.
>
> DANIEL KEMMIS : "The Last Best Place: How Hardship and Limits Build Community," in *A Society to Match the Scenery*

The popular image of the West is of wide open space and few people. In fact, the West *is* full of open space, but it also contains some of the fastest growing urban areas in the country. The 1990 Census reported that ten of the western states experienced above-average growth in their urban-area populations between 1980 and 1990. In Nevada, for example, urban populations grew by 52 percent during the 1980s. Arizona followed with a 37 percent urban population increase. The national average was 12 percent. Figure 1 shows overall population growth rates in the West compared with the rest of the nation.

Not all "urban" westerners live in the cities: most settle into nearby suburbs. The 1990 Census reported that more than half the nation's population now lives in suburbs, up from a quarter in 1950 and a third in 1960. Nineteen of the nation's twenty-five fastest-growing areas were suburbs, including Los Angeles–area suburbs Moreno Valley, Rancho Cucamonga, and Irvine; Phoenix suburbs Mesa, Scottsdale, and Glendale; and Dallas suburbs Arlington, Mesquite, and Plano. People are attracted to the natural amenities of suburban homes—like green lawns and swimming pools—which represent the new and changing demands on western water.

The rural westerner is changing, too. Small towns in Wyoming, Idaho, and Montana are attracting retirees, urban escapees, and "footloose industries" such as catalog order centers. For example, in 1988 the outdoor-clothing company Patagonia relocated about half of its mail-order operation from Ventura, California, to Bozeman, Montana. The company was drawn to the area for a number of rea-

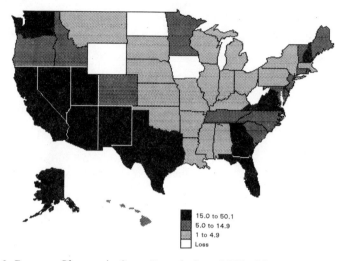

Figure 1. Percent Change in State Population, 1980–90
Source: U.S. Bureau of Census

sons: commercial rents were substantially lower (buildings in Ventura rented for $19–$45 per square foot, compared with $7.75 per square foot in Bozeman), and the terrain and climate of this western town offered excellent opportunities for testing Patagonia's sports equipment and clothing. For their part, the workers were attracted to lower housing prices. The average home in Ventura was selling for $250,000, compared with $63,000 in Bozeman. Even though Patagonia reduced hourly pay rates for workers who chose to relocate, nine individuals (of a total of thirty-five in the division) opted to make the move.

The lower cost of living and higher quality of life attract new residents, who are changing the nature of the rural West. In a recent study, University of Idaho researchers Gundars Rudzitis and Harley E. Johansen looked into the reasons that people move to small towns in the West. They found that newcomers seek towns accessible to undeveloped natural areas. These migrants to "wilderness communities" told the researchers that they favor protection of nearby natural resources over their own economic development; they came to these areas in order to enjoy a better quality of life made possible through the availability of amenities such as wilderness. In fact, in

the survey of people living in eleven counties with federally designated wilderness, 81 percent of the respondents agreed that wilderness was important for their county, both for the solitude and open
space it offers and for the tourists it attracts.

The Wilderness Society reported similar results in a study focused
on the area around Yellowstone National Park: the newcomers in
that region were drawn to the proximity of national forests and
parks, and most were not dependent on resource development activities for their livelihoods. In fact, the study found that income
from retirement and benefits and investment earnings made up almost 35 percent of personal income in the Yellowstone region, sur-
passing the combined income from agriculture, mining, and timber
harvesting. The researchers concluded that federal land management policies that still treat traditional extractive industries and agriculture as the region's economic mainstays are shortsighted, a
"view through the rear-view mirror." More realistic policies, they asserted, would recognize the value of the natural environment and
the growing importance of service industries and "non-labor income," including retirement and investment earnings. "It's a whole
new way of looking at our resources," Colorado Senator Tim Wirth
told the *Washington Post* in 1987. "People see that you can make more
money by leaving the forest alone and letting people hike through it
than you can by cutting down the trees and shipping out timber."

Ed Marston, publisher of the regional newspaper *High Country
News* (and himself a former New Yorker living in Paonia, Colorado),
expressed mixed feelings about these demographic and economic
changes. In a 1991 speech to the Grand Canyon Trust, Marston
noted that much of the rural inland West has experienced a "turned
over" population: "There has been a tremendous population outflow of rural people and an inflow of people from urban areas,
people with urban values. You don't see it because the populations
have stayed more or less the same. But the ways people make a living
and the values have changed." He compared the way newcomers
treat rural lands with the way a person might deal with a car that
doesn't run anymore: "You put it in your front or back yard or out on
the street, depending, you put it up on blocks and you run an ad saying 'Parting out 1957 Plymouth Fury.' Then your neighbors, or

whoever, come by and if they need a fender or if they need an air cleaner or a whatever, they just strip your car for you. It doesn't run anymore. It isn't worth anything. You've parted out the car." Marston expressed a fear that the newcomers in rural western communities threaten the region with a similar "parting out" if they fail to learn to live off the land in some way. "We have got to figure out," he concluded, "how to . . . turn the land back to being productive and resourceful rather than just something that is cut off and then sold for its space." In other words, westerners should recognize their own dependence on the land and resources that drew them to the region. Communities grow out of such a sense of shared needs. Ironically, water, the West's most important resource, has been eagerly "parted out."

Who lives in the region that includes these growing suburbs and metamorphosing rural towns? While there is no "typical" westerner, the 1990 Census provides some insight to western demographics. The census found that the region is more highly populated by younger people than the national average. All states but Oregon, Arizona, and Montana (which have drawn increasing numbers of retirees) reported lower than average percentages of people over the age of sixty-five. The census also reported that most westerners are of Anglo-European descent: the states reported above-average white populations and below-average African-American populations. Asian-American populations are above average only in Washington, California, and Nevada. There are relatively high percentages of Native Americans in every western state, and four western states (New Mexico, Arizona, California, and Colorado) reported relatively large Hispanic populations.

Census data also reveal a changing pattern of employment in the West. Figure 2 shows that more than one-third of the region's personal income is earned in service sector employment, while income from farming has declined steadily for most of this century. Today tourism is the fastest-growing industry in the West. Indeed, according to the Travel Industry Association, the travel and recreation industry is the largest private employer in Arizona, Colorado, Idaho, Nevada, New Mexico, Utah, and Wyoming. In a symbolic way, Idaho marked this transition in 1992 when it rejected the long-time

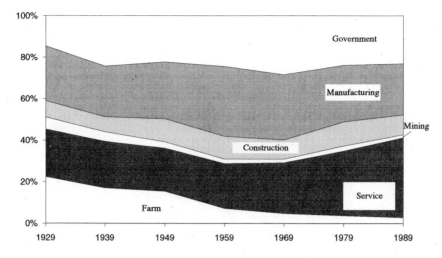

Figure 2. Percentage of Personal Income Generated from Selected Sources in the Western States, 1929–89

Source: U.S. Department of Commerce

automobile license plate slogan "Famous Potatoes" in favor of a colorful mountain and forest scene.

Other studies have made clear that westerners—even those most worried about future water supplies—are concerned about the quality of their environment. In 1990 the Field Institute polled Californians on the importance of eleven public policy issues facing that state in the next five to ten years. The survey indicated that the top two issues are controlling drugs and ensuring an adequate supply of water, both mentioned as "critical" by over 70 percent of the respondents. The same study found that Californians ranked environmental protection as the most important *use* of water; three out of four said that, in times of shortage, it is "essential" that enough water is allocated to this purpose. These opinions were expressed at the beginning of a fifth year of drought in the state, with no end in sight and water-use limits as strict as fifty gallons per person per day in some cities; these people were, in a sense, already making some of the choices that would be necessary to place environmental protection ahead of other water uses.

National polls have confirmed that environmental protection is a high priority. The *New York Times* and CBS asked a random sample of Americans whether they agreed that "protecting the environment is so important that requirements and standards cannot be too high, and continuing environmental improvements must be made regardless of cost." In 1981, only 45 percent of the respondents agreed with the statement; in 1990, 74 percent did. The same (1990) poll found that 71 percent of Americans said that they would be willing to pay higher taxes to clean up the environment, and 56 percent favored protecting the environment even if it meant lost jobs in their communities.

The new westerners, then, are more than statistical abstractions: they are the third-generation Wyoming ranchers who now raise llamas to carry the gear of wilderness outfitters; they are the retired executives who moved to Steamboat Springs to enjoy the fly-fishing and small-town lifestyle; they are the professional couples in eastern cities who spend vacations in southeastern Utah and have become concerned about federal land-management decisions affecting those lands. The new westerners have become a major agent of change in the region.

WATER IN TODAY'S WEST

> The United States west of the 100th meridian, which runs through the middle of the Plains states, really amounts to a distinct civilization, an empire grafted onto a landscape profoundly hostile to human habitation. If many Americans still do not fathom how arid the West is, that is because the graft has taken so successfully.
>
> MARC REISNER : "The Big Thirst," in *The New York Times Magazine*

Humans settled and put water to use first along natural waterways. Now, the West's water is pumped and piped throughout the land, making it possible for people to settle in areas far from reliable water sources. Consider the extent to which natural patterns of streamflow have been altered to fit human needs. In 1991 the Federal Emergency Management Administration reported that the seventeen western states have over thirty thousand dams, with the capacity to hold over 475 million acre-feet of water. That's nearly enough water to cover all the land west of the Continental Divide to a depth of one

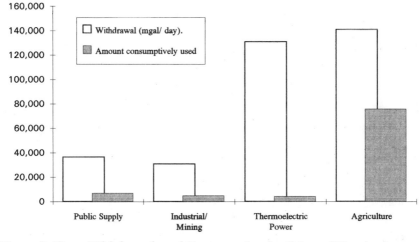

Figure 3. Water Withdrawals and Consumption for Selected Uses in the United States, 1985

Source: U.S. Geological Survey

foot. The water stored in dams is made available for use during dry seasons; many rivers that once flooded, then dried up, now flow more or less evenly throughout the year.

The water itself works unbelievably hard—diverted, used, and returned to a stream many times on its journey from the headwaters toward the sea. Much of the water never reaches the sea, though, but is lost in evaporation from reservoirs, transpired from field crops or lawns, or otherwise consumed. Water is said to be "withdrawn" or "diverted" when it is removed from its natural course or location through a ditch, canal, or other structure. The portion of withdrawn water that is evaporated, lost to evapotranspiration, or otherwise no longer in its original form is said to be "consumed." The rest of the withdrawn water—the water that flows back to a watercourse—is called "return flow." Figure 3 illustrates that consumption rates vary from small fractions to about half of water withdrawn, depending on the use of that water. The largest quantity of the water withdrawn in the West is for agriculture, almost entirely for irrigation of crops, with a small portion used for purposes such as livestock watering. The U.S. Geological Survey estimated in 1985 that agriculture constituted 88 percent of all water withdrawals in the West; that is a rate

Water sources and total withdrawals for eleven western states, 1985.

| State | Total freshwater withdrawals (acre-feet/year) | Water Source | |
		Surface	Groundwater
California	41,888,000	60%	40%
Idaho	24,976,000	78%	22%
Colorado	15,120,000	83%	17%
Montana	9,688,000	98%	2%
Washington	7,840,000	83%	17%
Oregon	7,324,800	90%	10%
Arizona	7,190,400	52%	48%
Wyoming	6,944,000	92%	8%
Utah	4,681,600	81%	19%
Nevada	4,188,800	76%	24%
New Mexico	3,684,800	54%	46%
West	133,526,000 (total)	77% (avg.)	23% (avg.)

Source: U.S. Geological Survey, 1985.

of about 102,300 million gallons per day—more water than Los Angeles uses in six months. The table above sets forth total water withdrawals and sources of waters in eleven western states.

As the western population and economy change, so too do the region's demands for water. Although agriculture played a critical role in the West's settlement and claims the largest portion of the region's water, today it competes with recreation, urban landscaping, and other, newer water uses. The changing, expanding demands for water are forming new ties—often by circumstance rather than by intent—that bind westerners in all corners of the West. For example, the consequences of water decisions in Los Angeles reach as far as the headwaters of the river systems that feed it and beyond, to the other communities that depend on or compete for the same waters in half the states of the lower forty-eight. The network of people who share an interest in Los Angeles' water use includes a farmer growing crops in California's Central Valley, a casino buying electricity in Las Vegas, a family floating the Grand Canyon, skiers in the Rocky Mountains, and an Indian tribe seeking drinking water for its reservation in southern Colorado. It also includes native trout and endangered squawfish; salmon and brine shrimp; eagles, whooping cranes, and ducks. L.A.'s "problem-shed" (to use a term coined by Harvard professor Peter Rogers) extends from the melting snows on mountaintops to ancient lakes, to deltas and estuaries far away from the sprawling city.

Despite these links of interdependence, the relationships among western water users historically have ranged from uneasy to hostile. The experience of Colorado's urbanized settlements east of the Rockies (the Front Range) illustrates the complicated nature of the ties that bind the region's water interests. Transmountain diversions—tunnels and pipes bored through the Continental Divide—have long been used to import water from the wetter, less developed Western Slope to the people of Denver and Colorado Springs. This water has been developed under pressure from these cities' expanding populations. The Denver metropolitan area, for example, has grown from 178,129 people in 1900 to nearly two million today. (These figures include the suburbs that have grown around the city at faster rates than the urban area.)

Public opposition to new transmountain diversions has forced city officials to look elsewhere for new sources of water supply. In addition to the well-publicized defeat of Two Forks Dam (which would have provided water for the Denver metropolitan area at the expense of a gold-medal trout stream), other recent water development proposals have been derailed. For example, Arapahoe County, near Denver, hoped to construct a network of diversions, reservoirs, and pipelines to import water from the Gunnison River watershed on the Western Slope. Local water users, Gunnison Basin citizens, environmentalists, and federal agencies all joined in opposition to the project. One new community-based organization, People Opposed to Water Export Raids (POWER), was formed specifically around opposition to the project. In a month-long trial in Gunnison in 1991, the judge refused to hear evidence offered on "public interest" issues like environmental and community impacts, but did consider issues ranging from the feasibility of the project to the adequacy of water. At the trial's conclusion, the water court judge ruled that the project proponents could establish legal rights to only a fraction of the water they had claimed. This has stalled the project for now. If the county presses an appeal, the opponents will appeal the exclusion of their public interest evidence.

Facing such opposition in any proposal to develop new water from Colorado's rivers, urban water suppliers are turning to other sources of water, particularly irrigated agriculture, with an eye to buying them out. Seeking nearby, reliable sources of water, cities have purchased Front Range farms for their water rights. The effects are obvious in places like Park County, a mountain valley 50 miles southwest of Denver. There the waters of Clear Creek historically were diverted to irrigate fields of alfalfa and wild hay, supporting large numbers of cattle, horses, and sheep. In recent years, Park County's irrigated acreage dropped sharply, as cities purchased ranches and transferred their water rights to municipal use. In 1969 there were over 35,000 acres of irrigated pasture and hay in the county. By 1982, that figure had dropped to 20,000. A 1990 study found fewer than 4,000 acres of irrigated land remaining.

Other rural areas in Colorado are feeling the pressure from thirsty cities. Some farmers find it nearly impossible to turn down the cities' offers. Reporters Mark Obmascik and Patrick O'Driscoll wrote in a 1992 *Denver Post* article on transfers of water from agriculture to urban use: "Though many farmers tend to be cash-poor, they tend to be water-rich." They told stories of several farmers who chose to sell their water to cities for many times more than other farmers would pay for it. "From a financial standpoint," remarked one farmer who made that decision, "it's very difficult to understand how I could not have sold." Others quoted in the *Denver Post* expressed concern that the movement of water out of farming communities will threaten their economies and futures. "When they move water out of an agricultural area, they absolutely destroy an economy," said long-time Colorado farmer Frank Milenski, who continued: "And for what? To grow green lawns and golf courses around Denver. I think a lot of these deals are plum stupid."

This sentiment was reflected in a 1992 initiative drive spearheaded by state Senator Bob Pastore, whose district in south-central Colorado includes several farming communities whose water is sought by growing cities. The initiative (which did not receive enough signatures to appear on the ballot) proposed an amendment to the state constitution that would require the vote of local residents before water could be moved from one river basin to another. Other measures to alleviate the impacts of agricultural-to-urban water transfers include requirements that the municipalities replant native grasses on the lands they dry up. This has occurred on a voluntary basis—with mixed success so far—on farms purchased in the lower Arkansas Valley.

Colorado's experience with water transfers illustrates the tremendous potential for reallocating existing supplies. Front Range cities have recognized that obtaining water from farms is less expensive and generally less contentious than building new dams and transmountain pipelines. But, as illustrated in Park County and other rural areas in the state, Colorado also offers lessons in the price of moving a resource away from a community without adequate safeguards for local interests.

Just as distant water users share interests in how water is distributed and managed, so, too, do water users competing within a single river basin for control over the resource. In Wyoming's Wind River basin, a battle between the state engineer and the Shoshone and Northern Arapaho tribes illustrates the emerging strength of Native Americans (and the persistently strong resistance of competing interests) in the complex tug-of-war among western water users.

The Wind River conflict traces back to July 3, 1868, when the United States and the tribes signed the Treaty of Fort Bridger, establishing a reservation where the Indians were expected to support themselves by farming. The treaty did not spell out how this would happen, but the 1908 U.S. Supreme Court decision *Winters v. United States* confirmed that such treaties implied a promise of adequate water supplies to fulfill the purpose of the reservation. Thus, the tribes had a right to water as early as 1868, putting them far ahead of farmers who came to settle the area in the early 1900s with the encouragement of the Bureau of Reclamation. The Bureau helped non-Indian settlers form the Midvale Irrigation District in 1906 and constructed the Wyoming Canal to deliver water to their fields.

In the 1980s the tribes went to court to confirm their legal rights to Wind River water. A 1988 Wyoming Supreme Court decision (later upheld by the United States Supreme Court) recognized the tribes' rights to 500,717 acre-feet of water, more than half the flow of the Wind River and its tributaries. The tribes immediately adopted a tribal water code and created an administrative body to implement it, the Wind River Water Resources Control Board. One of the Board's first decisions was to grant the tribes a water right to support a fishery in the river. In times of shortage, this permit would require upstream diverters (the Midvale farmers) to leave at least 252 cubic feet per second in the river in order to maintain the minimum streamflow for the tribes' fishery. However, when the tribes requested that the state engineer enforce this permit, he refused because he interpreted the tribes' water rights as requiring the water to be taken out of the stream for agricultural use. The tribes, however, expected far greater economic benefits from a thriving recreational fishery than from expanded agriculture.

The case went back to court in 1990. First, the district court upheld the tribes' use of water as within the scope of their reserved water rights. In that decision, the court ordered the state engineer to defer to the tribes on all matters of water rights administration within the reservation and declared that the tribes were entitled to use their water on the reservation for whatever purposes they saw fit, including restoring a fishery. The state appealed, and in the summer of 1992 the Wyoming Supreme Court sided with the state engineer. In a splintered opinion, the majority held that the tribes could develop water only for agricultural purposes (consistent, it said, with the intent of the treaty) and that the state engineer must continue to administer all water rights. In one of the dissenting opinions, Justice Brown argued that the tribes would lose control over their sovereignty if the state controlled their water rights. He concluded: "I cannot be a party to deliberate and transparent efforts to eliminate the political and economic base of Indian peoples under the distorted guise of state water law superiority."

The Wind River battle demonstrates the complexity of sharing western water. The Midvale farmers have invested many years' efforts in developing their lands, and only recently were forced to acknowledge the superior rights of their Indian neighbors. The tribes, on the other hand, for many years watched the non-Indian farmers enjoy the benefits of federal government irrigation projects, despite the fact that the same government had a legal duty to protect the tribes' interests. As one Indian irrigator commented in 1990: "There's as much pain on this side of the river as on the other." Water users throughout the West today are struggling with the sometimes painful realization that Indian water rights are here to stay.

Often fights over western water arise when there is a shortage, when people realize that they are competing for a scarce resource and seek to hold on to what they see as theirs. Tensions grow even higher when a shortage persists over a number of years, as was the case in California in the late 1980s and early 1990s. The fastest-growing state in the nation suddenly had to face the fact that its water supplies were not adequate for its needs. Its dilemma—and some of the promising responses—holds lessons for other parts of the West.

California depends on a complex system of water delivery facilities to move water from the relatively wet parts of the state (the northern coast and Sierra Nevada mountains) and the distant Colorado River to the agriculturally rich Central Valley and the arid, highly urbanized southern part of the state. The state leads the nation in water withdrawals, at 37,400 million gallons per day, of which about 80 percent is for agriculture. Yet the most pressing demand for new water supplies is for the thirty million people living in the cities and suburbs. The Association of California Water Agencies (ACWA) reported in 1991 that California is expected to gain another ten million people by the year 2005.

The state's precipitation varies widely. As the ACWA remarked in its report: "In California, a 'normal' water year is more of a statistical abstraction between uncomfortable extremes of drought and flood than something actually experienced." Analyses of tree rings show that the state experienced a sixty-year drought from 1760 to 1820, during which rainfall never exceeded the "normal" level assumed today. Moreover, a drought between 1865 and 1880 destroyed a thriving cattle-grazing industry in Southern California. The drought that began in 1987, then, was hardly unprecedented, but by that time the state had developed a far greater dependence on its unpredictable water.

By 1991, the fifth consecutive year of drought, the State Water Project halted all deliveries to its agricultural customers, but it cut deliveries to urban customers by only one-third. The federally operated Central Valley Project reduced deliveries by 75 percent to agricultural contractors and by 25 percent to others. Estimates of fallowed farmland ranged from 500,000 to 800,000 acres, and the annual economic losses suffered by farmers were estimated at $500 million to $1 billion—a large sum, but less than 5 percent of agricultural income. When cut off from surface water supplies, many farmers turned to groundwater. This huge reserve enabled most farmers to continue producing, but underground water tables in agricultural areas showed the impacts of depletion: from 1987 to 1991 groundwater storage in the San Joaquin Valley was depleted by 11 million acre-feet.

Fish and trees were among the most serious casualties of the California drought. State fisheries suffered from reduced streamflows. The Sacramento River's striped bass and winter-run salmon populations dropped to their lowest recorded levels. Forests throughout California felt severe impacts, too. The ACWA reported that ten million trees died as a direct result of the drought, including one-third of the trees in the northern Sierra Nevada and a higher percentage in the southern part of the state. Desiccated vegetation provided ready tinder for wildfires; the devastating Oakland–Berkeley Hills fire of October 1991 was attributed partly to the parched trees and shrubs in neighboring forests. The reduced freshwater flows in the Sacramento River exacerbated the water quality problems in the San Francisco Bay Delta, where depletions already had caused damaging saltwater intrusion and degraded water quality.

The drought opened many people's eyes to the tenuous nature of water supplies. When urban water users were asked to use less water, they complied with a burst of civic responsibility. For example, when the East Bay Municipal Utility District set a conservation goal of 15 percent, its customers responded by reducing water use by 30 percent. Marin County residents reduced their water use by 50 percent, Contra Costa by 47 percent, Santa Clara by 40 percent, and Los Angeles by 26 percent. For their part, agricultural water users were invited to participate in a state water bank (a voluntary pooling of water for temporary exchanges) and were offered $125 per acre-foot of water. In 1991 the state obtained over 800,000 acre-feet of water through this voluntary bank, about half of which came from fallowing. The remainder came from groundwater and stored water. The three largest water purchasers were the Metropolitan Water District (the major water supplier for Southern California), the Kern County Water Agency, and the City of San Francisco.

The drought—and fears it has spawned about future water supplies—prompted some water suppliers to seek unlikely new sources of water from farther sources. The City of Goleta (in Santa Barbara County) proposed to import water from Canada using ocean-going tankers, at an estimated cost of $2,000 per acre-foot. Not far away, the City of Santa Barbara built the largest desalination plant in the nation, capable of converting 6.7 million gallons per day of sea water to fresh water. According to the International Desalination Association, the average cost of desalted water in the United States is $1,300 to $5,000 per acre-foot. As other coastal communities are exploring this approach, one manufacturer of desalination equipment concluded that the drought is not the only impetus. "Population growth is the main thing," Randy Truby told the California-based Water Education Foundation, which published an issue of *Western Water* focused on desalination. "The drought has done nothing more than offer us a peek into the future, and what we see is that by 2010 our water transfer and import facilities won't be adequate to meet the growing demand."

A NEW WESTERN COMMUNITY?

> At the very heart of [the concept of public rights in water] is the idea of a community of people endowed with a limited source of sustenance upon which they are mutually dependent. Because the survival of all of them depends upon the continuing ability of their resources to sustain them, their relationship is invariably one of mutual dependence, common enterprise and joint responsibility.
>
> JOSEPH L. SAX : *The Constitution, Property Rights and the Future of Water Law*

From fights over water transfers and water management to crises of supply, westerners are more aware than ever about the water in their regions. Organizations including the League of Women Voters, the Center of the American West, and the Denver Museum of Natural History have developed public education programs focused on water and have found eager audiences. Articles on water resources in the regional newspaper *High Country News* reach readers throughout the nation. Popular books such as Marc Reisner's *Cadillac Desert* have drawn into the debate people who otherwise would not be interested in water policy. Water has become a political and social issue throughout the West.

We have described the tremendous diversity of people living in the western United States. In the past, evolving uses of water brought people together in communities of interest—irrigators, miners, and others. Each community worked toward its goal of securing adequate water supplies, whether through building storage and diversion works or by establishing legal rules determining the rights to use the resource. Today's uses of water, and the laws and policies that guide them, reflect the influence of each of these communities.

Those living in the West today are linked firmly to those who were there before and made choices about how water and other natural resources should be put to use. It has become increasingly clear that many of those decisions now conflict with contemporary interests, that new choices will become necessary as the limits of resources and the complexity of public values are better understood.

Just as historical uses of water and other resources formed communities of interest, so, too, does the region's shared interest in a sustainable future. Today's community of interest could emerge out of a better understanding of the shared nature of western water. Communities of interest in the past accomplished joint development through cooperation. Similarly, a western community could enable the region to control its own destiny, to avoid the "parting out" of land and resources that Ed Marston decried. This will require cooperation and coordination on a scale that has never been achieved in the region.

Chapter Five

River Basin Stories

A whole river is mountain country and hill country and flat country and swamp and delta country, is rock bottom and sand bottom
and weed bottom and mud bottom, is blue, green, red, clear,
brown, wide, narrow, fast, slow, clean, and filthy water, is all the
kinds of trees and grasses and all the breeds of animals and birds
that men pertain and have ever pertained to its changing shores, is
a thousand differing and not compatible things in-between that
point where enough of the highland drainlets have trickled
together to form it, and that wide, flat, probably desolate place
where it discharges itself into the salt of the sea.

JOHN GRAVES : "Goodbye to a River," in *River Reflections*

Ariver basin starts with
mountain peaks where snowpack feeds the cold, clear streams in the
headwaters where the river is born. It takes in the thick, green forests that carpet the mountainsides or the arid desert lands traversed
by running water. It is all the fish and other creatures that live there.
And so it includes the people who live along the river, whose present
and future depend on adequate water supplies to meet their physical, material, and spiritual needs.

We look closely now at the major western river basins, at their
mountain streams, their forests and deserts, their people, and their
fish. Each story illustrates how these basins are unified by their many
parts, and each shows how the whole basin suffers when humans iso-
late and elevate one part above the others. Often that single part is
the water itself—diverted from the river, stored to be used at a more
convenient time, or transported to faraway locations. This approach
may threaten the entire ecosystem. Decisions and commitments

about water use may sometimes find economic justification but sacrifice values that lack easy economic measures; may help one part of the basin to the detriment of another; or may promote short-term benefits without regard to long-term effects. The price of focusing on a single part of a watershed is high indeed, as demonstrated by the stories of these western river basins.

THE COLUMBIA: HYDRORIVER

> There were some sockeye in Mason Lake, south of Hood Canal (Puget Sound area). These ran up Sherwood Creek from Allyn on Case Inlet. They'd hang around the lake till ripe, then run up the creeks from there. The Squaxon got them with a weir in Sherwood Creek. Finally a pioneer named Sherwood built a little dam in the creek and stopped the fish, and they named the creek after him.
>
> HENRY ALLEN : a Twana Indian born about 1865,
> quoted in "Pacific Salmon at the Crossroads."

The Pacific Northwest. Stretching from waterlogged rainforests on the Olympic Peninsula to desolate plains formed from primeval lava flows. Land of ancient cultures, ancient forests, and an ancient river that once burst through a frozen ice age dam and created potholes hundreds of feet deep and many miles wide. Home of the salmon.

The large, strikingly colored fish that evoked beautiful descriptive names—sockeye, coho, chinook—the salmon has long mystified humans with its fantastic anadromous life journey. A young salmon is hatched in a high mountain stream or lake, drifts and swims hundreds of miles downstream and out to the open sea, travels north to the fertile coastal waters of British Columbia and Alaska, and then after several years—grown, nourished, and ready to procreate—makes one final journey back upstream to the very place it was hatched, to spawn and die. Salmon are so specialized in their adaptation that biologists identify "stocks," or interbreeding populations of fish that live in relative isolation from others. Thus, the Columbia River basin is home not only to various species of the salmon, but also to hundreds of stocks of those salmon: Hood River spring race chinook, Umpqua River chum, and Redfish Lake sockeye, to name three.

Salmon meat once supported populations of some fifty thousand

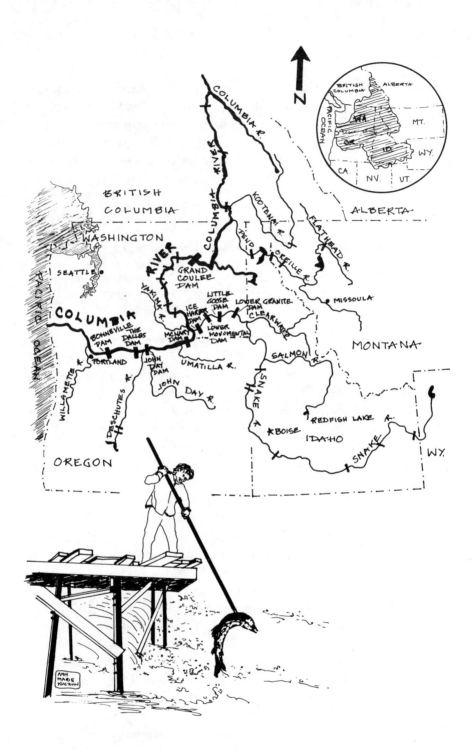

Northwest Indians who ate it, traded it, and expressed their appreciation by celebrating the first salmon to arrive each spawning season. The very presence of salmon defined the Pacific Northwest. Sent to explore the United States' new territory, Lewis and Clark knew they had arrived on the Pacific side of the Continental Divide when the Shoshone Indians fed them fresh salmon at a camp near the Lemhi River (a tributary of the Salmon River, which is itself a tributary of the Snake and thus the Columbia). As they drew closer to the ocean, the explorers enjoyed rich feasts of salmon, oysters, and clams. They observed Indian fishing stations along the entire length of the lower Columbia River. At one point Captain Clark wrote of "great numbers" of stacks of dried and pounded salmon, each stack comprising about 1,200 pounds of fish: "Great quantities as they inform us are sold to the whites people who visit the mouth of this river as well as to the nativs below."

The fish could reach enormous size. On the Elwha River in Washington, for example, the spring chinook lived ten to twelve years and sometimes grew to one hundred pounds, apparently an adaptation that ensured their survival navigating the river's narrow canyons and fierce rapids. Other chinook in the river averaged about twenty-two pounds, still a sizeable fish.

Salmon once seemed as bountiful as the enormous waters of the Columbia River; neither appeared vulnerable to control or depletion. Yet this perception was wrong. The river that had formed over twenty million years to drain 260,000 square miles of land was harnessed and subdued in the course of just a few decades by ambitious engineers driven by war and a national frenzy of growth and development. Fish that had thrived in its abundant waters for millennia fought valiantly against obstructions but inevitably dwindled in numbers and well-being. Though the story is not over for the Columbia River, for an estimated one hundred stocks of salmon and steelhead it ended in extinction.

The first structures on the Columbia River were wooden scaffolds from which Indian fishermen speared, netted, and trapped as many as eighteen million pounds of fish annually. The most important Indian fishing site was the spectacular Celilo Falls, 200 miles from the Pacific Ocean, where the river narrowed and gushed through 8 miles of cascades and waterfalls. Fish struggling to navigate this stretch were relatively easy to catch; as many as three thousand Indians would gather at the falls during spawning runs. The stacks of salmon prepared for trading that Captain Clark described were from Celilo Falls. Celilo Falls was more than a source of physical sustenance; it was a religious and cultural touchstone.

Non-Indian fishing became a major industry in the Pacific Northwest. In the early years, fish were dried, salted, and packed in wooden barrels. In 1866, when the new process of canning came to the Columbia River basin, far greater numbers of salmon could be packed and shipped to distant markets. Within twenty years, commercial canners were packing about thirty million pounds of salmon annually. More efficient fishing methods were invented or adapted from Indian practice, including large fish traps and fish wheels that scooped up fish by the ton. The commercial fishery grew even more valuable when refrigerated shipping was developed around the turn of the century. Commercial harvests went almost unregulated until the 1930s.

In addition to the fishermen, early non-Indian settlers came to the Yakima, Willamette, and other Northwest valleys in the 1800s, drawn by glowing descriptions of the region's salubrious climate and fertile soils. Their small diversion dams in the Columbia's tributaries were supplemented by larger irrigation projects financed by the federal government under the auspices of the Reclamation Act of 1902. Eventually, irrigated agriculture became the largest diverter of water from the Columbia River, withdrawing over 30 million acre-feet each year (of which approximately half was used in such a way that the water was lost to the river).

At the same time that farmers were harvesting their first crops with Columbia River water, business and political leaders were putting their heads together to figure out how to improve the navigation on this inland waterway. Ocean-going vessels could penetrate as far as the mouth of the Willamette River near Portland, but at that point they were stymied by narrow channels, steep drops, and other obstacles. That was frustrating: other than those impediments, the river offered the widest, deepest, and longest navigation route west of the Mississippi. It seemed inevitable that engineers would re-shape the river to fit human needs.

The Bonneville Dam, completed in 1938, was the first of the federal multipurpose water projects on the Columbia River. It was built to provide a safe channel for ships to reach inland ports, to control floodwaters coursing down the river channel, and to generate hydroelectric power. Its system of locks lifts ships as much as 67 feet each and sets them into magically placid waters to continue their journeys undisturbed by rocks, rills, and other dangers of natural river flow. Bonneville was followed in short order by dozens of other dams, some intended to extend navigation farther inland, others more directly focused on the generation of electricity for homes and industry. The result has been described as a "stairstep series of slackwater reservoirs," a far cry from the surging flows of the river that had flushed young salmon smolt seaward for centuries.

Navigation was an important historical use of rivers such as the Columbia. But as the Depression spurred the need for public works projects to create jobs and World War II and the subsequent economic boom demanded expansion of manufacturing, engineers were more keenly attracted by the hydroelectric generating capacity of large federal dams. The mighty Columbia was an irresistible target. The river was huge by western standards—its volume ten times more than that of the Colorado River and second only to the Mississippi River in the lower forty-eight. The basin's cities were poised for growth and industrial expansion. The stage was set for massive development.

Within a few decades, the Columbia River basin was plugged from top to bottom with dams. By 1985 there were 19 mainstem dams and 128 hydropower and multipurpose projects in the basin, with a total storage capacity of over 67 million acre-feet of water, including the Grand Coulee Dam, which holds over 5 million acre-feet. The projects made the river navigable for 500 miles by tug and barge from the mouth up to central Idaho on the Snake River.

One of the most tragic episodes in the creation of the Columbia-Snake hydroelectric complex involved the inundation of Celilo Falls in 1956. Seventy-five feet of water buried more than a hundred centuries of cultural and historical traditions when the Army Corps of Engineers closed the gates at the Dalles Dam. The Indian tribes received cash settlements, but few believed that their loss could be measured in dollars. Hydropower—and raw political power—won out over tradition and treaty-promised fishing rights.

The Columbia-Snake fishery has suffered from these assaults. From estimated runs of 10–16 million salmon and steelhead before non-Indians arrived, today's numbers are around 2.5 million (only about one-quarter of which are native stock). Entire stocks have been wiped out, and others are nearly gone. Dams make access difficult to much of the salmon's original spawning habitat. An estimated one-third to one-half of the habitat is now completely inaccessible to migrating fish. But the adult fish swimming upstream may have it easier than the smolts heading for the sea. The highly regulated flows in the Columbia River fail to flush those young fish at anywhere near the speed of the unharnessed river. It now takes young chinook salmon an additional forty to fifty days to reach the ocean during low-flow years, increasing its susceptibility to predation and impeding its ability to convert from a freshwater to a salt-water environment. Until fish screens were installed, many of the young fish perished in hydroelectric turbines.

In the spring of 1991 the American Fisheries Society published a comprehensive report on the status of Pacific salmon. It concluded that, in addition to one hundred now extinct stocks, seventy-six native salmon and steelhead stocks in the Columbia River basin are in danger of extinction or otherwise deserve "special concern." Some of the remaining stocks, it acknowledged, may already be extinct; many others are in danger of losing their genetic identity through interbreeding with hatchery stocks. The report attributed the declines to a variety of factors: loss of and damage to habitat, plus inadequate passage and flows caused by hydropower, agriculture, logging, and other developments; overfishing; and negative interactions with other fishes, including non-native hatchery salmon and steelhead. Among these, historical overfishing and hydroelectric dam operations are likely the most important.

The plight of the salmon is perhaps best understood from the vantage point of a single spawning site. Idaho's Redfish Lake was named for the brightly colored migrating fish that returned each October to spawn on its shores. Before the dams, tens of thousands of Snake River sockeye salmon would navigate the 7,000-foot climb through 900 river miles to reach the lake. In the 1950s (after passage was impeded by a dam), adult counts ranged from 55 to 4,400. In the fall of 1991, only three males and one female made it to the lake. Finally, the National Marine Fisheries Service has listed the Snake River sockeye salmon as an endangered species. The few remaining fish are not allowed to risk the vicissitudes of nature, but are guarded and artificially spawned in a state hatchery. The American Fisheries Society concluded that "[t]he Snake River sockeye is now considered to be functionally extinct."

Columbia River salmon have suffered a tremendous decline as a result of hydroelectric generation, overexploitation, timber harvesting, irrigation diversions, and other development in the basin. Yet there is some reason for hope. The Northwest Power Planning Council, an interstate organization formed after Congress passed the Northwest Power Act in 1980, is pursuing an innovative effort to restore the anadromous fishery, as well as to ensure adequate power supplies for the region. Among its approaches, the Council has designed a "water budget" that releases water from the dams in a sequence that mimics natural surges during runoff periods. The Council hopes this hydrologic push will reduce smolt mortality and revive the fishery. The Indian tribes along the Columbia River have formed their own association, the Columbia River Inter-Tribal Fish Commission, whose cooperation is integral to the effectiveness of the Council.

Perhaps most important, there are proposals to remove some dams from tributaries of the Columbia, thus restoring the fishery to an extent that otherwise would not be possible. Thomas Bigeater, of the Warm Springs Tribes, expressed a long-term view in a special 1991 issue of the *High Country News*: "This is not forever. Dams break. Rivers never do. Two salmon can spawn a thousand. The salmon are an old and patient people."

THE RIO GRANDE: "WHERE THUNDER IS SACRED AND THE RAIN IS A GOD"

> Who is this that cometh?
> People of the dark cloud,
>   Let your thoughts come to us!
> People of the lightning,
>   Let your thoughts come to us!
> People of the blue-cloud horizon,
>   Let your thoughts come to us!
> Rain! Rain! Rain!
>
>   MARY AUSTIN: "Rain Songs from the Rio Grande Pueblos,"
>   in *The American Rhythm*

At some times and some places the Rio Grande is not a "river" in the ordinary sense of the word: its entire flow is diverted or evaporated out of the shallow riverbed. Rainfall is scarce—as little as 8 inches per year in much of the basin—and when the rains come, they come in flood-producing torrents that turn the river into a raging monster. The earth around the river has been trampled into submission by hooves. All the Rio Grande's natural runoff is controlled by dams, and supplemental flows are piped in from the Colorado River.

At the same time, the Rio Grande is more than a river. It's an international boundary, an interstate boundary, and—until humans arrived—it was the fundamental agent of change in this arid southwestern country. "Above all," wrote Harvey Fergusson in describing the Rio Grande valley in 1933, "it is a land where water has always been scarce and therefore precious, a thing to be fought for, prayed for, and cherished in beautiful vessels—a land were thunder is sacred and rain is a god." This is more than a desert with a river running through its middle; it is, in historian Paul Horgan's words, a "riverscape." And, in this riverscape, humans are an indelible part of the watershed.

The earliest settlers of the Rio Grande were the Indian irrigators—the descendants of the Anasazi who moved south from the Four Corners region in the thirteenth century. By all accounts, the Pueblo Indians used the water from the Rio Grande modestly. Unlike Anglo-European farmers who came later, the Indians tended to farm close to the river and to use simple ditches to reach their crops.

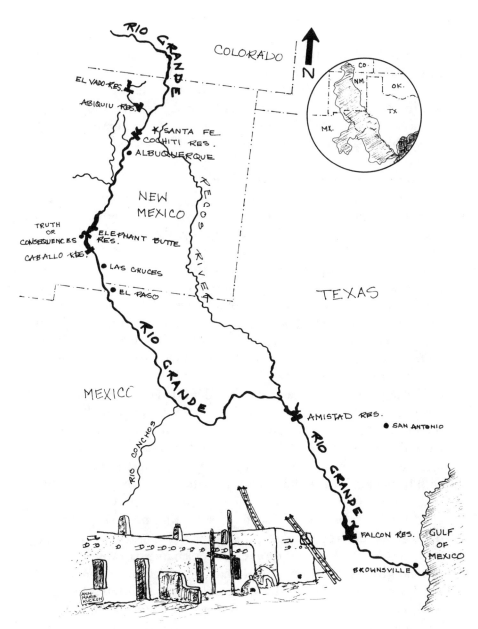

RIO GRANDE

COLORADO

N

CO.
NM.
OK.
MX.
TX.

EL VADO RES.

ABIQUIU RES.

SANTA FE
COCHITI RES.

ALBUQUERQUE

NEW
MEXICO

PECOS RIVER

TRUTH
OR
CONSEQUENCES

ELEPHANT BUTTE
RES.

CABALLO RES.

LAS CRUCES

EL PASO

TEXAS

MEXICO

RIO GRANDE

RIO CONCHOS

AMISTAD RES.

SAN ANTONIO

RIO GRANDE

FALCON RES.

GULF
OF
MEXICO

BROWNSVILLE

ANN MARIE KUCZUN

Floods and droughts had little but short-term effect on their livelihood, since these farmers adapted their methods to fit the dynamics
of the river. Their reverence for the value of water was demonstrated in their ceremonies and creation stories.

The Pueblo Indians still farm in the Rio Grande basin. In the sixteenth century they were joined by Spanish settlers, who brought
the acequia system of community ditches to the area. Mexican settlers subsequently came north into the area. Then settlers from the
eastern United States migrated to the Rio Grande in the 1800s,
quickly settling into the fertile bottomlands. They proved to be
much less adaptable to the river's changing moods, more willing to
exert brute force to tame its course. As more people moved into the
basin and began to exploit its resources—land and water—the basin
itself began to change.

The human footprint lies heavy on the Rio Grande. Perhaps we
should say the "hoofprint," for much of the physical change has
come from the cows, sheep, and other livestock first introduced to
this arid region by the Spanish and Mexicans and continuing with
the nineteenth-century settlers. The hoofed creatures made life easier for humans, but in excessive numbers they wreaked havoc on the
desert vegetation in the Rio Grande watershed. First, they ate most
everything they could reach and thus denuded entire hillsides. The
newly exposed earth dried out in the hot sun and was unable to resist
the eroding effects of heavy rain showers. Topsoil simply washed
away, the runoff first creating narrow gullies and then wide arroyos,
tearing off any remaining vegetation in the flood and filling the river
with heavy loads of sediment. Second, the sheer weight of the animals was death to desert soil structure; once compacted and hard-
ened, the soil's ability to absorb moisture and nourish plants was
damaged or destroyed.

Over time, the Rio Grande's vegetation changed dramatically. Perennial grasses (those that grow back from permanent roots each
year), which were so valuable as forage and as soil stabilizers, gave
way to annual grasses (grasses that reproduce from seed each year
and never develop extensive root systems) and shrubs. Entire plant
communities migrated upward to higher elevations, a typical reaction to severe stress. And the land's capacity to accommodate hu-

mans and their domesticated beasts was nearly destroyed. The river filled with silt from the heavy erosion, but heavy spring flows flushed the silt downstream—that is, until the new federal Reclamation Service built the first mainstem dam on the Rio Grande in 1916 and effectively placed a concrete stopper right in the middle of the river.

Elephant Butte Dam, a project intended to expand irrigated agriculture in the middle Rio Grande Valley (the section of the river between Albuquerque and El Paso), was not welcomed with open arms by local farmers. Valley residents, especially Hispanic farmers with small plots who had lived there for generations, resisted the federal government's insistence that they form a water-users association to assume partial responsibility for repaying the costs of the dam's operation. Their resistance was overcome, however, by enthusiastic proponents of reclamation and development.

When it was built, the Elephant Butte Dam was the largest water storage facility in the United States, with a capacity of 2.6 million acre-feet of water. It worked. It held spring flows from melting snow for use later in the dry summer and fall. But this success bred a host of new problems. First, the silt-free waters pouring from the dam ran at a high velocity, scouring and deepening the riverbed downstream from Elephant Butte and dragging more sediment from its banks. Second, silt dropped out of the water where river flows crawled to a near halt at the inflow to the reservoir, forming huge shallow deltas and flooding upstream farms and communities. Finally, the lifespan of the reservoir itself is now threatened by the accumulation of silt behind Elephant Butte Dam; it has already lost nearly a quarter of its original capacity.

In short, the dam may have created more problems than it solved. As waters backed up behind the dam and as the growing delta pushed water outward from the river, upstream farmers were forced to abandon their lands. Some built levees to hold the river back, but it kept rising. The total number of irrigated acres in the valley actually dropped—from 125,000 acres in 1880 to 40,000 acres in 1924—due in part to the spreading river and waterlogged soils. Farmers and public officials complained, and the Army Corps of Engineers stepped in to help. Shortly the Rio Grande was straightened, dammed further, and otherwise manipulated to keep the water in the course most convenient to its human users. The Corps even built several dams on tributaries specifically devoted to trapping silt. By the end of the flood control campaign, the river was about 300 miles shorter than its original length.

In an effort to share the expenses of flood control measures and to obtain additional water supplies, Albuquerque officials urged the formation of a regional conservancy district. After much administrative wrangling and pressure on local farmers to cooperate, the Middle Rio Grande Conservancy District was created in 1925. Looking back in 1951, historian Albert Williams proclaimed that the District "saved Albuquerque and the surrounding farm lands upon which the city must feast from a grave of mud and swamp." In so doing, though, this new creature (following in the footsteps of the cattle and sheep that preceded it) left its mark all over the river basin, on its geography, economy, culture, and wildlife.

First, the District assumed broad land-use, taxing, and condemnation powers. What Albert Williams called a shining example of "Democracy in Action," was viewed differently by those who suddenly found themselves financially liable for its operations. Seventy acequia associations were absorbed into the District, which was funded by assessments demanded of those beneficiaries. Hispanic farmers who owned small plots divided to subsistence size by many generations of inheritance, were burdened with assessments to pay the costs of District operations and projects. If farmers fell behind in payments, the District could exercise its liens on their property. In a 1941 decision, *Tondre v. Garcia*, the New Mexico Supreme Court upheld the District's authority to sell properties whose owners failed to pay their assessments.

Second, the District had a voracious appetite for water. It sought to irrigate an area 7 miles wide and 125 miles long—a goal requiring more water than the river reliably could provide, even with the guaranteed deliveries of water in the 1938 Rio Grande Compact, an agreement among the states that share the river's water. The District's thirst was more than matched by that of the growing city of Albuquerque, which sought water to fuel its expanding defense industry. Out of those two pressures for more water, and other political motivations, was born the San Juan–Chama Project in the 1950s.

The idea of the Project was about as far as one could deviate from the Pueblos' attitudes toward water. It said, in effect, "This river's not big enough for what we want to do here; we'll make it bigger." There were, in fact, many reasons this idea was attractive to political leaders at the time. In the 1948 interstate compact dividing the Upper Colorado River basin water, New Mexico had been guaranteed 11.25 percent (an average of 647,000 acre-feet) of the Colorado River's flow annually. The only natural source of that water reaching the state was the San Juan River, a tributary of the Colorado River running through the sparsely populated northwest corner of New Mexico. The state wanted to claim its entitlement, and move it to where the people were, even if not all the water was needed yet. Moreover, the Middle Rio Grande Conservancy District saw the San Juan–Chama Project as a source of water to fill its growing number of irrigation reservoirs and ensure irrigation water during dry years.

The Project was completed in 1974. It now moves 110,000 acre-feet of water from the Colorado River basin to the Rio Grande basin, dropping it into Heron Reservoir at the confluence of Willow Creek and the Rio Chama, a tributary of the Rio Grande. The project includes three diversion dams, two siphons, and a tunnel through the watershed divide.

The "new" water piped into the Rio Grande created a whole new set of problems. On its way downstream to the thirsty farms and cities, the water flows past four Pueblos, that have used Rio Grande water for centuries for irrigation and domestic needs. Until recently, however, the quantity of the Pueblos' water rights had not been recognized by a court. Thus, when the Conservancy District and Albuquerque asserted their rights to the San Juan–Chama water, the Pueblos objected that those claims would interfere with their use of the river. After years of expensive and divisive litigation, the conflict remains unresolved.

In addition, it became clear that the proponents of the project had overestimated their needs for this water. As the full project went into operation, excess water began to fill reservoirs behind flood control dams—such as Abiquiu and Cochiti—that were never intended to be used for water storage. At Abiquiu, rising waters began to inundate a stretch of the Rio Chama that was highly valued for whitewater rafting; it also began flooding adjacent privately held lands. As the reservoir behind Cochiti Dam rose, it flooded the archaeological sites at Bandelier National Monument—burying relics of ancient cultures under silt and water. Though there was no foreseeable use for all that water in New Mexico, state officials preferred to store it to keep the water from flowing to Texas or Mexico.

What will become of the riverscape of the Rio Grande? Its history reveals a constant theme of human dependence on water. Those who lived on the river earliest showed how to adapt to the limitations of the arid country—they incorporated deeply held values for the scarce water into their use of it. Those who came later dismissed such practices as primitive and sought to subdue the river's unpredictability. As the river continues to dump its silt behind concrete dams and threatens to overcome human controls, the values of the original residents of the Rio Grande still may prove viable.

THE SACRAMENTO: RIVER OF SEASONS

> The finest striped and black bass fishing in the world is found in these waters. Numberless, also, are perch, crappy, and catfish. Otter slides and beaver dams abound. Quail and doves thrive. At the end of summer come clouds of ducks and geese and snipe.
>
> JULIAN DANA : *The Sacramento: River of Gold*

It must have been about as close to paradise on earth as humankind has seen. Joaquin Miller, nineteenth-century poet and adventurer, gave his first impression of the Sacramento River valley: "Silver rivers run here, the sweetest in the world. They wind and wind among the rocks and mossy roots, with California lilies, and the yew with scarlet berries dipping in the water, and the trout idling in the eddies and cool places by the basketful." He described a fantastic scene in late spring when spawning salmon were so thick "that it was impossible to force a horse across the current."

The valley floor runs about 200 miles long, from the solitary volcanic cone of Mount Shasta ("the most comely and perfect snowpeak in America," wrote Miller) to the Sacramento–San Joaquin Delta, a labyrinth of marshes and channels in which the waters of the Pacific Ocean mix with Sierra snowmelt. In its historical path the river

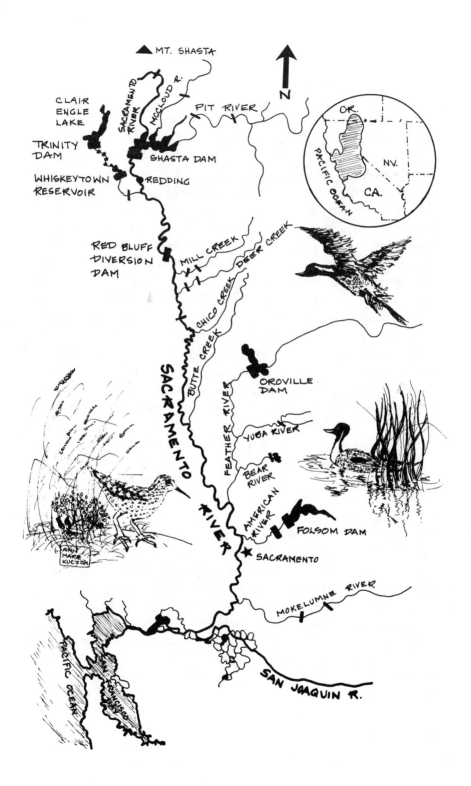

MT. SHASTA

N

OR.

PACIFIC OCEAN

NV.

CA.

CLAIR ENGLE LAKE

TRINITY DAM

WHISKEYTOWN RESERVOIR

SACRAMENTO RIVER

MCCLOUD R.

PIT RIVER

SHASTA DAM

REDDING

RED BLUFF DIVERSION DAM

MILL CREEK

CHICO CREEK

DEER CREEK

BUTTE CREEK

SACRAMENTO RIVER

FEATHER RIVER

OROVILLE DAM

YUBA RIVER

BEAR RIVER

AMERICAN RIVER

FOLSOM DAM

SACRAMENTO

MOKELUMNE RIVER

PACIFIC OCEAN

SAN FRANCISCO BAY

SAN JOAQUIN R.

ANN MARIE KUCZUN

ebbed and flowed with the seasons, creating rich "little edens" that delighted Joaquin Miller.

During the winter the Sacramento River valley was soaked by heavy rains, which fed the lush grasses and grains that made the valley green. The valley was filled with millions of ducks, geese, and other waterfowl—finding in this marshy paradise the food, warmth, and shelter they needed to thrive on their annual migratory loop. Early visitors described grasses tall enough to brush horsemen's knees and skies darkened with "clouds of geese." In the rolling hills above the river, specially adapted plants in rain-fed vernal pools (seasonal marshes) greeted winter storms with a flush of color. Winter, a dormant season in most of the country, was a celebration of life in the Sacramento Valley.

In the spring, swollen with melted snow, the river spread to cover as much as a quarter of the Sacramento Valley. Its flooding waters carried nutrient-rich sediment to build the fertile soil. Migrating salmon traveled upward during this runoff season, seeking gravel beds in the clear headwater streams in which to spawn. At the other end of the river, heavy freshwater flows pushed through the Sacramento–San Joaquin Delta and into the San Francisco Bay, literally moving the ocean back from its path up the estuary.

As the rains tapered off in the summer and fall, the Sacramento River slowed, warmed, parted into separate channels, and more closely resembled the languid "silver rivers" that Joaquin Miller described. The burning valley sun parched the foothills a tawny gold. The meandering, braided river nourished cottonwoods and other riparian vegetation, creating a 5-mile-wide green swath across the valley floor. As freshwater flows dwindled, the salt water of the Pacific Ocean moved upstream, bringing marine organisms into the vast mixing zone of the estuary.

These seasonal fluctuations were the very essence of the Sacramento River: water flows that varied by as much as 750 percent between fall and spring, seasonal floods that watered and enriched the soil, a serpentine river path that offered shelter and sustenance to fish and wildlife, an artery between the water-rich coastal mountains and the dry Central Valley.

That all changed rather suddenly. Historian Julian Dana put it well when he wrote that, "American history began latest and ran fastest along the Sacramento." It wasn't that the river had been ignored before the discovery of gold on one of its tributaries in 1848, but earlier non-Indian settlers had more or less adapted to the river's seasons, grazing cattle on the lush grass or growing dryland wheat irrigated only by winter rainfall. Two related developments changed the course of the river forever: hydraulic gold-mining and Delta farming.

The forty-niners must have been disappointed to learn that much of the Sierra gold did not lie in neat deposits, ready for the taking. Some of it was buried in the gravel along the streambeds, often in hard-to-reach small deposits. The miners soon invented a sluice box, which worked on the same principle as gold washing through mountain streams—running water, over time, will carry materials downhill, and heavy minerals such as gold will settle out if obstructed—on a much accelerated timescale. But the sluice box was labor-intensive, demanding movement of huge quantities of gravel. After several frustrating years, two miners named Joe Wood and Jack Payne built the first hydraulic mining device, which washed soil and gravel from a hillside into a sluice box with water under pressure from a hose. This sped the process up tremendously. Hydraulic mining caught on, and soon nearly every stream in Northern California was carrying mud from washed-out hillsides.

Miners' fortunes were more than balanced by the resulting devastation suffered downstream. At the height of the hydraulic mining boom, Joaquin Miller mourned the death of rivers he remembered as clear and strong, "that since have become turbid yellow pools with barren banks of boulders, shorn of their overhanging foliage, and drained of flood by ditches that the resolute miner has led even around the mountain top." Miller also lamented the destruction of salmon spawning grounds, buried beneath the sediments of mining wastes.

Farmers suffered when the slick mud filled the riverbed and sent floodwaters flowing over banks and levees to inundate their fields. Ultimately, it was legal action by those farmers that brought an end to the practice of hydraulic mining thirty-five years after it began, but not until over 2 billion cubic yards of mining wastes were deposited downstream.

Sacramento Valley farmers readily blamed miners for the destructive floods that ravaged their lands. Indeed, there is no question that the waves of mud took their toll. But the farmers were not without responsibility for the disasters. In their efforts to "reclaim" the fertile soils of the Sacramento River basin, farmers first settled on the flat lands where the river had deposited nutrient-rich silt. Then they edged onto the fertile lands that had historically been flooded by the river, repelling the river's seasonal floodwaters with earthen levees, ever larger and ever subject to defeat by the course of the river.

The first levee was a small affair, about 3 feet high and 12 feet across at the base, built by a vegetable farmer several miles downstream from Sacramento in 1850. Although it was washed out by the rain-swollen river within two years, the idea caught on, and settlers throughout the lower Sacramento River basin began creating curious sunken "islands" by diking river water from fertile bottomland. The river continued to deposit sediments (supplemented considerably by the mining debris washing downstream), thus building up its base, so the diked-off lands soon lay below river level.

The rains returned, as they periodically had, and a series of levee-breaking years followed: 1861, 1868, 1876, 1877, and 1881. Each time the levees broke, the Sacramento River lowlands filled with water. Cattle were stranded on broken levees, hundreds of people drowned, and the tops of trees in orchards bobbed like apples in the water. With astounding persistence, the settlers rebuilt the levees after each flood, finally erecting them over 100 feet wide and dozens of feet high.

Today there are over 1,000 miles of levees and fifty-seven diked-off islands in the lower Sacramento River. And, on a much grander scale, the Army Corps of Engineers has constructed a massive flood control project in the river that includes ninety-five miles of bypasses (channels that divert water around the river's course), fifty miles of drainage canals, and three major drainage pumping plants; over one-third of the lower river's banks are now denuded of vegetation and lined with wire-covered (or "riprapped") rocks.

Upriver, the Sacramento's headwaters are stopped up behind the Shasta Dam, completed in 1945. The dam has the capacity to hold 4.5 million acre-feet of spring runoff, which is then released during the historically dry summer months to provide water for irrigated agriculture throughout the Central Valley. The Shasta Dam is the linchpin in the Central Valley Project, or CVP, operated by the Bureau of Reclamation. In addition to the Shasta Dam, the CVP includes dams on the American, Trinity, and San Joaquin rivers. Water stored upstream is conveyed through the Sacramento River and through the Delta, pumped into the Delta-Mendota Canal, and sent to farms in the San Joaquin Valley to the south. The State Water Project (SWP) also uses the Sacramento River as a channel for water delivery. The SWP begins at the Oroville Dam on the Feather River, which releases water down the Sacramento River, through the Delta, and into the 444-mile-long California Aqueduct to Southern California.

Excited about the Central Valley Project, Julian Dana wrote in 1939 that the Shasta Dam "will leash forever the fury of the springtime floods and prevent the sluggish currents and low water of late summer. . . ." A promotional brochure published by the Southern Pacific Railroad in 1905 was equally rhapsodic about the coming flood control projects, concluding that "the great valley will be enhanced in beauty and enriched a thousand fold."

One has to wonder how Joaquin Miller would react to the now disciplined Sacramento River. He surely would decry the destruction of over 95 percent of the "little Edens" of wetlands that once carpeted the valley—now filled, drained, and no longer inundated by seasonal overflowing river water. The valley still provides wintering habitat to about two-thirds of the waterfowl on the Pacific Flyway, but the bird populations have declined to a small fraction of their original numbers, and they crowd together on the few remaining wetlands protected in national wildlife refuges. The sky no longer grows dark with geese.

Miller might marvel at the expanse of irrigated agriculture in the valley, but one speculates that he would miss the wide corridors of riparian vegetation that once surrounded the river. Of an original 500,000 acres of foliage, less than 5 percent remains.

At the headwaters of the Sacramento River, where he lived with Indians for a time and periodically worked on mining claims, Miller's eyes would pop at the 600-foot-high Shasta Dam. Just as he railed against the miners' pollution of salmon spawning grounds, he likely would protest the fact that the dam now blocks salmon from reaching over half of their cold-water spawning grounds. Just twenty years ago the winter-run species of Sacramento River chinook salmon numbered over eighty thousand (at that, well short of the horse-blocking multitudes that Miller observed); in 1990 only about five hundred fish made the trip up the Sacramento River to the Red Bluff Dam, and the National Marine Fisheries Service listed it as a threatened species (the first ocean-going fish to be listed) under the Endangered Species Act. Despite the legal protection, the 1991 count found only 191 adult fish in the river. The American Fisheries Society attributes the winter-run chinook's decline "to inadequate dam passage for adults; poor water flows and high water temperatures; and pollution and habitat damage from mining, irrigation diversions, river channelization, and bank stabilization."

Miller most certainly would be flummoxed by the legal and political battles now underway over the waters that flow through the Sacramento–San Joaquin Delta (much of which is siphoned south through the Central Valley Project's plumbing system). Hydrologists are battling over exactly what percentage of historical Sacramento River flows are now diverted upstream of the Delta and thus lost to the estuary. Experts on one side of the table have produced elaborate calculations to show that average annual freshwater flows (about 22 million acre-feet per year) are undiminished. They cannot dispute, however, that the timing and intensity of the flows are profoundly changed by the hundreds of diversions and impoundments on the river. Nearly all agree that the Sacramento River's spring flows are less than half of their original levels.

Perhaps the conclusion that Joaquin Miller would draw from all this is that the Sacramento River has simply lost its seasons. The price of this loss is still being calculated.

THE COLORADO: A RIVER DIVIDED

> Just four hundred years from the time the first white man sailed into its
> mouth, the wildest and most violently beautiful river in the world had
> been broken to the needs of man.
>
>   Man at last has conquered the land. But to what ultimate end no one can
> say. There is only a vague, inquiet feeling that in all his scheme of domina-
> tion there is something he might have forgotten. It may well be that the
> river itself will have the last word, after all.
>
>   FRANK WATERS : *The Colorado*

No other large western river is asked to do as much with so little
water. Few other rivers are tortured to the extent that their waters
seldom reach the river's mouth. Frank Waters captured its importance when he wrote of the Colorado River that it is "the greatest single fact within an area of nearly a quarter million square miles." Despite being sucked dry and manhandled throughout its course, the
river remains a mighty force on both the land and the society in the
American Southwest.

In its 1,400-mile path to the sea, the river runs from the Never
Summer Mountain Range in the Colorado Rockies to the hottest,
driest lands in the United States. Although many cities depend on
the river's water, not many are near it. It is the most sparsely populated large river basin in the lower forty-eight. The river is managed
by the Bureau of Reclamation under the guidelines specified in the
collection of laws and agreements that constitute the "law of the
river."

Much of the river runs a steep course, dropping precipitously
through narrow canyons carved into an ancient sea floor, carrying
heavy loads of silt and sand in its speeding waters (thus the Spanish
name *Colorado*, which refers to the reddish color of the river's muddy
water). For all its force and grandeur, the river carries a relatively
small amount of water, about 13.5 million acre-feet in the average
year. But, as Frank Waters commented, the Colorado River is "bigger than its statistics."

It is a place where history is measured in geologic periods, written
in the layers of the exposed rocks. It is a vast, open country, but the
river itself is sometimes hidden from sight in thousand-foot-deep
chasms. John Wesley Powell, exploring the river in 1869 and again

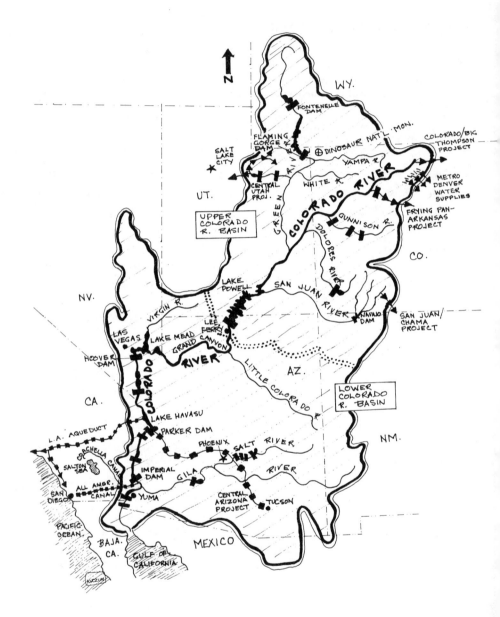

in 1871, found it both daunting and beautiful: "Wherever we look there is but a wilderness of rocks—deep gorges where the rivers are lost below cliffs and towers and pinnacles, and ten thousand strangely carved forms in every direction, and beyond them mountains blending with clouds." Edward Abbey, writing a century later, simply called it "earth in the nude."

Today's Colorado River was created by the marriage of two rivers, the Hualapai and the ancestral Upper Colorado, which joined together thirty-five million years ago. The river cut deeply through the up-lifting Kaibab Plateau to create the Grand Canyon—the mile-deep gash in the earth that would frustrate Spanish fortune-seekers and inspire urban thrill-seekers in future centuries. As it sliced through the rock to create those spectacular canyons, the river carried the earthen materials downstream, depositing some along occasional wide floodplains but dumping most of its load when it entered the Gulf of California.

The Colorado River Delta grew to cover an enormous area, more than 150 miles long and 100 miles across. Although much of it was a tidal plain, covered intermittently with sea water, a sufficient river channel existed to support a commercial steamship operation from 1865 to 1878. (The company went out of business when a railroad connected its upstream port city of Yuma with other trading posts.) Canoeing on the Delta in 1922, naturalist Aldo Leopold found an expanse of "green lagoons," through which the river meandered, and geese, quail, doves, egrets, bobcats, raccoons, and deer thrived. Leopold and his companions found those creatures "too abundant to hunt" and "of incredible fatness." The river, which spread its waters everywhere, seemed "reluctant to lose his freedom in the sea."

Leopold decided never to return to the Colorado River Delta, fearing that the loss of the green lagoons as the river was developed would tarnish these rich memories. Indeed, it has changed tremendously: the Delta is no longer part of the Colorado River, and only in rare, high-water years does any fresh water approach the mouth of the river. Of course this desiccation has changed the place. A more recent visitor, Philip Fradkin, described the Delta as "the most inhospitable terrain on the North American continent." Far upstream from the Delta, just below the last diversion structure, he observed that the "limp water" of the Colorado River "simply evaporates from shallow ponds." Fradkin concluded, it is "a river no more."

How has the Colorado River been lifted from its bed? Where does the water go if not to the sea? The story of the Colorado River is one of competition for a scarce resource. It might best be illustrated by imagining a pack of thirsty dogs all pulling on a wet towel, each gaining a few drops to slake its thirst but growing more famished for the effort of defeating the others. The dogs in this metaphor represent the seven states through which the Colorado River runs, as well as the Indian tribes located near the river and Mexico at the end of the river. All are seeking water and seeking to maintain a measure of control over the river. The river loses in this battle. Much of the water is removed from the Colorado River basin, evaporated from large reservoirs, or seeped through salt-laden soils before returning to the river. The river is divided in more ways than it can stand. Each division has been contentious and difficult, yet the resulting "law of the river" provides the unifying thread among the many who share the river's water.

The first official division of the river took place in 1922, when the basin states signed the Colorado River Compact. The compact was an effort to sort out competing claims to the river and to ensure that the slower-developing states would not be left without rights to use water as Southern California grew and demanded more diversions, particularly a large dam in Boulder Canyon.

This agreement apportioned the water roughly equally between the Upper Basin states (Colorado, Wyoming, Utah, and New Mexico) and the Lower Basin states (Arizona, Nevada, and California). This was the first time an interstate compact was used to apportion an interstate stream. Not all the parties were satisfied. Arizona, in particular, objected to being left to argue with California over rights to the Lower Basin's share, and thus refused to ratify the compact. After six years of wrangling, Congress resolved the impasse in 1928 with passage of the Boulder Canyon Project Act. This statute authorized construction of what would be called Hoover Dam, provided that the 1922 Compact could become effective with the ratification of only six of the seven basin states, required California to agree to a limit on its consumption of Colorado River water of 4.4 million acre-feet per year, and provided figures for the other Lower Basin states' shares of river water. With this accomplished, Hoover Dam construction proceeded, and California constructed a system of aqueducts to move its share of the water to farms and cities.

In 1944 Arizona finally ratified the compact, but the Lower Basin states never did agree on an allocation among themselves. That required a decision by the U.S. Supreme Court in 1968, ruling in *Arizona v. California* that the 1928 Boulder Canyon Project Act effected a congressional apportionment of the water. In the meantime, the Upper Basin states divided their share in 1948 through another interstate compact and formed the Upper Colorado River Commission.

There were some serious shortcomings in the 1922 division. First, the compact negotiators assumed that the average annual flow of the Colorado River was about 18 million acre-feet. In fact, 13.5 million acre-feet is closer to the average flow, and tree-ring data indicate historical annual flows of less than half that in especially dry years. This hydrologic error would ever after haunt the basin. The mistake works to the particular disadvantage of the Upper Basin, which is obligated to deliver a set quantity of water to Lee Ferry, the dividing point between the Upper and Lower Basins. If flows drop below the assumed level, the Upper Basin must forgo part of its allocation in order to satisfy the Lower Basin's entitlement.

There were other shortcomings. For example, the compact negotiators did not consider water entitlements of Indian tribes located in the Colorado River basin. Today, as courts are recognizing and quantifying those rights, it appears that the tribes may control a large proportion of Colorado River water. The Supreme Court's 1968 ruling held that Indian water rights should be charged against the entitlements of the states in which they are located.

The 1922 Compact negotiators acknowledged but did not fully address Mexico's water needs. Farmers in the fertile Mexicali Valley, just across the border from California's Imperial Valley, depended on flows from the Colorado River. For many years U.S. and Mexican negotiators argued about the United States' obligation to allow water to flow downstream to satisfy Mexicali farmers' growing demands. California, in particular, was concerned that Mexico's entitlement might infringe on its rights. Finally, in 1944, the United States signed a treaty with Mexico guaranteeing that at least 1.5 million acre-feet per year would remain in the river as it flowed across the southern border in the last part of its journey. Not long after that, when irrigation of salty soils and near total depletions of river flows sent the river's salt levels skyrocketing and poisoned the water flowing as far as Mexico, the United States was pressured to guarantee that water deliveries would be cleaned up enough for irrigation uses. That has turned out to be an expensive concession.

Meanwhile, the river tries to flow toward the sea. At the headwaters of the Colorado River in Rocky Mountain National Park, the Grand Ditch (built in 1892) siphons water from the snowmelt stream to carry it across the Continental Divide and on to farms down on the plains. Farther down the river, Colorado River water is diverted to irrigate crops in the Grand Valley, an ancient seabed thick with natural salts. The return flows add about 580,000 tons of salt per year, raising the river's salt level by about fifty-three parts per million, roughly double the river's salt level in its headwaters. After the federal government promised Mexico it would clean up the Colorado River water, the Bureau of Reclamation began working on major projects to intercept natural salts and to prevent addition of salts by improving irrigation methods and lining ditches. These efforts are estimated to cost about $250 million.

Onward the river flows and into the first of the big mainstem reservoirs, Lake Powell. (The Green River, which joins the Colorado upstream of Lake Powell, has already been stopped up in the Flaming Gorge Reservoir at the Utah-Wyoming border.) Lake Powell, which inundated Glen Canyon, can hold close to 27 million acre-feet of water—more than twice the river's annual flow. This dam was constructed in part to make it easier for the Upper Basin to meet its delivery obligations at Lee Ferry, just a few miles downstream from Glen Canyon, but the operation of the dam for hydroelectric power generation has been the dominant objective since it was completed. Colorado River hydropower generates over $500 million in revenues each year. The Western Area Power Administration (WAPA) is responsible for marketing this power to power suppliers serving sixteen million people in fifteen states. Until recently, WAPA ordered water releases based entirely on consumer demands for electricity, so the river's flows downstream of Glen Canyon (in the Grand Canyon) fluctuated as much as 13 vertical feet during the day. The river's "tides" are disruptive and even dangerous for boaters, but they are deadly to the fragile beaches and vegetation along the river's edge. Now that the river's heavy load of silt is backed up behind the dam, there is nothing to replenish the soil and sand washed away in these frequent mini-floods. Under growing pressure from biologists, boaters, and others, the Secretary of the Interior in 1991 ordered that the releases be modified to reduce the fluctuations. The Department of the Interior is preparing an environmental impact statement on dam operations.

Down beyond the Grand Canyon the river backs up again, this time behind the landmark Hoover Dam. It was California's pressure to build this dam (and thus make use of greater quantities of water than it previously had) that prompted the other basin states to convene and hammer out the 1922 Compact. This reservoir, Lake Mead, holds a bit more water than Lake Powell, 28 million acre-feet. A lot of that water is lost to evaporation—at least 7 vertical feet each year. (All told, about 2 million acre-feet evaporate from the river's mainstem reservoirs—more than Los Angeles' share of the river.) Below Lake Mead is Parker Dam, where the Colorado River Aqueduct diverts 1.2 million acre-feet per year to the Los Angeles metropolitan region and a few other points along the way. The Central Arizona Project has the capacity to divert 1.5 million acre-feet per year in the other direction, flowing to Arizona's cities and farms.

Farther down is the Imperial Dam, where the All-American Canal takes 3 million acre-feet annually to irrigate vegetable, alfalfa, and cotton in the Imperial Valley. In 1905 the Colorado River flooded, breached its banks, and flowed for sixteen months into this sunken valley. The massive infusion of water into a basin with no outflow created the Salton Sea, now saltier than the ocean after many years of irrigation return flows and evaporation. The wayward Colorado River was finally set back in its course after hundreds of trainloads of rocks and wood were dumped in the breach.

The river runs on, past the Laguna and Morelos dams. It takes a turn for the worse at the Wellton-Mohawk Drain, where highly saline soils were lined with tiles and dewatered with scores of wells to drain salty water away from the crops and back to the river. The sudden influx of salty water in 1961 damaged crops in the Mexicali Valley, prompting an international crisis and eventually leading to the United States' construction of the gigantic Yuma desalting plant, at a cost of a quarter of a billion dollars.

Finally the river ends at a diversion ditch to Laguna Salada, in Mexico. Just downstream of this structure, Philip Fradkin observed that the water remaining in the river actually appeared to flow back upstream, toward the final diversion: "The end of the river," he wrote, "was now all too apparent."

The Colorado River is a good example of a resource stretched too far and among too many. In recent years the stakes have grown higher. California has enjoyed its position near the end of the river to use water that belongs to upstream states that have not yet built the projects that would allow them to develop their allotments. Now that the Central Arizona Project has been completed (the final extension began delivering water to Tucson in 1991) and part of this "surplus" water is no longer available, California is scrambling to secure reliable supplies for the future. One proposal is to establish an interstate water bank into which states could deposit quantities of unused water for which others could pay to use the water temporarily. This proposal has met with skepticism from Upper Basin states, fearing that even the briefest release of control over their allotment may result in its loss. The Colorado River Indian tribes, on the other hand, appear amenable to the prospect of leasing their water entitlements.

Perhaps the scrapping dogs metaphor holds a lesson. So long as the fighting dogs grow thirstier and fiercer, the only possible outcome is a destroyed towel and a lot of injured, thirsty beasts. Cooperation among the basin states—as difficult as that may be to imagine—may be the only way to save this divided river. There is a community of shared interests in the Colorado River basin, but its members are practically strangers.

THE MISSOURI: RIVER OF SACRIFICE

> The Missouri was a devil of a river . . . it was no river at all but a great loose
> water that leaped from the mountains and tore through the plains, wild to
> get to the sea.
>
> A.B. GUTHRIE, JR. : *The Big Sky*

It's a river with wanderlust. It's an erratic river. It's a river that has been developed—often for not much more than the sake of development—at the expense of societies that had been living on its banks for centuries, and thus it is a river of sacrifice.

Asked to identify the longest river in the United States, most people would name the Mississippi, which runs 2,340 miles from headwaters to the Gulf of Mexico. But they would be wrong. The Missouri River—the massive tributary to the Mississippi that runs from the Rockies to St. Louis—is even longer, at 2,540 miles. The single waterway formed by the confluence of these two rivers is the longest in the world.

On its long journey toward the sea, the river flows over ice age debris—plains of "high loess," a loose conglomerate of packed dust left behind as the glaciers moved through. Running uncontrolled across this dusty floor for centuries, the river easily shifted from side to side, rather than carving deeply into the earth in the mode of other western rivers. The big Missouri regularly shot its banks, cutting and swerving all over its broad valley. The river's twists and turns confounded settlers hoping to farm on its banks; they would suddenly find their land washing toward St. Louis, the river having changed course by as much as a half mile in a single day.

The restless river literally carried the farms downstream. Mud was its primary cargo. The river gained its nickname of "Big Muddy" from the naturally heavy loads of sediment it washed down from the ancient plains, well over two hundred million tons per year. When the rains were heavy enough, the river uprooted trees and shrubs and carried them many miles away. An early non-Indian visitor to the Missouri River basin, Jesuit missionary Father Jacques Marquette, was awed by the sight of uprooted trees washing downstream at the mouth of the Missouri; he wrote in his journal, "I have

seen nothing more frightful . . . we could not, without great danger, expose ourselves to pass across."

Father Marquette's visit in the seventeenth century barely touched the half-million square miles of the Missouri River basin. The first major United States incursion did not occur until May 1804, when Meriwether Lewis and William Clark set out from the mouth of the river with orders from President Jefferson to inventory the lands, peoples, and resources of the recent Louisiana Purchase. Lewis and Clark traveled to the headwaters of the Missouri and from there crossed the Rockies to descend the Columbia River. On the first part of their trip, the explorers stayed with the Mandans and other Indians living along the Missouri River. The Indians guided their journey; one, a Shoshone woman named Sacajawea, traveled with them and (together with her French fur-trapper husband) guided them all the way to the sea.

Ancestors of the Mandans began farming in the Missouri River basin as early as A.D. 800, building villages and tilling soil on terraces above the river's floodplain. They grew corn, squash, beans, sunflowers, and tobacco, sometimes using the river water for irrigation. They hunted game on the plains and fished the Missouri River for catfish, sturgeon, turtles, and mussels. Around the year 1400, other groups began moving into the area, and by the 1700s the basin's Indians had horses and were dealing with non-Indian traders. As the United States settled the eastern plains, other tribes moved into the Missouri River basin and brought their traditions of ranging over wide areas to hunt bison and other game. The influx of trappers in the early 1800s nearly exterminated the beaver from the basin's tributaries and the bison from the plains. Moreover, those newcomers brought smallpox, a disease to which the Indians fell by the thousands. More outsiders came to the basin to hunt gold in the 1860s; others moved in to farm the fertile lands. The Indians were in the way. The United States Army battled the Indians into submission and eventually forced them onto reservations. Many smaller bands were grouped together with others—often their historical enemies—and the reservations typically were located on poor land with little potential for irrigated agriculture.

The Mandans, still enjoying rewards for having hosted Lewis and

Clark, were relatively fortunate in receiving fertile river bottomland when they were grouped with the Hidatsa and Arikara bands in the Fort Berthold Reservation in 1851. Originally, the reservation included 12.5 million acres of land, but that was whittled down to only 430,000 acres by settlement legislation and other incursions over the years. Nonetheless, the Three Affiliated Tribes of the Fort Berthold Reservation enjoyed access to plentiful timber for building and firewood, lignite for heating fuel, and abundant deer and other game. Most important for their livelihood, the reservation's lands included fertile Missouri River bottomland with plenty of good cattle forage.

As the Indians were settling into their reservations, the non-Indian newcomers were confronting the challenges of agriculture west of the 100th meridian, where average annual rainfall drops below the critical level of 20 inches and most crops are unable to grow without supplemental water. The Reclamation Act of 1902 brought a few irrigation projects to the upper river basin, but they were plagued with problems. For instance, project water was delivered to lands containing soils unsuited for irrigation because of their high alkaline levels and poor drainage. There was little support for large-scale irrigation until the drought and dust storms of the 1930s. Suddenly the Bureau of Reclamation had an interested constituency in the Missouri River basin. The agency responded by preparing a plan for ambitious irrigation projects in the Upper Basin. Prepared by William Glenn Sloan, an assistant engineer with the Bureau, the plan proposed ninety dams and reservoirs, seventeen power plants, and irrigation of over 5 million acres of land. The Sloan Plan was submitted to Congress in May 1944.

Meanwhile, downstream from the high loess plains of the Upper Basin, the Army Corps of Engineers was aching to do its work on the wandering river. The river's periodic floods were devastating to human settlements in the Lower Basin, and its habit of changing course on short notice made commercial shipping nearly impossible. The Corps wanted to straighten the river, shore up its banks with concrete and rock, and control its surging flows with regulating dams upstream. Again, it took an act of nature to bring this dream closer to reality: serious floods in 1943 encouraged the Corps to deliver a brief but ambitious plan to Congress. The Pick Plan, named for

Colonel Lewis A. Pick, who prepared it, included the construction of thirteen new dams, eleven others already authorized, and 800 miles of levees. The Pick Plan did not even consider irrigation potential in its proposed dam sites.

The two plans were fundamentally inconsistent, but refusing an "either-or" choice, Congress chose "and." The Pick-Sloan Plan, as incorporated into the Flood Control Act of 1944, was sold as a compromise but in fact was an impossible attempt to satisfy the competing agencies. The legislation contained nearly every project proposed in both Pick's and Sloan's plans. Writing shortly after the act was passed, historian Albert Williams termed it "a majestic pork-barrel and log-rolling spree." Perhaps because it aimed at pleasing everyone, there was little opposition to the legislation. Almost immediately upon passage, the Corps embarked on hundreds of mainstem river projects. The Bureau agreed to wait; many of its projects remain unbuilt today.

It seemed, at the time, that nearly everyone got something from the Pick-Sloan Plan. But that was not the case. The plan proposed mainstem reservoirs that would inundate hundreds of thousands of acres of Indian and non-Indian lands in the Upper Basin, displacing thousands of people from their homes and communities. Yet Congress did not see this as too high a price for development of the river's potential. At the time, the federal policy toward Indians was one of "assimilation"; the goal was to dissolve the reservations and encourage Indians to integrate with the larger society. The proposed reservoirs would simply speed the process. A project supporter seeking to justify the government's action, writer Richard Baumhoff in 1951 explained that "officials . . . regard this enforced removal from the reservoir areas as a challenging opportunity to make a fresh start with a large group of Indians."

The human price of this "fresh start" was a steep one, as evidenced by the tragedy at the Fort Berthold Reservation. There, where the Mandans, Hidatsa, and Arikara cultivated their fertile bottomlands, the Corps proposed its Garrison Dam. This 210-foot-high dam would flood most of the valuable land in the reservation and thus destroy the Indians' homes, timberlands, rangelands, and game habitat. The tribes objected to the project, but without support of their guardian agency, the Department of the Interior, their pleas fell on deaf ears. On May 20, 1948, in a ceremony in which the tribal representative broke into tears, the tribes signed a sales contract and settled for a payment of $33 an acre to give up 160,000 acres of their most valuable lands.

Soon thereafter, more than 90 percent of the Three Affiliated Tribes' two thousand members were relocated to arid plateaus above the Missouri River. Looking back recently, tribal members expressed bitterness at the move. "The tragedy is that we gave up a way of life," tribal council chair Alyce Spotted Bear said in a story reported by UPI in 1986, attributing a panoply of social and health problems to this historical dislocation. The statistics are grim: unemployment levels on the reservation have long exceeded 50 percent, diabetes and alcoholism are rampant, and infant death rates are about ten times the national average. Some additional compensation was promised in a 1991 congressional bill that established an economic recovery fund for the tribes from power receipts earned in the basin. The programs it funded will help address some of the problems, but none will bring back the fertile Missouri River bottomlands.

What was gained from this sacrifice? One might expect that the improvements would be impressive indeed, to have been exacted at such a high cost. In fact, the flood control works (which primarily benefit the Lower Basin states) have been successful; the Corps estimates that several million dollars in flood damage have been saved since the mainstem dams were built. But the other components of the Flood Control Act have not been as successful. The Missouri River has never become a thriving center of commercial river travel, for example. Barges run for just over 700 miles between St. Louis and Sioux Falls. At about two million tons annually, the Missouri's commercial shipping is a mere shadow of the six hundred million tons per year shipped on the Mississippi. This relatively insignificant business commands a huge volume of water from the upper river basin. Unlike the shipping channels on the Columbia River, where ships rise and fall through locks and float easily through slackwater reservoirs, Missouri River ships are carried by enhanced flows of water released from dams upstream—about 17 million acre-feet of water each year. This demands water from the Upper Basin, taking nearly all the natural flow in normal years and depleting reservoirs in dry years.

Moreover, the Upper Basin states never received the promised irrigation water. Although the Sloan Plan was to benefit over 5 million acres of farmland, less than one-tenth of the water has been developed. Montana, North Dakota, and South Dakota, each of which lost farmland when mainstem flood control reservoirs were filled, have gained only tiny fractions of the newly irrigated lands that were promised; some Upper Basin states have suffered a net loss of farmland. Upper Basin states have found that recreational use of the reservoirs is a far more significant source of revenues. Thus, the drawdowns for Lower Basin navigation (particularly in drought years) exact steep costs on the Upper Basin states. During a recent drought, for example, the Corps turned to reservoir releases to support Lower Basin navigation, lowering the levels of some artificial lakes in South Dakota by 30 feet or more. As boat ramps were marooned and fish habitat destroyed, fewer people chose to visit the area. The state saw a drop in income from reservoir tourism from $41.9 million in 1989 to $37.9 million in the following year. At the same time, the Corps' releases from the Oahe Dam threatened the valuable fishery in that reservoir. The Upper Basin states sued the Corps in an effort to keep water upstream.

How will these conflicts be resolved? Is there any opportunity for cooperation between the states, federal government, and tribes, or must the Missouri River's history of sacrifice continue? A nearly defunct interstate organization, the Missouri River Basin Association, has been revived, and the Northern Lights Institute (a nonprofit organization based in Missoula, Montana) has helped organize a Missouri River Assembly. These forums may help bring together the ten states, twenty-five Indian tribes, and various federal agencies that share an interest in the future of the basin, but it depends on setting aside bitter rivalries and making a rare interstate commitment to cooperation. Just as the Pick-Sloan Plan followed periods of droughts and floods, it may take a crisis to bring significant change in the Missouri River basin.

Chapter Six

Losing Sight of the Headwaters

> There are many ways to allocate scarce resources, and the
> triumph of prior appropriation was not inevitable.
>
> DONALD PISANI : *To Reclaim a Divided West*

T HE PRESENT condition of the
West's beleaguered river basins is no accident. The dams, the diversions, the depletions, and even the degradation are the direct results of laws and implicit policies adopted, for the most part, well
over a century ago to meet the needs of a frontier society. The dominant rule for allocating western water (the prior appropriation system), and then the reclamation laws enacted at the beginning of the
twentieth century, turned water into a tool of economic development. These laws and the policies they represent reflected the dominant priority of a nineteenth-century America, in which land and
minerals were in unparalleled abundance; only water, it was believed, was needed to realize the wealth. They were utilitarian laws
in which the sole function of water resources is to do a particular
kind of work for human benefit. And leave no doubt about it: rudimentary though they were, those early laws were effective in
achieving their goal: the creation of an extraction-based economy
to support the newly arriving American citizens in the era of Manifest Destiny.

Western water decisions continue to be dominated in many ways
by the early prior appropriation and reclamation laws. But perhaps
even more important, the use of most of the West's water still is governed by the rights that were established and the projects that were

128

built under those early laws. That legacy is now under challenge. Many of those water-use decisions, and the laws and policies that supported them, are being reconsidered; some are now viewed as inequitable and, often, as just plain wrong.

Law is sometimes painted as value-neutral, but in most cases law is value-laden, and it ought to be, for societies lodge many of their highest philosophical ideals, collective objectives, and passions in their laws. Surely this is evident in statutory law, the direct product of the political process. It is also true of judge-made law. In elaborating on his adage that "The life of the law has not been logic: it has been experience," Oliver Wendell Holmes explained, "The felt necessities of the time, the prevalent moral and political theories, intuitions of public policy, avowed or unconscious, even the prejudices which judges share with their fellow-men have had a great deal more to do than the syllogism in determining the laws by which men should be governed."

Because law can be described as societal values codified or decreed, careful students of law and public policy never study the face of a law in isolation. Instead, they look to the interests and ideas that propelled the law into existence. They understand law and public policy by understanding their sources as well as their text.

Western water law is surely a product of the era that created it, though not broadly representative of the values of society, even then. The historical prior appropriation doctrine is often presented as if it were a self-evident set of immutable principles leading inexorably to a neutral system of private property rights. But read carefully the words of Colorado Supreme Court Justice Helm in the seminal 1882 decision, *Coffin v. Left Hand Ditch Company*. Prior appropriation, he wrote, arises out of "the imperative necessity for artificial irrigation of the soil." More to the point, however, he explained:

> Vast expenditures of time and money have been made in reclaiming and fertilizing by irrigation portions of our unproductive property. Houses have been built, and permanent improvements made; the soil has been cultivated, and thousands of acres have been rendered immensely valuable, with the understanding that appropriations of water would be protected. Deny the doctrine of priority or superiority of right by priority of

appropriation, and a great part of the value of all this property is at once destroyed.

Legal historian James Willard Hurst characterized early western water law as "instrumental," directed at achieving immediate economic benefits but lacking any "clarifying legitimated long-range values." In fact, however, this instrumental view of water contains its own implicit ideology, its own values, its own policies. It emphasizes economic growth ahead of any other values. Individual initiative is rewarded, even at the expense of collective concerns. Short-term returns drive decision making, with little regard for long-term consequences. The product of transient social and economic forces, these policies continue to have great force and effect in the West today. The dominance accorded to certain interests, particularly to the exclusion of other valuable interests, has taken us far from the headwaters—from the life source of the resource.

This chapter explores three concepts that have fundamentally shaped water law and directed the use of water resources in the West: the "policy" of free water; the "policy" of capture; and the "policy" of water as property. Rarely articulated as the basis of early western water law, these de facto policies have in fact dominated decisions about water. They developed for the most part not through conscious deliberation, but as the result of ad hoc choices made by early water users, courts, and finally legislatures to achieve "the felt necessities of the time." Though altered somewhat over the years, they have taken us far from a broad consideration of the values of their own era, let alone a sound water policy that reflects today's values.

THE POLICY OF FREE WATER

> When irrigation first began, little attention was paid to the economical
> use of water or to the just division of rivers among irrigators. The area
> watered was so small that the owners of ditches did not need to consider
> how much was used or how much was wasted. They had all they wanted,
> and because it cost nothing and they were free to take it as they pleased
> they failed to realize its coming scarcity and importance. Every transac-
> tion which had to do with the disposal of streams was marked by a lavish
> prodigality. Ditches diverted more water than was used. Their owners
> claimed more than they could divert, while decrees gave appropriators
> titles to more water than ditches could carry and many times what the
> highest flood could supply. Little was known of the quantity of water
> needed to irrigate an acre of land, and in the absence of such informa-
> tion the ignorance and greed of the speculative appropriator had its
> opportunity.
>
> ELWOOD MEAD : *The Use of Water in Irrigation*

From the Louisiana Purchase in 1803 to the Alaska Purchase in
1867, the United States more than tripled its land area. Though
land sold for as little as twelve and a half cents an acre, many viewed
even small cash payment requirements as inhibiting the settlement
of the vast empire. Thus, in 1862 Congress enacted the Homestead
Act, granting individuals the right to claim up to 160 acres, paying
nothing to the United States except modest application fees. In a
similar manner, Congress jettisoned earlier policies of selling or
leasing mineral lands: in 1866, and again in the General Mining Law
of 1872, it confirmed the right of miners to claim areas of the public
lands containing valuable minerals and to develop those minerals
without payment to the United States.

As owner of most of the lands in the West, the United States controlled the water. There was no policy respecting its use, however,
until 1866, when Congress simply recognized water-use rights that
had been established under "local customs"—customs established by
the miners in California. As with mineral claims on the public lands,
it was a policy of first-come, first-served. Water was needed for mineral development and was freely available to the earliest to claim it.
Later, water necessary for agricultural development in many areas
of the West was used on the same basis. The "first in time, first in
right" custom that miners had adopted to sort out rights among

themselves in waters on federal lands was extended to waters on private lands in most western states.

The development imperative that ruled resources policy in the 1800s dictated not only that water (and land and minerals) be free, but also that it be readily accessible. The first territorial legislature for Colorado enacted a statute in 1861 authorizing one water user to build a ditch across the others' land as necessary to bring water from a stream. Virtually all western states now have constitutional and statutory provisions authorizing the creation of such rights-of-way. Such provisions were remarkable for their day and still are unique in authorizing an individual essentially to take over the use of the property of others for an entirely private use. Ordinarily, authority to use the property of another is limited to public entities and only for public purposes with just compensation. Courts have upheld the constitutionality of these right-of-way laws, however, reasoning that ditches are public uses, since irrigation is viewed as essential to the economic welfare of the state. Irrigation law expert Wells Hutchins explained, "Under typical western conditions, the irrigation of one's own land is so important to the welfare of the community and eventually to that of the State as to justify the declaration that it is a public use."

Making water free and providing special right-of-way authority marked only the beginning of public encouragement of water use in the West. Getting water out of streams and to a place it could be used often was very expensive, exceeding the financial and technical resources of individual users. States encouraged water users to band together by authorizing the formation of "mutual" irrigation companies as nonprofit corporations with authority to issue stock and to assess that stock as a means of raising revenue, to incur indebtedness such as by issuing bonds, to construct and operate irrigation works, and to acquire water rights. Even greater advantages to irrigators became available when states authorized the creation of special water districts. Water districts have the authority to tax lands within their boundaries to raise revenues. Both mutual companies and water districts are generally exempt from federal and state income taxation and often from property taxation. Interest paid on bonds issued by districts (although not mutual companies) is tax-exempt.

But even the special advantages of mutuals and districts could not induce enough water development to irrigate all the West's potential farmlands. Farmers eyed the abundant springtime flows fed by snowmelt from the mountains, but they lacked ways to capture and hold the runoff for use later in the summer and into the fall when natural streamflows were low. Ambitious plans then arose for large dams on the mainstems of rivers, not just on small tributaries. Stored water could be moved to fields and farms far from the streams, sometimes even in different water basins. Promoters of western development argued that it would be wasteful not to capture this water and use it to realize the economic potential of the lands.

Large-scale irrigation could be accomplished, however, only with massive financial and technical assistance from the federal government. Convinced that the future of the West depended on irrigation, politicians justified major public investments in building dams. The result was the Reclamation Act of 1902.

The 1902 Act, even given the many sweeping laws designed to open the West, was perhaps the most decisive action in the history of the region. Under its auspices billions of dollars from the federal treasury were spent to build perhaps the world's most extensive hydraulic systems, allowing manipulation and control of water resources to a degree and on a scale never before realized. Structures such as the Hoover, Grand Coulee, and Shasta dams rank among the engineering marvels of the world.

Only in the years following World War II did the nation begin to question the costs and benefits of the reclamation program. Beginning in the 1970s, studies revealed the astounding subsidies associated with the construction and operation of those facilities—subsidies that continue today. Reclamation water users were required to pay for only a portion of the construction of the facilities and for the operating costs of the projects, nothing for the water itself. Further, many users have paid only a small part of those construction and operating costs. Economist Richard Wahl calculated that only 14 percent of the total construction costs incurred in building Bureau of Reclamation facilities for irrigation use will ever be repaid to the federal treasury. A 1981 study by the U.S. General Accounting Office found the construction cost subsidy exceeded 90 percent for the six Bureau projects it examined.

Landowners benefitted handsomely from the program. The

value of the reclamation subsidy for irrigated agriculture, according to Wahl, averages $1,900 per acre of land irrigated. The Economic Research Service in the U.S. Department of Agriculture determined that about 80 percent of the water supplied by the Bureau of Reclamation costs the irrigator under $20 per acre-foot—less than six cents for one thousand gallons. The Soil Conservation Service determined that 45 percent of the acreage irrigated with Bureau-supplied water in 1981 grew surplus crops—crops that other government programs would pay farmers *not* to grow. Statistics like these led Tim Palmer to write in his book about the Snake River: "The western irrigation system is perhaps our finest example of social welfare for a class of people who are not homeless, not jobless, and not handicapped." Furthermore, it encourages the waste of water. The Department of Agriculture reported that the price of water is so low that it does not justify "economically . . . the adoption of water saving practices. . . ."

Underpricing of water supply in the West is not restricted to agricultural use. Diana Gibbons, in *The Economic Value of Water*, pointed out that the price of city water in arid Tucson, Arizona, in 1979 was only half the price of water in humid Raleigh, North Carolina. And the definitive Water Industry Data Base, prepared by the American Water Works Association, corroborates that the average charge for residential water supply is considerably lower in the western states than in the eastern states. Cheap water is viewed as a tool of promoting urban expansion in the West, just as it has been for agricultural development; but economists such as Charles Howe have challenged the conventional wisdom that low-cost water is an important factor in economic growth. Some amount of water is necessary for economic activity, but water is a relatively minor consideration in most new business undertakings today.

Irrigated agriculture requires large amounts of water, and subsidizing the costs of that water has led to what many now regard as an over-expansion of irrigated agriculture. Howe and Easter pointed out that much of the development of irrigated agriculture in the West was made possible through major crop subsidies and that subsidized irrigated agriculture displaces production in other regions of the country. The costs of this subsidy are measured in part by the painful adjustment process underway in parts of the region where irrigated agriculture is no longer economically viable due to increasing production costs and low crop prices. Artificially cheap water helped to build a rural economy that has not proved to be sustainable in some areas. The lure of cheap water caused many farmers to develop agriculturally marginal lands. Now water is being transferred from farmlands to cities, leaving places like Colorado's Crowley County, where only about 5 percent of historically irrigated lands remain in irrigation, with few economic options.

The real costs of this subsidized water development also can be measured in the dewatered streams and aquifers in many parts of the West, with the attendant widespread loss of wetlands, fisheries, and ecological values. Consider the fate of wetlands in the Sacramento–San Joaquin Delta, deprived of sustaining freshwater flows by pumps that lift water into the Central Valley Project's canals. The state's economically important commercial salmon fishery is also suffering from this reclamation project's dams and diversions.

Water development subsidies contribute to the water quality problems plaguing western streams and aquifers. "Nonpoint source" pollution (polluted runoff from diffuse sources) from agriculture is now the most widespread cause of water quality degradation in the West. Much of it comes from ditches carrying irrigation return flows and from uncontrolled runoff and seepage. The water is laced with residues of fertilizers and pesticides, as well as salts and other chemicals naturally in the soil that are picked up as excessive amounts of cheap water is spread on fields.

A basic rule of economics is that when something is priced at less than its cost, it tends to be overused. The development of western water makes this rule painfully evident. As the West moves from an era when conservation of water meant enough *storage* to cover shortage to an era when conservation means *efficient use* of scarce resources, the policy of free water is one of the greatest obstacles. The illusion of plenty hides the consequences of waste.

THE POLICY OF CAPTURE

> In a dry and thirsty land it is necessary to divert the waters of streams from
> their natural channels, in order to obtain the fruits of the soil, and this
> necessity is so universal and imperious that it claims recognition of the law.
> The value and usefulness of agricultural lands, in this territory, depend
> upon the supply of water for irrigation, and this can only be obtained by
> constructing artificial channels through which it may flow over adjacent
> lands.
>
> COLORADO SUPREME COURT : *Yunker v. Nichols*, 1872

Early western water users adopted what lawyer Moses Lasky in 1929
called "the mining doctrine of water": rights to water are based
solely on capture and possession (appropriation); and, if there is not
enough water, the earlier (prior) users have better rights than later
users. The rivers were thrown open, first-come, first-served, without restriction. These were rough and ready rules that emulated the
rules allocating rights among miners claiming minerals on the public domain.

The notion that rights to water derived solely from possession and
use—not, for example, from ownership of land along the stream or
from some sort of watershed planning—matched well the needs of
miners. The land was public domain, where the only riparian owner
was the United States itself. Possession as the basis of the water right
also matched the policy of allowing miners to claim a piece of public
land to exploit its minerals. And, since the major needs for water in
mining involved its diversion from the stream, there was little doubt
about who first possessed it. Consistent with the teachings of John
Locke, rights were established through the acts of individuals; government's role was to confirm these private rights and help resolve
disputes.

Possession eventually translated into a requirement that the water
be diverted out of the stream; this was partly aimed at providing others with notice that there had been an "appropriation," but it also
provided evidence of the bona fide intentions of the diverter to
make productive "beneficial" use of the water. The investment of
time and money in the construction of diversion works represented
such a commitment. Thus, the diversion requirement fit the production ethic of the times. Only later did the value of protecting

free-flowing water for such things as fisheries and recreation become apparent, and by then the diversion requirement was basic law.

The policy of capture explicitly separates the right to use water from the ownership of riparian land. The appropriation itself establishes the use. Water may be removed completely out of its natural watershed, leaving no return flows for those who may later wish to use water downstream. In Colorado, early rules recognized both riparian rights (as they existed in the eastern states) and rights established by appropriation (according to the miners' customs). In *Coffin v. Left Hand Ditch Company*, a direct conflict arose between downstream riparian farmers and upstream appropriators who had taken much of the natural flow of St. Vrain Creek to irrigate lands in a neighboring watershed. In upholding the rights of the upstream appropriators who began using water first, the Colorado Supreme Court provided this rationale for not following a territorial statute recognizing rights of riparian owners:

> The doctrine of priority of right by priority of appropriation for agriculture is evoked, as we have seen, by the imperative necessity for artificial irrigation of the soil. And it would be an ungenerous and inequitable rule that would deprive one of its benefit simply because he has, by large expenditure of time and money, carried the water from one stream over an intervening watershed and cultivated land in the valley of another. It might be utterly impossible, owing to the topography of the country, to get water upon his farm from the adjacent stream; or if possible, it might be impracticable on account of the distance from the point where the decision must take place and the attendant expense; or the quantity of water in said stream might be entirely insufficient to supply his wants. It sometimes happens that the most fertile soil is found along the margin or in the neighborhood of the small rivulet, and sandy and barren land beside the larger stream. To apply the rule contended for would prevent the useful and profitable cultivation of the productive soil, and sanction the waste of water upon the more sterile lands.

The policy of capture did more than simply separate water from riparian lands: it removed water from the stream itself, from the watershed, and even from the river basin. It said that water, as an instrument of economic activity, had value only as a means of promoting that activity. Though a river is, by nature, a shared resource serving many purposes, the law made water a distinct, private commodity that could be taken wherever desired to serve the exclusive economic interests of the appropriator, without regard to other uses that were being satisfied without an "appropriation."

"Water flows uphill to money" is a familiar saying in the West. Indeed, water users living on the Front Range of Colorado draw an important part of their supply from sources on the other side of the Continental Divide; more than half of Denver's water supply comes over the mountains from the Colorado River. Similarly, people in coastal Southern California depend almost entirely on water imported from sources hundreds of miles away, including the Colorado River, the Owens Valley, and the Sacramento–San Joaquin Basin.

The Owens Valley saga is a compelling illustration of the policy of capture. Around the turn of the century, Los Angeles' population more than doubled in just four years. Water engineers working for the city realized that the desert city (the Los Angeles Basin receives less than 6 inches of rainfall per year) would soon exhaust the pool of underground water that had supported its growth. At the time it seemed infeasible to pump water over mountains from the Colorado and Kern rivers. But Fred Eaton, superintendent of the Los Angeles City Water Company, saw potential in the Owens Valley, a high valley on the eastern side of the Sierra Nevada mountains about 250 miles northeast of Los Angeles. The city could pipe water from the valley using gravity alone, and the Owens River (which ran through the valley and terminated in a remnant ice age lake) could provide water for thousands of people. Eaton and his cohort at the water company, William Mulholland, gave little thought to the social and economic impacts this massive water export would have on the Owens Valley watershed and the communities dependent on a thriving irrigated agriculture economy in the valley. And the law did not require any such consideration.

Eaton and Mulholland bought land and water rights along 40 miles of the Owens River and covertly undermined a proposed Bureau of Reclamation project that would have competed for the valley's water. The aqueduct linking Los Angeles and the Owens Valley was completed in 1913. About ten years later, when a drought brought valley ranchers face to face with how much water had left the valley, protestors dynamited parts of the city's aqueduct. The protest was quelled, and the valley continued to dry up. Eventually, as water demands grew heavier and supplies scarcer, L.A. also pumped out the valley's groundwater, and the dried-up Owens Lake bed, no longer held in place by vegetation or moist sub-surface soil, turned to alkaline dust. Until a recent L.A.–Inyo County settlement, the Owens River had not run in its bed for decades (except in the rare occasion when pipes burst or renegade protestors dynamited the pipeline); for many years the valley's economy has been tenuous at best.

By the 1950s Los Angeles extended its aqueduct upstream to the Mono Lake basin, where the city extracted water from streams that fed that large saline lake. Years later, when ecologists sounded the alarm about severe drops in Mono Lake water levels (and the consequent decline of brine shrimp and the gulls and grebes that depended on the unique water body), California courts turned to the historical "public trust doctrine" in a last-ditch effort to remedy the environmental damage. But, according to the basic rules of western water law, Los Angeles' desiccation of Mono Lake and the Owens Valley was perfectly legal—in fact, it was exactly the type of "beneficial use" that the early miners and irrigators had already made of streams in many locations across the West.

The policy of capture encouraged construction of the plumbing systems that move water from watershed to watershed and basin to basin throughout the West. Reflecting on this legacy, Gary Weatherford characterized the waters of the West as a "hydrocommons":

> The transwatershed diversion breaches one drainage and bonds it, in a utilitarian sense, to another. Whether the exporting drainage can ever be left better off is a matter of dispute. Whether the bonding amounts to bondage, in a colonial sense, depends on the social and political condition surrounding the diversion, the benefits exchanged and costs incurred, and the long-term impact of the exportation on the watershed of origin. What is certain is that, after the linkage, neither drainage is an isolated catchment.
>
> [As applied, t]he policy of appropriation made water a commodity and placed decisions about its use in the hands of those with the means to capture that water and take it to the desired place of use.

As illustrated by the fate of Owens Valley and Mono Lake, traditionally little or no consideration has been given to the adverse effects of transbasin diversions on the so-called "basin of origin."

Those effects can be substantial, both economically (lost jobs, property taxes, and opportunities for future development) and environmentally (destruction of fisheries, riparian vegetation, and the wildlife that depends on it for shelter and food). The people whose demands are responsible for the diversions typically are unaware of these costs. Los Angeles is a good example: How can one water user among several million identify distant impacts in the Owens Valley or Mono Lake when turning on a faucet or filling a pool? Furthermore, water suppliers traditionally have not included any of these costs in the price charged to customers.

The National Water Commission in its 1973 report concluded that transfers of water from one river basin to another should be limited to those that can be demonstrated to be the lowest economic cost source of water supply and with benefits that exceed all costs. Other analysts have added the condition that the area of origin be adequately compensated for its losses. Certainly a transbasin diversion may be undesirable for social or cultural reasons that are not reflected in the economic balance proposed by the Commission: Can the value of a Hispanic farming community's traditional way of life be compared fairly with the economic benefits of moving its water to a distant growing city?

The policy of capture also encouraged users to maximize their claims on the water resource. Initially there were no explicit limits to these claims. Users determined the size and nature of their claims through their actions in diverting the flows of water. Concerns about accommodating the needs of subsequent users caused courts and then legislatures to revisit the concept of "beneficial use." The meaning of that concept—only partly realized even now—provided a general standard by which to evaluate and limit the quantity of water necessary for an appropriation. Beneficial use was early said to be "the basis, the measure, and the limit of water rights." But limits were slow to be imposed.

Elwood Mead was one of the most illuminating sources on the consequences of the policy of capture. Mead had a long and distinguished career between 1882 and 1936; he was the first professor of irrigation engineering in the United States (at what is now Colorado State University), the first state engineer in Wyoming, chairman of the State Rivers and Water Supply Commission of Victoria, Australia, and commissioner of the U.S. Bureau of Reclamation. In his authoritative 1903 book, *Irrigation Institutions*, Mead deplored the excessive claims accommodated by the appropriation system—water users who asserted rights to all the water flowing past a certain point in a stream, some claiming rights to more water than flowed in the stream, often more than their own ditches could carry or they could put to use. He criticized the wasteful practices of taking water from streams continuously even though it was used for irrigation only periodically: "The results of this lavishness do not warrant its continuance. It led farmers to substitute water for cultivation, and to injure their land and exhaust streams by wasteful and careless methods." The policy of capture, in his view, led to excessive litigation and necessitated the need for elaborate state administrative processes to manage conflicts among water users.

Elwood Mead and others have eschewed the waste allowed in the operation of the early prior appropriation system. Yet, in the nineteenth century, the "first in time, first in right" principle offered an apparently simple means of sorting out disputes to a resource on public lands that, like minerals, was up for grabs. In the event of an inadequate supply of water, the rights of appropriators are protected according to the order in which they were established. The earliest appropriators may fully satisfy their demands to the extent an adequate supply is available, even if that means that junior appropriators may take nothing.

The resulting clarity of rights among users was intended to encourage investments in facilities needed to make full economic use of water. Investors wanted to be sure that the water supply on which these facilities relied would not be reduced by subsequent water development. Historian Donald Pisani found some roots of the prior-right principle in an 1844 Massachusetts court decision that he criticized as placing "economic development ahead of equal access. Water had become property detached from land, and prior appropriation offered businessmen a monopoly subsidy just as special franchises and charters did."

A person holding a senior water right has little incentive to use water efficiently. On the contrary, the user is primarily concerned about making full use of the entitlement. Because appropriative rights arise from use, they may be lost if they are not fully used. Stephen Williams, now a judge on the United States Court of Appeals, accused the "Rule of Capture" of stimulating unneeded development: "A project may be economically attractive only because it has the side effect of transferring a water right from the public domain to the developer. Because racing to win under the Rule of Capture requires construction of facilities to apply the water to use, it consumes and wastes real resources."

The policy of capture was modified in a number of ways to try to repair its worst effects. Every state couched its permission to appropriate water for a "beneficial use" in the context of a declaration that all water belongs to the public. Early state statutes introduced supervision and order over the laissez-faire practices of water users. Originally, appropriators established rights simply by their actions. In the 1880s, western states began providing for administrative control of the appropriation and use of water. They required the posting of notices at the intended point of diversion with information concerning the quantity of water claimed, the purpose and place of use, and the means of diversion. Copies of notices also were to be filed with the county recorder. Such modest steps were inadequate, however, in addressing the conflicts raised by the unboundaried policy of capture, leading states to set up administrative systems and agencies.

For example, Colorado's water rights system developed, in part, out of conflicts on the Poudre River in the northern part of the state. In 1874, after constructing two main ditch systems at great expense and difficulty, Union Colony members found no water to divert from the river. A drought coincided with new diversions of water into canals 25 miles upstream, near the city of Fort Collins. The colonists called for the establishment of a river superintendent who would allocate streamflows according to the priority of the rights involved, and, in return for dropping a lawsuit they had filed, they obtained an agreement from the upstream irrigators to release additional water. As expressed by one of the colonists, David Boyd (in *A Hundred Years of Irrigation in Colorado*), the bitter dispute provoked calls for a more ordered system of water rights:

[The upstream diverters] were told that if their policy of the ditches highest up stream taking what they wanted was the one to be pursued, then we could go above them, and there would result an interminable and exhaustive race in which the greatest numbers and largest purses would come out winners. . . . [The upstream diverters] would not hear to moderation and justice. Force must meet force. We outnumbered them, and many of us had seen as rough service some ten years ago as we were likely to experience in an encounter with these water thieves, etc. Then some one arose and moved an immediate adjournment. Every man to his tent, to his rifle and cartridges. But gradually voices of conciliation were heard above the storm. . . . It was finally agreed that they would let us down some water to save the most valuable things in Greeley. A promise they did not keep nor meant to keep. They were too intent on running the water out on the cactus plain in order to boom the "Agricultural Colony," which was to be our great rival. A general rain-storm came in about a week afterwards and saved us; but from this day forth we had set our hearts on having some regulations looking towards a distribution of waters of the state in harmony with the principle of priority of appropriation.

Shortly after this dispute, Colorado enacted statutes establishing a system for the courts to clarify priorities and for a water commissioner to administer the use of those rights in times of shortage. Donald Worster characterized those statutes as "the first steps toward declaring that the rivers of the West are in some sense public property and that any private appropriation can only be made under public rules and at public sufferance."

Wyoming took another step forward in 1890, when it established a system by which new appropriations could be obtained only through a state-administered permit system. Actual appropriation of water was subject to certain requirements including the demonstrated availability of unappropriated water, evidence that the water would be used in a valuable (beneficial) manner, and satisfaction of a public interest review. Once established, these rights were then subject to state supervision in their use. This kind of state involvement in the creation and administration of water rights reflected the belief that such actions were necessary to ensure that limited water resources could meet the expanding needs of the rapidly growing West. But these requirements were modest in every way. The idea of a public interest review remained just that—an idea—and was rarely enforced. The state record-keeping and enforcement system actually reinforced the original private appropriations. The rule of capture, deeply imbedded in prior appropriation from the beginning, continued as a key policy of the new state administrative systems.

THE POLICY OF WATER AS PROPERTY

> The whole system is wrong. It is wrong in principle as well as faulty in procedure. It assumes that the establishment of titles to the snows on the mountains and the rains falling on the public land and the water collected in the lakes and rivers, on the use of which the development of the State must in a great measure depend, is a private matter. It ignores public interests in a resource upon which the enduring prosperity of communities must rest. It is like A suing B for control of property which belongs to C. Many able attorneys hold that these decreed rights will in time be held invalid because when they were established the public, the real owner of the property, did not have its day in court.
>
> ELWOOD MEAD : *Irrigation Institutions*

Western water law is heavily freighted with property notions. Two ideas have been especially influential. First, the water within the boundaries of a state has been called the "property" of the state or of the people of the state. Second, the private right to use water is regarded as a property right, capable of ownership, use, and transfer, as with other kinds of property. These apparently unrelated property notions concerning water have caused considerable confusion. Though they have been partially modified or rejected, they nonetheless remain important elements of a mythology about western water that continues to influence modern policy debates. Today, an understanding of the property concepts directing water use is central to such major tasks as sorting out the role of states in relation to the federal government and Indian tribes, and defining the rights of governments to regulate private uses of water to promote conservation, economic, environmental, and other objectives. Reading the two notions of property together is the key to comprehending reforms that are afoot in western water policy.

State "Ownership" of Water

> To put the claim of the State upon title is to lean on a slender reed.
>
> JUSTICE HOLMES : *Missouri v. Holland* (1920)

Many western state constitutions enacted during the nineteenth century asserted state or public "ownership" of the water within their boundaries. For example, the Wyoming constitution says that "the waters of all natural streams, springs, lakes or other collections of still water, within the boundaries of the state, are hereby declared to be the property of the state." An Oregon statute declares that "all water within the state from all sources of water supply belongs to the public."

Over time, the limitations of state ownership doctrine became apparent. As development pressure increased, states on the larger western rivers began to contest each other over the allocation of water. Could Wyoming and Colorado, for example, really claim ownership over all the waters of the Colorado River arising within their boundaries (most of the flow of the entire watershed) as against the other five states in the watershed? Could states claim ownership of waters arising on or flowing through Indian reservations that had been established as a result of federal and tribal sovereign prerogatives, usually long before statehood? Was the federal government prevented from protecting the waters of the national parks, forests, refuges, and wild and scenic rivers?

The provisions declaring state ownership of water were written in a time in which many legal theories were expressed in terms of property concepts. For example, the U.S. Supreme Court, in the 1896 *Geer v. Connecticut* case, declared that state "ownership" of wildlife permitted states to prohibit hunters from interstate trade in game birds. Dissenting from that decision, Justice Field said, "It is pure fantasy to talk of 'owning' wild fish, birds or animals," and pointed out that the Commerce Clause of the U.S. Constitution prohibits state regulations limiting interstate commerce. In a 1979 decision, *Hughes v. Oklahoma*, the Supreme Court overruled *Geer*, adopting the dissent's view that the state ownership of wildlife is "no more than a 19th-century legal fiction. . . ." In the 1982 case, *Sporhase v.*

Nebraska, the Supreme Court rejected a state law prohibiting the transport of water across state lines, holding that the "demise of the public ownership theory" applied to water as well as wildlife.

Thus, states do not *own* water in the sense of holding property, but they do possess broad jurisdictional and regulatory authority over the water within their boundaries, subject to the supreme authority of Congress to preempt, or overrule, state laws. Under the Constitution, valid congressional statutes are the "supreme law of the land." Federal statutes override state laws, including constitutional provisions, if they are within some delegated power of Congress. Congress' regulatory power under the Commerce Clause is extraordinarily broad and probably reaches virtually all waters of every state. Congress also has extensive power over Indian affairs and federal public lands, areas in which control of water is also at issue.

It bears reemphasis that, while states may not "own" water, it is a scarce resource, critical to western states, and they have broad authority to regulate it. One side of the coin, therefore, is that Congress can override state water laws; the other side of the coin is that state water laws control until Congress does exercise its superior authority. In the case of western water, the federal government has left most areas of regulation to the states—major exceptions include federal water pollution laws, large water development projects, and federally guaranteed Indian water rights. The states may not possess ownership of the water, but, in practical terms, they have made most of the laws regulating it. That regulation, as the following section shows, has been previously to grant to private users vested property rights in the use of water. The states' interest has thus become a context for allowing and limiting property rights in water.

Private Rights

> When property rights are well defined, individuals have a clear idea of what actions they can take regarding resources.
>
> TERRY L. ANDERSON : *Water Rights: Scarce Resource Allocation, Bureaucracy, and the Environment*

One of the most distinctive characteristics of western water law is that prior appropriation grants permanent property rights to private water users. Riparian principles prevailing in the eastern

United States also recognized private property in water rights, but they belonged to all landowners along that stream, not necessarily the earliest users. Rights were not fixed in quantity based on past usage, but depended on all the other owners' demands and the natural supply. Appropriative rights, however, granted the user an exclusive right to a constant amount of water so long as it was available in the stream. The water need not be shared by the senior appropriator with others, even in the severest drought. These are rights based on possession and use of water, not rights arising out of ownership of land, and carry the highest reverence for the earliest uses. According to the Colorado Supreme Court in *Coffin v. Left Hand Ditch Co.*: "Water in the various streams . . . acquires a value unknown in moister climates. Instead of being a mere incident to the soil, it rises, when appropriated, to the dignity of a distinct . . . right of property."

When courts characterized those rights as property, they implied that the water user has certain legal rights and protections. Most important, others are prevented from interfering with the appropriator's use of water—at least to the extent that their rights are junior in priority. Since those rights are regarded as real estate, they pass by inheritance and can be sold. Subject to certain limitations, their use may be changed. And, as property, appropriative rights are protected by the Fifth and Fourteenth Amendments to the U.S. Constitution.

The notion that a right to use water is a form of property is deeply entrenched and has been a controlling force since the mid-nineteenth century. But what, exactly, did the early courts mean when they characterized the right to use water as property? In the common law of the 1800s water law was but a part of the property law applying to riparian lands. Rights based on use rather than land ownership separated the legal right from its historical property moorings. Having thus recognized the miners' customs, it then became the task of California and other western state courts to explain the legal rights they had created.

Initially, the courts focused on protecting the appropriators' investments in constructing water diversion and carriage works. Eventually, judicial decisions made it clear that the property was in the possession and "beneficial use" of water and not in the ownership of the ditch through which the water is diverted or the ownership of the land on which it is used. Thus, the person using the water holds exclusive rights and is protected against harmful interference with that use by others. That is true even if the appropriator's use requires all the water of the stream. As the federal circuit court for Idaho said in a 1906 decision concerning a conflict between two appropriators on the Snake River: "Beyond question, under our laws, a party may be protected in the use of all the water he actually appropriates and uses, even if it be every drop that flows in as great a river as the Snake."

Those private property rights to use water have long dominated western rivers, most of which were fully or mostly appropriated by the late nineteenth or early twentieth century. Some have argued that those water rights are such secure property rights that they are immune even from government conservation efforts that are so critical in preventing widespread waste of water. That perspective is illustrated by the 1939 Nebraska Supreme Court decision, *Enterprise Irrigation District v. Willis*. In 1911, the Nebraska legislature adopted a conservation law prohibiting any irrigator from diverting more than 3 acre-feet per acre per year. The legislature tried to strike a balance between achieving conservation objectives and not imposing too burdensome a requirement on farmers. An irrigation district that had first diverted water in 1889 and was using 3.5 acre-feet per year challenged the conservation statute.

The Nebraska Supreme Court recognized the importance of water conservation and acknowledged that beneficial use "shall not exceed the least amount of water that experience indicates is necessary in the exercise of good husbandry for the production of crops." The court, however, would not permit regulation in a case where the irrigation district's diversion predated the conservation statute and evidence showed that it was not wasteful. The Nebraska court found that "any interference that limits the quantity of water or changes the date of its priority to the material injury of its holder is more than regulation and supervision and extends into the field generally referred to as a deprivation of a vested right."

The court's statement, though limited to the context of the case, reflects the conviction of many water rights holders in the West that their diversion rights cannot be altered in any way and that regulation of water use is simply impermissible. Consider, for example, the perspective of water lawyers Gregory Hobbs and Bennett Raley in a 1989 law review article:

> [A] senior right to use water in priority for beneficial uses cannot be denied or restricted in order to protect junior appropriators or interests that are not represented by an appropriation. . . . The application of the police power to conflicts among uses or classes of uses would be nothing other than a reallocation of the right based on something other than the priority of the competing uses, and would therefore be completely inconsistent with the constitutionally mandated doctrine of prior appropriation. . . . If a state wishes to restrict an appropriator's exclusive right of use to his allocated quantity of stream water in priority, it must pay compensation for doing so.

By comparison, Professor Joseph Sax has argued that water rights have *less* protection than some other kinds of property rights because of substantial inherent public claims on water. In Sax's view:

> Water, as a necessary and common medium for community development at every stage of society, has been held subject to perceived societal necessities of the time and circumstances. In that sense water's capacity for full privatization has always been limited. The very terminology of water law reveals that limitation: terms such as beneficial, non-wasteful, navigation servitude, and public trust all impart an irreducible public claim on water as a public resource, and not merely a private commodity.

Perhaps the single most influential development in western water law during this century has been the rediscovery of the public nature of water. The permission for private use is, at last, being read together with the declaration of public "ownership." Much, if not most, of the conflict concerning use of water relates to protecting values of water often disregarded in the creation of property rights for water, a subject taken up in the next chapter.

THE LEGACY OF WESTERN WATER LAW

> We can say this: That what we call "development" is not a uni-directional
> process, especially in a semi-arid country. To develop this land we have
> used engines that we could not control, and have started actions and reac-
> tions far different from those intended. Some of these are proving
> beneficial; most of them harmful. This land is too complex for the simple
> processes of "the mass-mind" armed with modern tools. To live in real
> harmony with such a country seems to require either a degree of public
> regulation we will not tolerate, or a degree of private enlightenment we do
> not possess.
>
> ALDO LEOPOLD: "The Virgin Southwest"

The policies that arose from laws of prior appropriation and federal
reclamation made water rights easy to obtain and scarce water plentiful for certain purposes in an otherwise dry region. The policy of
capture allows a property right to attach as soon as water is diverted
and put to a beneficial use. The policy of free water means that there
is no fee or other payment that must be made to state or federal governments. And the policy of water as property says that those water
rights are permanent: they remain in effect forever, unless intentionally abandoned by the user or forfeited through non-use under
a statutorily established requirement.

Those policies suited the early development era of a frontier society. They maximized incentives to take and use water resources,
ironically encouraging activities that utilize water in an arid environment. They were aimed at immediately and directly benefitting
those first to make use of the water, allowing those users indirectly to
determine and limit future water uses. They made sense in a historical setting, given past understandings of society's needs. Yet today
they are incomplete. They are policies that place no value on water
as part of a vital, functioning natural system, but rather see water
only as a tool for economic activity. They do not assure that rivers,
lakes, and aquifers will be sustained. They treat an inherently mul-
tidimensional resource in a fundamentally one-dimensional manner.

The West is a different place today than it was in the mid 1800s.
Though now modified in some respects, the policies that grew out of
that era continue to determine the manner of water use in the West,

because they governed the appropriation and development of most of the water; nearly every western river is controlled by water rights and dams established under the old policies. Yet, it now seems inevitable that western water policy is changing in fundamental ways, in spite of the legacy of the prior appropriation doctrine and the reclamation program.

Chapter Seven

The Journey to Rediscovery

The arid West has entered a new era. What was once an endless frontier is now a vital, populated region fully integrated with the rest of the country. What were once seemingly endless stores of natural wealth—water, land, forests, blue skies—are now resources under stress. Water, one of the West's most essential resources, is no less physically abundant today than it was decades ago, but it is now oversubscribed and, in many cases, polluted.

MOHAMED T. EL-ASHRY AND DIANA C. GIBBONS:
Water and the Arid Lands of the Western United States

THE PIONEERS who shaped the prior appropriation doctrine would be stunned by the rhetoric of today's discussions of western water. By the late-twentieth century, westerners see definite limits to rivers and aquifers that seemed inexhaustible a century earlier. Today, state engineers are preoccupied with the concerns of anglers and boaters, while a few years ago they heard only from water rights holders. Modern Indian tribes assert their historic water rights with force and are becoming players in many of the key decisions. In the 1990s, Americans worry about how to save squawfish and wetlands, yet many people remember federal programs to poison "trash fish" like squawfish and to drain swamps. Contemporary water rights, once granted, may be laden with conditions requiring use of measuring and water-saving devices, fish screens, and limits on the manner of use. The architects—politically and physically—of the great federal water projects would shake their heads in disbelief at the lack of appreciation for their handiwork. Built to facilitate the economic development of the

152

West, those projects now are viewed by many as subsidized causes of environmental degradation. The mission of the Bureau of Reclamation is in transition; indeed, the necessity for the Bureau's continued existence is under examination.

Still, actual water-use practices would give some comfort to the old timers. Practice has not yet caught up with modern values. Most water uses in the West are still tied to decisions made according to policies of capture, property, and subsidy.

Western water policy today is under pressure to respond to a world of new technology, a society of newly realized values, and an economy of changing demands. In some important ways, prior appropriation rules have evolved and developed: the policy of capture, for example, has been modified by some states' recognition that not every beneficial water use requires diversion of water from a stream. But a separate body of law is also beginning to cause major changes in the allocation and use of western water. Though much of the law has developed at the federal level, states and local citizens also have been active. The primary significance of these legal developments has been to recognize and protect water uses and water-related values and interests not considered under traditional prior appropriation principles. In short, diverse communities of interest are shaping a new western water policy.

Some states have adopted innovations to protect streamflows, to review new uses for consistency with the public interest, to encourage transfers of rights to more productive uses, and to allow wider participation in water proceedings. Federal water supply agencies are beginning to require more efficient and environmentally protective uses of project water. An array of environmental laws, mostly federal, deal with water quality, wetlands, and wildlife protection. And local communities have demonstrated remarkable initiative in developing cooperative approaches to protect and manage their resources. Underlying all of these changes is a new understanding of and appreciation for the fundamentally public nature of water.

REDISCOVERING PUBLIC INTERESTS IN WATER

> Few public interests are more obvious, indisputable and independent of
> particular theory than the interest of the public of a State to maintain the
> rivers that are wholly within it substantially undiminished, except by such
> drafts upon them as the guardian of the public welfare may permit for the
> purpose of turning them to a more perfect use. . . . The private right to
> appropriate is subject not only to the rights of lower owners but to the
> initial limitation that it may not substantially diminish one of the great
> foundations of public welfare and health.
>
> JUSTICE HOLMES : *Hudson County Water Co. v. McCarter* (1908)

Water is a quintessential public resource, and societies throughout
time have recognized the public nature of water in many ways. The
Institutes of Justinian, perhaps the most important statement of Roman civil law, declares: "By natural law these things are common to
all: air, running water, the sea, and as a consequence, the shores of
the sea." Spanish, French, and Italian law—influenced directly by
Roman law—regard water as *res communis* (common property) and,
therefore, not susceptible to private ownership.

In the Orient, public uses of water were acknowledged well before
the birth of Christ; the earliest Chinese water laws, dating to the
Ch'in Dynasty (249–207 B.C.), called upon water users to enhance
the public welfare. African nations held similar traditions: in Nige-
ria, T. Elias wrote, "From time immemorial the people . . . have enjoyed the right to fish the sea, with its creeks and arms and navigable
rivers within the tides." In Moslem countries, according to a United
Nations report, "[T]he fundamentals of Islamic water law purport
to ensure to all members of the Moslem community the availability
of water." The Indian Code of Manu, which dates back to at least 200
B.C., regarded water as public and prohibited individual monopoly
of a particular water source. Spanish and Mexican laws and institutions in the New World evinced a powerful tradition that large portions of the water supply must be dedicated to the community good.

Governments outside of the American West typically protect public rights to water by limiting the duration of a water right. In some
countries water uses remain in place for a fixed period, subject only
to revocation for violation of the terms of the grant; in others, water
uses are less permanent and last either for a relatively short term or

at the grace of the government. In the United States, approximately twenty states following the riparian doctrine have adopted permit systems, and most retain the right to revoke water rights. About half of them provide for perpetual permits; in the others, a permit is issued for a fixed term ranging from ten to fifty years.

Perhaps the most profound change in western water law in this century has been the recognition of a diverse set of values and demands often characterized as the "public interest." There were stirrings in the late nineteenth and early twentieth centuries. The creation of Yellowstone National Park "as a pleasuring ground for the people" in 1872 preserved the "wonders" of its geysers as well as special scenic areas like Yellowstone Lake, the deep gorge of the Yellowstone River, and others.

In the late 1800s Elwood Mead and others advocated state control of the appropriation of water and subjecting the grant of an appropriation to, among other things, a rudimentary public interest or public welfare standard. This ideal was embodied in the declarations of "public ownership" in western state courts and statutes. But those declarations lay dormant for years, sometimes misunderstood, almost always ignored. Finally, state legislatures, state water administrators, and courts are giving meaningful content to the public interest. The recent ascendancy of the public interest reflects a rediscovery of the fundamentally public nature of water. The prior appropriation doctrine, with its almost exclusive emphasis on private rights, simply does not acknowledge or protect many valuable public water uses, such as recreation and fisheries.

The public interest represents a broad set of interests. Inevitably, there is a public interest in *all* uses of a shared resource like water, even private uses. Certainly a water utility can argue persuasively that providing water to its customers is within the public interest. From there it is a short step to seeing a public interest in other water uses, like power generation, cattle feeding, and sewage disposal. But all these uses have representatives to speak for them, water rights to support them, and measurable economic value. So the concept of the public interest in water implies a use that is widely valued, has a diffuse constituency, and is difficult to express in traditional economic terms.

The public interest requires an interested public. Until the environmental consciousness-raising of the 1970s and 1980s, members of the urban public thought little about water. Municipal water supply efforts have been so successful in the United States that the availability of water has been taken for granted. Water generally is clean enough to drink, and the cost has been too low to worry about. Most people do not know or care where their water comes from. Only when they begin to see and hear about the consequences of water use—dammed canyons, pollution, dry riverbeds, declining fish and wildlife populations, dry or contaminated wells—do they begin to worry about water. As awareness has developed, national political support for water development has waned. The public has become interested in protecting its use of water. But what does this mean for the water rights holder?

The idea of vesting private water users with permanent property rights arose at a time when water policy was simple: the only real objective was to get water out of the streams to mining claims and crops, and to the communities whose material well-being depended on them. Today, however, the public makes more complex demands on its water. People expect water to be available for a wide variety of instream uses and for new users, including not just growing cities but also the Indian tribes who legally have the oldest rights on many rivers, though they have not seen their rights fulfilled. Further, many people are calling for existing users to create "new" water supplies by conserving water in order to avoid large new water development projects that are widely viewed as too expensive and too environmentally destructive.

Yet even these widely accepted objectives seem difficult to achieve. Virtually all of the West's surface water and much of its groundwater is tied up in water rights representing vested property interests. How can water rights based on nineteenth-century notions of capture and development be reconciled with contemporary interests in water? Fortunately, private property rights in water do not necessarily impede the fulfillment of modern policy goals; in some cases, those very attributes of water rights actually promote public goals.

Consider the promise of water marketing, by which existing rights to use water can voluntarily be made available for another to use.

The transfer of water rights to a new user is an area in which permanent vested property rights serve the transition to new needs for water exceptionally well. All western states now allow water available under existing rights to be used in new locations and for new purposes. Such changes of use are an especially effective means of allowing economic values to be better reflected in the uses of water. Those promoting valuable new urban and industrial uses can purchase water rights now being applied to uses with lower economic return. These are voluntary transactions involving willing sellers and buyers.

To be sure, there are difficulties in transferring the rights to use a shared resource such as water. Protection of all other water rights in the same source of supply requires a court or administrator to determine how much water may be transferred—usually the amount historically consumed by the use under the original water right. The laws and procedures that govern water rights are not always conducive to efficient transfers, however. Some states, such as New Mexico, have established administrative procedures in recent years that promote quick transfers, with relatively few costs (such as attorneys' and engineers' fees), based upon generally sound state administrative determinations on technical matters such as crop consumption of water. Other states have less well-developed procedures in place, with the result that transfers proceed more slowly and less predictably. In Colorado, one of the most active states for water marketing, cumbersome court procedures often result in extended (and thus expensive) proceedings. In virtually all western states, moreover, inadequate attention is given to address adverse effects of such things as water quality or the local economy. If these difficulties could be resolved, treating water rights as permanent property rights could be advantageous, promoting reallocation of water by making rights to its use saleable, leasable, and otherwise transferable to more socially desirable uses.

The new uses that seek to obtain water rights by transfer need not be traditional consumptive uses. Environmental organizations have begun to purchase senior water rights now being used out of the stream and apply them to instream uses such as fisheries enhancement and wetlands protection. For example, irrigation uses in the

Newlands Project of Nevada are being transferred to improve valuable wetlands habitat in the Stillwater National Wildlife Refuge.

Transferring a water right to a use that yields higher economic benefits does not always ensure that the full range of interests associated with that water will be served. The existing user will be compensated, other water rights will be protected, and the new user will have the benefit of the transferred water. But incidental beneficiaries such as the environment and others in the existing user's community may not be considered and be heard in this process. Moving water to a new place of use, for example, could affect water quality by changing the amount and timing of streamflows. Wetlands created by the availability of water for irrigation could be lost. Lands removed from irrigation are likely to have a lower assessed valuation, thus lowering property tax revenues upon which counties rely to provide community services. Weeds can grow up in formerly irrigated croplands, spreading onto adjacent lands still in irrigation. Water marketing must occur in a context that respects those interests if it is to be a primary means of comprehensively meeting new water demands in the West.

University of Arizona professor Helen Ingram has focused attention on the fundamental importance of water to communities in the West—an importance that transcends purely economic considerations. As she and F. Lee Brown wrote in *Water and Poverty in the Southwest*: "The community value of water should be regarded as the broad context within which economic values may be pursued. Unless community values of water are satisfied, debilitating attitudes of hopelessness persist, fostered by perceptions of injustice, lack of efficacy, and loss of opportunity." They went on to suggest, "the acquisition of secure control of water through a community's own initiative and effort may supply the key ingredients of participation and belief in the possibilities of the future that are essential to sustained economic improvement."

Transfers should aim at improving rather than undermining the area from which the water comes. In a case often described as a model transaction, the Metropolitan Water District of Southern California agreed to pay $110 million to upgrade irrigation facilities and practices in the Imperial Irrigation District in return for use of the more than 100,000 acre-feet a year of water that the District should be able to save by operating with the system improvements. The Imperial Irrigation District is the largest single user of water from the Colorado River. Most of its irrigation facilities were built in the early part of this century and are grossly inefficient by modern standards. Metropolitan's investment will strengthen the agricultural productivity of this extremely fertile area, reduce costs to the users, and greatly improve irrigation practices. At the same time, the "new" water will help to fill the needs of the densely populated southern coastal areas of California.

As demonstrated by the Metropolitan Water District–Imperial Irrigation District arrangement, water marketing and other kinds of voluntary transfers can satisfy the public values of water while preserving the private property rights recognized by the prior appropriation doctrine. Yet, in some instances, the environmental harms caused by the exercise of water rights have required more disruptive remedies.

The destruction of environmental values allowed by absolute prior appropriation have given rise to an expanded interpretation of the public trust doctrine. This legal doctrine, rooted in the public nature of water, asserts that states have a duty of continuing supervision over the property rights that they have recognized in water. The duty requires the states to protect certain public trust values in the process of letting property rights be established in the public's water. In 1983 the California Supreme Court relied upon this doctrine in determining that Los Angeles' forty-year-old water rights in tributaries to Mono Lake could be altered by the state if necessary to preserve trust values in this resource. Diverting water under the rights awarded to it, Los Angeles had caused the lake to shrink, become more saline, and lose much of its brine shrimp population— leading to the deterioration of its once rich bird habitat. The court articulated the public trust doctrine as "an affirmation of the duty of the state to protect the people's common heritage of streams, lakes, marshlands and tidelands, surrendering that right of protection only in rare cases when the abandonment of that right is consistent with the purposes of the trust." Thus, Los Angeles' old, established water rights were vulnerable, because the state failed to consider various public values in granting them to the city.

A doctrine that apparently permits direct revision of property rights to protect public trust values is controversial. The courts in several other western states have cited it in water-use disputes, but, in spite of predictions to the contrary, the public trust doctrine has not been invoked to make wholesale changes in water rights—even in California. It suffers from a number of deficiencies as an instrument of public policy in its present form: it is essentially a remedy to be applied after harm is proved, not an effective preventive measure. But, at the very least, the public trust doctrine is a harbinger of a rising tide of public interest concerns in western water matters.

In recent years, the most important assertions of the public interest in water have come in the form of environmental regulations, state instream flow programs, and federal and state water conservation programs and requirements. Federal environmental laws including the Clean Water Act and the Endangered Species Act express a public policy that values such as water quality, fish and wildlife habitat, and wetlands should be protected. They express the federal government's new willingness to be involved in managing the nation's natural resources—a reaction to public outrage over environmental crises and a response to changing public values. Just as the prior appropriation doctrine embodied the ideals of an expanding nation in the late nineteenth century, these federal environmental programs express society's values in the late twentieth century.

The Clean Water Act calls for all of the nation's waters to be fishable and swimmable; it mandates the protection and restoration of the physical, chemical, and biological integrity of those waters. The Act successfully attacked pollutant discharges from discrete "point sources," such as pipes, through a national permit program. It has been less successful in dealing with runoff from streets and parking lots, mine drainage, livestock feedlots, irrigation return flows, and erosion from timber harvesting and grazing. Such nonpoint sources of pollution are not regulated by the Clean Water Act. In 1987, Congress took one small step forward by requiring state management plans to address nonpoint sources. But much remains to be done to deal with what is now acknowledged to be the most widespread source of water quality degradation.

Another important federal environmental law, the Endangered Species Act, has focused attention on the relationship between water development and use and the water-based needs of plant and animal species. The Act provides strong protection for species that the U.S. Fish and Wildlife Service has identified as threatened with extinction. Activities such as water development projects requiring a federal permit fall within the Act's provisions, which prohibit federal officials from taking or authorizing any action that will "jeopardize" a protected species. Indeed, water use has radically altered the region's rivers, sometimes eliminating species whose habitat was destroyed by water projects. Reflecting a new awareness of these environmental costs, the Endangered Species Act says that activities causing the permanent extinction of species are no longer acceptable. Federal agencies are now developing recovery plans for protected species, seeking ways to permit water use to continue in a manner that allows natural systems and the species that depend on them to be sustained. Although researchers still do not fully understand the needs of such systems, they are gaining important new information in these efforts to accommodate water use and species preservation.

The Endangered Species Act has been interpreted strictly. In 1978, the U.S. Supreme Court upheld a decision to halt completion of the Tellico Dam in Tennessee because of the likely jeopardy to the continued existence of the snail darter, an endangered minnow. "It may seem curious to some that the survival of a relatively small number of three-inch fish . . . would require the permanent halting of a virtually completed dam," wrote Justice Berger in the *Tennessee Valley Authority v. Hill* opinion, but the Act "admits of no exception." Similarly, possible impacts 200 miles downstream on the habitat of the endangered whooping crane prevented construction of the Wildcat Reservoir in Colorado. The strict requirements of the Endangered Species Act press water managers to consider new ways to operate water storage facilities across the West to protect endangered fish habitat.

While comprehensive federal pollution and species-protection laws are a relatively recent development, the states and the federal government have long recognized the value of maintaining water "instream," or in its natural place. In 1915 Oregon enacted legislation prohibiting water diversions above many of its scenic waterfalls in the Columbia River gorge. The modern instream flow preservation programs, which began in Oregon in 1955 and spread to most western states, mark a shift in views about the value of water in the West. Such programs explicitly recognize the importance of maintaining at least some minimum quantity of water in streams and lakes to support such things as fish, water quality, and recreation. They pursue this goal through various means: setting minimum streamflow levels, authorizing the appropriation of instream flow water rights, and reserving unappropriated waters from further development. These programs help to address the needs of western rivers and to protect many important public values not historically considered under the prior appropriation system.

Yet, important as these programs are, they have made little impact in most parts of the West. The policies of free water, capture, and property ensured that much of the West's water was fully appropriated long ago. Little has been done in most places to improve stream conditions beyond what the existing patterns of water use incidentally provide. New reservations of water to preserve streamflows are junior in priority to all existing uses. Moreover, the purposes for which water is protected generally are very limited—in most states, protection of fish is the only authorized purpose for establishing instream flows. And the flow levels protected are typically the minimum that can sustain the use. Finally, most states have limited the right to seek and hold instream flows to a single state agency, so that others who want to preserve them have to work through that agency.

There are other opportunities to remedy the consequences of past water policies. Since the mid-1970s, western state legislatures, Congress, and the courts have become increasingly active in programs related to water-use efficiency. Their motivation is simple: As withdrawals under prior appropriation mount, water supplies become increasingly tight. There is less water for traditional extractive uses, such as irrigation, power generation, and industrial and urban demands. The stress on the rivers has been accentuated by the necessities of fulfilling promises made to Indian tribes and of maintaining acceptable levels of instream flows. Further, water withdrawals have caused serious water quality problems. Return flows from farm and ranch lands bring with them soil, salts, and, in many cases, agricultural chemicals. Water quality is altered as the warmer return flows raise temperatures in the streams, thus affecting wildlife habitat. Problems of soil erosion raise disturbing questions of long-term agricultural sustainability and of loss of reservoir capacity as sediments build up behind dams.

States are pursuing improved water-use efficiency through a number of avenues. On the one hand, water administrators are beginning to impose specific limitations on water uses in some circumstances to encourage greater efficiency. For example, Arizona's 1980 Groundwater Management Act sets up specific limitations on certain agricultural water uses and encourages greater urban water-use efficiency. And the California State Water Resources Control Board has brought legal actions against users such as the Imperial Irrigation District to curtail wasteful or unreasonable use of water. Some states are enacting plumbing codes that require installation of water-efficient fixtures in newly constructed buildings.

Other approaches are voluntary, offering incentives for more efficient water use. The California legislature enacted a law clarifying that a water user may conserve water then sell or put the saved water to other uses without fear of losing the water right. Oregon has specifically provided for the right to transfer conserved water, coupled with a requirement to dedicate up to 25 percent of that water to the state to enhance streamflow. Federal programs funded under the 1985 and 1990 farm bills and section 319 of the Clean Water Act pay part of the costs of installing more efficient water-use systems on farms to improve water quality by reducing polluted return flows.

State courts have long held that "the right to use water does not give the right to waste it." Indeed, western water law is replete with admonitions against waste of water. The beneficial use doctrine limits users to the amount of water necessary to accomplish the beneficial use for which their water rights were established. The Oregon Supreme Court, in the 1911 decision *Andrews v. Donnelly*, put it this way:

Before the country was so thickly settled as it is now, the practice for the appropriator of water "to keep all you get and get all you can" was in many cases tolerated; but, yielding to reasonable justice to all, the later authorities have established a different rule. We conceive it to be the law, except as modified by statute, that the right of a prior appropriator is paramount, but the right is limited to such an amount of water as is reasonable and necessary for such useful purpose and project as may be fairly within contemplation at the time the appropriation is made.

This well-accepted standard makes clear that there is an objective, quantifiable amount of water available to the appropriator: not necessarily the amount of water claimed, nor the amount of water capable of being carried through the diversion structure, nor even the amount of water historically diverted. Rather it is, in the words of the Colorado statute, "that amount of water that is usable and appropriate under reasonably efficient practices to accomplish without waste the purpose for which the appropriation is lawfully made." In spite of its clarity, the beneficial use doctrine's antiwaste mandate has been honored more in its breach.

How might western states encourage water-use efficiency *and* protect other water rights holders, new uses, and the streams themselves? A comprehensive state program can provide incentives to conserve water, including the right to transfer saved water, and access to low-interest loans to fund conservation projects; it can also support other marketlike mechanisms. Most notably, if western states abandoned their practice of allowing free private use of public water and imposed charges for water extraction, there would be incentives for water conservation, and the proceeds could be used to provide funding to water users for water conservation measures.

Sensible regulation—the setting of reasonable water-use standards and a phased-in schedule to achieve those standards—must also be part of the comprehensive program. Conservation of western water and protection of western watercourses are essential goals in the modern West, and regulation is one appropriate and necessary method to move water users toward those objectives.

We have described a variety of ways in which the public interest has gained protection in laws and policies affecting western water users.

These are signs of genuine change, and signs that the values represented by the public interest need not be buried beneath unfortu-
nate decisions of the past. There are opportunities to expand on
many of them and to share successful experiences among states.
Given the "irreducible public claim on water as a public resource," in
the words of Professor Sax, and the inherently limited nature of an
appropriative water right, private rights will continue to evolve in
order to accommodate legitimate public needs. As Dan Tarlock observed, recent western water adjudications demonstrate "that state-
created water rights are not different from any other property
rights despite the vast energy dissipated by western water lawyers to
will a contrary result." In the context of the Endangered Species Act,
Professor Tarlock concluded that "state water rights are not immune from the retroactive application of state police power or of
federal constitutional authority." The policy of water as property
provides an effective means of establishing private rights, but property has always been a flexible institution, responsive to changing societal values within a constitutional framework. Following are examples—national, regional, and local—of opportunities for the
public interest to be infused into specific areas of water policy in order to revitalize decision making and the rivers themselves.

RECONSIDERING WATER PROVIDED BY
FEDERAL WATER PROJECTS

> Water policies need to be changed to permit recognition of and accommo-
> dation to the demands of the new West. Many such changes have already
> been made through state legislation and court decrees and the pace of
> change is accelerating, particularly in the northern tier of states. Changes
> in federal policies are being forced by the growing federal deficit. When
> the present round of federal reclamation projects is completed there may
> not be any more. Policy makers in the Bureau of Reclamation have already
> announced their intention to change the Bureau from a construction
> agency to a water management agency. It is time for this change.
>
> THEODORE M. SCHAD : *The Changing Scene in the American West:*
> *Water Policy Implications*

The great plumbing systems that collectively control about a fifth of
all water in the West are operated either directly by federal agencies

or by local districts under legal obligations to follow certain federal dictates. When water is transferred from present project uses to new ones, the transaction is subject to federal guidelines. Operation of the projects—how much power is generated, the level of regard for fish and wildlife, the degree of efficiency in water use, and the terms of contracts with individuals who use project water—all can be determined by federal agencies.

The government, therefore, has an opportunity to use its authority over federal project contracting and operations. In this way it can alter existing patterns of dam releases to prevent damage to a fishery, control irrigation of certain lands to reduce pollutant-laden runoff, and curtail inefficient water uses. Discretionary federal authority can also be used to promote beneficial transfers of water from one use to another. The federal government has not exerted all of the power and influence at its disposal to insist that projects be operated to achieve fuller public benefits. Even the statutory requirement that districts operating federal water projects develop water conservation programs is not fully enforced.

The Department of the Interior, which oversees the Bureau of Reclamation, adopted principles in 1988 to guide the Bureau in its treatment of voluntary transfers of project water. In issuing the principles, the Department acknowledged that "to an increasing degree, [the Department of the Interior] will be asked to approve, facilitate, or otherwise accommodate such transactions that involve or affect facilities owned or operated by its agencies." The principles appear to be a positive step toward favorable transfers of project water, but they fall short of articulating a federal policy to encourage transactions that would improve water use from a public interest perspective. To date, the principles have produced little change.

The legacy of federally subsidized water development seems literally "set in concrete," but there are some remarkable possibilities on the horizon that could roll back earlier decisions. In 1991, Interior Secretary Manuel Lujan ordered a new operating regime for the Glen Canyon Dam, expressing the federal government's willingness to temper releases and thus forgo lucrative power generation in order to protect fragile beaches in Grand Canyon and give boaters on the Colorado River a better ride. In the meantime, the Bureau of

Reclamation marshalled the efforts of 140 scientists and 300 volunteers to prepare a comprehensive environmental study of impacts of operating the dam for hydroelectric power generation.

The recently enacted Elwha River Ecosystem and Fisheries Restoration Act, aimed at tearing down two small hydroelectric dams on the Elwha River (which runs into the Pacific Ocean in Washington) that have driven local salmon to extinction. The Act explicitly states as one of its purposes: "to restore, protect, and enhance the value of the Elwha River anadromous fishery and other resources" for the benefit of local Indian tribes and citizens. The Federal Energy Regulatory Commission soon will review dozens of other privately built dams whose fifty-year permits are up for renewal in coming years; environmentalists, tribes, and others are lining up to participate in the agency's review.

Already the U.S. Fish and Wildlife Service and the Bureau of Reclamation have cooperated in changing release patterns from the Flaming Gorge Dam on the Green River in northeastern Utah, sacrificing hydroelectric power generation flexibility in order to restore habitat conditions for four endangered fish species. When the dam was operated solely on the basis of consumer demand, it was "like a flush toilet," according to environmentalist Dan Luecke. The surging releases (highest during peak demand times) bore little resemblance to the river's historical flow patterns. Now, however, the dam operates under a new regime aimed at recreating natural flows, particularly in the spring (when the fish spawn) and summer (when the young fish swim downstream). Whether this new pattern will save the bonytail chub, humpback chub, razorback sucker, and Colorado River squawfish remains to be seen, but the federal agencies have demonstrated initiative in pursuing this goal.

In 1992 Congress enacted the sweeping Reclamation Projects Authorization and Adjustment Act. This bill included a section that will bring major changes in the operation of California's largest water delivery system, the Central Valley Project (CVP). The federal government built the CVP in the 1930s; today the system includes 20 reservoirs, 500 miles of waterways, and 12 million acre-feet of storage capacity. The CVP irrigates about 3 million acres of farmland and provides water to more than 2 million urban residents. The

1992 legislation established a $50 million annual fish and wildlife habitat restoration fund and instructed the Bureau of Reclamation to allocate annually 800,000 acre-feet of water (600,000 acre-feet in a dry year) to the environment. This reallocation of water may be one of the most significant signs of change in federal water project operations.

ACCOMMODATING INDIAN RESERVED RIGHTS

> In the history of the United States Government's treatment of Indian tribes, its failure to protect Indian water rights for use on the Reservations it set aside for them is one of the sorrier chapters.
>
> U.S. NATIONAL WATER COMMISSION : *Water Policies for the Future*

Many of the West's Indian reservations have very limited water resources available to them, yet federal policy favored farming as the best means for Indians to support themselves on reservations. The need for irrigation water on the Fort Belknap Indian Reservation in Montana, together with the prior appropriation doctrine's failure to protect the Indians' needs, led to the U.S. Supreme Court decision in 1908, *Winters v. United States*, establishing the "reserved" water rights doctrine.

The Fort Belknap Reservation was set aside in 1888 as a permanent homeland for several tribes who agreed to give up vast areas of their neighboring ancestral lands. The United States initiated a project ten years later to provide water from the Milk River to irrigate reservation lands. By that time, however, non-Indian settlers who had homesteaded on nearby lands relinquished by the tribes had constructed water diversions upstream of the reservation, leaving insufficient water for the Indian irrigation project. The United States belatedly brought an action in federal court claiming that the tribes had a better right to the water. In what would eventually be recognized as a crucial victory for tribes, the Supreme Court in 1908 found that the federal government had implicitly reserved enough water to carry out the purposes of the reservation. The Indians were assured of this water right even though they had not put the water to use before the neighboring non-Indians.

Despite the explicit recognition of tribal water rights and the need for protection of those rights, for the fifty years following the *Winters* decision the United States did virtually nothing to protect and develop water resources for tribes. It wasn't until 1963 that the Supreme Court reaffirmed the existence of Indian reserved water rights and established a standard for determining the quantity of water associated with those rights based on the "practicably irrigable acreage" existing on the reservation. This decision marked the date the reservation was established as the effective priority date of the reserved water right and clarified that the right is not subject to loss because of non-use. Subsequent decisions have recognized that Indian reserved rights can be based on flows necessary for fisheries and wildlife if the reservation was established for those purposes; other cases have concluded that reserved water rights quantified for irrigation purposes can be used for maintaining streamflows.

State court adjudications and negotiated settlements implemented through Congressional enactments are finally beginning to make water available to the tribes. The Ak-Chin Tribe in Arizona has been able to expand its irrigated agriculture by over 10,000 acres as a consequence of two settlement acts passed in 1978 and 1984 by Congress. A 1990 settlement act permits the Fort McDowell Tribe in Arizona to expand irrigated agriculture on that reservation from 730 to 4,000 acres and for the tribe to develop 18,350 acres for urban and other uses within the reservation. Other tribes whose water rights have been settled recently by statutes or compacts include the Southern Ute and Ute Mountain Ute tribes in Colorado; the Assiniboine and Sioux tribes of the Fort Peck Reservation in Montana; the Tohono O'odham and Salt River tribes in Arizona; the five Mission bands along the San Luis Rey River in Southern California; the Shoshone-Bannock tribes of the Fort Hall Reservation in Idaho; and the Fallon and Pyramid Lake Paiute tribes in Nevada. Most of these settlement acts include funding to help construct new irrigation facilities. Indian law experts Reid Chambers and John Echohawk have predicted that Indian use of water for agricultural and other purposes will expand by as much as 20 to 30 percent over historical uses when the rights are all quantified.

Recognition of tribal water rights is becoming a reality in the West. In some cases those rights have been defined only after prolonged conflict. In other cases negotiations have produced settlements acceptable to the tribes and other parties. Courts across the West are faced with claims for adjudication of tribal reserved water rights. Many tribes have not yet decided whether or when to pursue claims for reserved rights, and they are uncertain about the benefits and flexibility of negotiated settlements versus the leverage of courtroom litigation. The United States has a duty to assist the tribes but currently has a policy of measuring its financial commitment and obligation by its exposure to litigation costs.

One point is clear: tribes, as holders of substantial rights to use water resources, are now important participants in water-use decisions of the West. Validation of Indian claims gives them the opportunity to seek financing for water projects and to initiate new uses. It may also cast them in the position of a water supplier for existing and future non-Indian uses.

RETHINKING THE GOVERNANCE OF WESTERN WATER

> There are many signs of the rediscovery of a sense of place—the importance of being consciously related to and respectful of a setting.
>
> GARY D. WEATHERFORD : *From Basin to "Hydrocommons"*

The prior appropriation doctrine promoted individual water uses through the creation of private rights to use water. Over time, as the water rights established under the policies of free water, capture, and property began to threaten important public values, a new set of considerations developed—largely developed outside of the prior appropriation system. Today's western water policy has broadened considerably through judicial decisions, environmental programs, and new approaches to managing water facilities. Yet there is another trend worth noting: a rediscovery of the importance of broader, water-based values to individuals and local communities. These are values of water as part of a natural system, a watershed, and a living community—and they are linking people in new and exciting ways. Often focused on the areas defined by watershed boundaries (river basins, for example), these efforts are re-orienting people around the resources they share.

This is not a new idea. John Wesley Powell advocated the commonality of interests and the logic of decision making at the river basin level, as opposed to the state or federal government level, as have others since him, but the advice has rarely been heeded. Today the idea is attracting attention and respect. Local and regional neighbors have come together in river basins around the West to understand their shared resources and manage them for the future. Because each effort is unique to the community behind it, we illustrate this trend by recounting the stories of several local initiatives.

A Home for the Salmon: Mattole River, California

> The first thing we learned from salmon was the importance of the watershed as a unit of perception. If salmon organize themselves so clearly by watershed, wouldn't it make sense for us to organize our efforts similarly?
> FREEMAN HOUSE: "To Learn the Things We Need to Know"

On its way to the Pacific Ocean the Mattole River drains a 306-square-mile basin near the northern end of California. The river historically supported healthy annual runs of native king salmon; as recently as 1965 yearly runs were estimated at thirty-five thousand fish. But massive timber cutting in the last twenty years (90 percent of the old-growth redwood is now gone) and consequent erosion and siltation of the river ruined many traditional spawning sites and blocked fish migration routes up smaller tributaries.

Residents of this sparsely populated river basin organized in the early 1980s in an effort to restore the salmon runs. (The salmon, by that time, had grown so scarce that state fisheries officials had declared them too far gone to save.) The organization's early work focused on the spawning process: They trapped salmon and removed eggs for fertilization and incubation in fish hatch-boxes, then released the smolt into the Mattole River. The salmon rescuers soon realized that their efforts would be futile if the watershed continued to decline. So they formed a new organization, the Mattole Restoration Council, and began by mapping the watershed and its resources, using a mostly volunteer force of local watershed residents. The Council then embarked on a series of watershed-wide projects of erosion control, reforestation, salmon enhancement, and public education. It sought to bring together all two thousand watershed residents—a diverse mix ranging from traditional ranchers to hippie farmers, from loggers to fishermen—to devise a watershed protection strategy that reflects local wisdom and priorities. As one participant reflected, local residents were best situated to take on such a challenge: "Who else had the place-specific information that locals had? Who else could ever be expected to care enough to work the sporadic hours at odd times of the night and day for little or no pay?"

Today the Council's work extends far beyond hatch-boxes, although salmon propagation remains at the core of its priorities. Its other activities include extensive education programs for local elementary school students (the children help release tiny fish each year, then learn about their migratory path to the sea and back); planting new trees on eroded hillsides; opposition to any further removal of old-growth timber in the watershed; and lobbying in favor of more protective forest management initiatives. For more than ten years, the Mattole Restoration Council has worked to build cooperative relationships with commercial fishermen (whose livelihood depends as much on good land management in the headwaters as access to coastal water) and with small-scale loggers interested in sustainable forestry practices. The Council's target of restoring salmon runs is moving ahead more slowly than expected—it seems that the fish populations were even lower than biologists estimated—but the community restoration occurring in the Mattole River basin already has produced valuable and far-reaching lessons.

Farmers, Ranchers, and Anglers Cooperating: Clark Fork River, Montana

> The challenge, not only on the Bitterroot but throughout the Clark Fork basin (and in other basins too), is to get the people who are involved with the river to understand that what divides them is less important than what they have in common.
>
> DANIEL KEMMIS : "How the River Taught People to Talk"

Montana's Clark Fork River flows northwest into Lake Pend Oreille in Idaho and eventually joins the Columbia River. Early residents of the Clark Fork River basin found the river full of fish, thriving on its cool waters, meandering curves, and shady, overhanging vegetation. But recently, after many decades of channelization, tree-cutting, and irrigation diversions, the fishery was in a serious decline. Anglers hoping to restore the river approached valley farmers with a request that they reduce diversions for irrigation when natural streamflows were lowest in late summer.

At first, the farmers wanted nothing to do with the fishing interests. They repeated the basic principle of western water law: "We were here first." But several local conservation district members set about trying to bring the two factions together. Through repeated meetings with state agency officials, farmers, and anglers, they designed a new allocation of the river's water to meet the needs of farmers (by allowing full diversions during June and July when it is most needed for irrigation) and the fish (as irrigators agreed to leave a large proportion of their allocation in the river in August).

Today, the fishery is recovering, and the cooperative spirit has spread beyond water allocation. For example, local members of Trout Unlimited are volunteering to assist farmers with nonchemical weed removal from irrigation ditches. And, with the assistance of the Northern Lights Institute and several foundations, representatives of all the major interests with a stake in the river basin pool their time and talents in the Clark Fork Project. The Project is an effort to bring basin residents together "to gain a deeper understanding of one another's interests and of how those interests might be balanced for the good of the river system and the people who inhabit it."

Daniel Kemmis, now the mayor of Missoula, coined the phrase "basin citizenship" to describe this process. He noted that the Clark Fork agreement represented more than a technical solution to an old water fight: "It was also an example of the civilizing influence of the river. As people mature in their relationship to nature, some of them learn to appreciate the integrity of a river itself, as opposed to their own narrow rights to it." By gaining an appreciation for the needs of others within the watershed (and by cooperating to come up with an approach to meet those needs), the anglers, farmers, and local government leaders learned to focus on their shared interests rather than their differences.

A River Runs through the City: Urban Stream Restoration Efforts

> There's an increased awareness of the ecological importance of streams as
> links between the ocean and the upper watershed. There are more people
> who understand these connections. They are realizing that cities can and
> need to be more livable.
>
> BRUCE VAN ALLEN : "Consciousness of Streams"

Westerners first lost sight of the course of western rivers in the burgeoning urban centers. Streams running through some cities were
channelized or buried in concrete tunnels, or just filled with trash.
Many city residents were hard pressed to name the streams running
through their neighborhoods. Increasingly, however, there is a new
consciousness of urban rivers; the geographic feature most responsible for the boundaries of western cities is being rediscovered.
Streams are being cleaned up, river walks and parks created, and
habitats restored.

Between 1985 and 1990 the California Department of Water Resources' Urban Streams Restoration Program awarded $1.4 million
to cities, counties, and nonprofit community groups for environmentally beneficial streambank stabilization and natural flood
control projects. One of those projects is Wildcat Creek in the low-
income community of Richmond, just north of Berkeley, California. When government officials proposed channelizing and burying the creek to prevent floods, local citizens (with the help of a
statewide group, the Urban Creeks Council) proposed an alternative to the concrete solution: They wanted to see the creek's natural
meandering path restored, flood terraces constructed, and riparian vegetation planted on the streambanks. With a grant from the
Urban Streams Restoration Program, and a lot of citizen volunteer
effort, the Wildcat Creek Project became a model for urban initiative.

Urban stream restoration efforts are important to inner-city residents who have no other sustained contact with the natural environment. Funding sources like California's Urban Streams Restoration
Program provide the means by which local residents can actively improve their watershed.

*   *   *

These examples show that neighbors sharing a common source of water can overcome fragmented political boundaries to plan for sustainable use of water and other natural resources. On a larger scale, the basin-wide Northwest Power Planning Council has embarked on an ambitious effort to restore the Columbia River basin's salmon fishery. And the 1990 Truckee River water rights settlement in Nevada, which enables transfers of water from irrigation to environmental enhancement, demonstrates the possibilities for preserving wetlands and an Indian fishery through cooperation with irrigation water users. Although each of these watershed-oriented approaches is unique, they share some similarities. Each was organized out of shared perceptions of the need for action—information gathering, planning, and consensual decision making. Each has recognized that gathering information about a watershed is a difficult but necessary starting point for taking action.

These approaches tend to look to existing government structures for administration and direction, rather than advocating the creation of new government entities or legal authorities. One participant in the Mattole Restoration Council concluded that "building from the bottom up, preferably on a previous base of mutual interest and cooperation, is infinitely preferable to a mandate from on high." Even the Northwest Power Planning Council, a new entity created by interstate compact, does not possess independent legal authority over other government agencies.

Most important, perhaps, all these efforts shared a simple sense of belonging—belonging to a region or area defined by a body of water and the interests it serves or affects; belonging to a community of people dependent on the resources in that watershed; and belonging to the complex of living and nonliving things that make up the ecosystems that rely on the water.

Water use in the American West is breaking free of the prior appropriation doctrine and reclamation law. Today, institutional protections for the public interest, environmental statutes, instream flow programs, incentives for water conservation, Indian water rights, and local initiatives are all influencing water decisions. What is driving these changes, and where are they headed?

Western water policy, with its strata of decisions, laws, and programs of earlier eras influencing the shape of today's policies, was the product of relatively few people and entities. Those few are the ones who have been best served by the policies and who have been the participants in most policy decisions. The prior appropriation doctrine and federally subsidized water projects were originally designed to meet rather discrete needs. But the goals of encouraging mining on the public lands and making the arid West productive for family farmers lacked the broad appeal needed to sustain sufficient political commitment to the underlying policies. As isolated ideas or decisions, neither prior appropriation nor federal water projects would have been such powerful or enduring influences without the support and advocacy of others besides miners and farmers.

Early farmers wanted the security that the prior appropriation doctrine gave, so they embraced the miners' idea. Land developers and speculators also recognized that attaching legal rights to water so that it could be used on parcels away from streams was the key to land sales. They supported and still defend the prior appropriation doctrine as a convenient tool to promote development. States liked the idea of controlling water allocation, even on federal lands. Water projects—some of the country's largest public works undertakings—found eager backing from construction and engineering firms, local boosters, unions, and many others that have benefitted from subsidized water. And politicians were attracted to policies that enabled them to procure big spending programs for their home districts.

Taken as a whole, the interests traditionally served by western water policy are not numerous, at least compared with those who were and are affected by the policies. They are, however, economically and politically influential. Nearly every person in the West experiences terrain shaped by the legacy of early water laws. They are concerned about the consequences. They see and care about the environmental impacts of water use. As new commitments and decisions are made—dams built, drought plans made, trade-offs among resources discussed—these people want to be involved. They know there is a lot of water "out there," but have no means to decide what is done with it because the water is controlled by others. Though everyone has always had a stake in water policy, only recently have people begun to realize it.

The water policy that westerners want today is the policy founded on long-established values. Both the number of people and the diversity of interests to be served by water have expanded. People are less likely to be intimidated by water agencies and water "experts" and are beginning to stand up for their positions. They are willing to challenge proposals that are offensive to the interests of substantial groups of the public. Thus, for example, the people of Colorado's rural San Luis Valley voted to increase their taxes to fund litigation against a private development company's scheme to pump groundwater from beneath their valley and sell it to distant growing cities. And they won.

Policy decisions in western water are more susceptible than ever to public influence. First, the overlay of environmental law has already opened the process so that there are public hearings before most big decisions. Second, the public and groups representing it (citizen associations, water-user groups, and environmental organizations, for example) are increasingly informed and skilled at participation and advocacy. Still, the issues are growing in complexity, since the basic public demand is for more comprehensive water policy.

A comprehensive water policy will require a coherent vision for the future and a rationale for making decisions. Without these, western water will remain the captive of powerful interests, despite the gains in public participation and environmental protection that have occurred in recent years.

Chapter Eight
———————————
Change and Rediscovery in Western Water

As birds have flight, our special gift is reason. . . . Should we choose, we could exercise our reason to do what no other animal can do: we could limit ourselves voluntarily; choose to remain God's creatures instead of making ourselves gods. What a towering achievement that would be, so much more than the largest dam—beavers can build dams—because so much harder.

BILL MCKIBBEN : *The End of Nature*

WATER RESOURCES are needed by the whole community, not just those parts that were there first or that have money or power. This is especially critical in areas where water is scarce, such as the western United States. Recent changes in water law and policy soften the hard edges of the old system. But if those changes are no more than political responses to the newest set of special interests, the emerging policy will have little lasting value.

Meaningful and enduring change in western water law and policy must be rooted in a set of principles that reflect westerners' core values and concerns. These principles must represent a coherent vision of why people *care* about water—a framework defining what makes policy "good" or "bad," "right" or "wrong." They must reach a fundamental level of belief so that they can guide change and not merely respond to it. They must form a water ethic that will be at the base of all decisions concerning water use.

It is rare to think about water in ethical terms, when it has historically been viewed as a commodity, as an instrument, as a conve-

178

nience. People tend to take water for granted, expecting it to be where they want it, when they want it. Westerners have been willing to fight about water, especially when they believe that someone is interfering with their use of it. But it is unusual to talk about principles directing uses of water instead of short-term expediency, to talk of what is "right" instead of who has rights.

Laws in other areas—civil rights, due process, torts, free speech—tend to reflect basic ideals of right and wrong. Not so in water law. Beyond the simple appeal of first-come, first-served, the prior appropriation doctrine is not tied to any widely held principles. Indeed, many are unhappy with water decisions precisely because water policy lacks such principled anchors.

We believe that western water policy must be based on three fundamental principles: the principle of conservation, the principle of equity, and the principle of ecology. Together, these principles represent the emergence of a water ethic that provides a coherent and lasting basis for water policy. These are principles of fundamental importance. While they have always influenced water use, their importance has been greatly obscured by the dominant role of water as a tool of western economic development over the last 150 years.

The changes described in the preceding chapter reflect a rediscovery of the importance of these principles. They represent the emergence of a new sensibility about water, a new awareness of its broad importance to the whole community of the West. They are steps in the direction of defining a water policy that meets this vision of the role of water in relation to the society and community of which it is an integral part. We turn now to a discussion of these principles and how they relate to the changing water policy of the West.

THE PRINCIPLE OF CONSERVATION:
WATER SHOULD BE USED WITH CARE

> The period when the West could satisfy much of the country's rapacious
> appetite for natural resources is drawing to a close. . . . Over the long run,
> certainly by the time our children's children are grown, our culture must
> come to grips with the inherent inconsistency of sustained growth on a
> finite planet.
>
> STEWART L. UDALL : *Beyond the Mythic West*

Stewardship of resources is a basic value of most societies, certainly
of our own. Parents teach children not to waste. The Old Testament
says: "Is it not enough for you to feed on the good pasture, that you
tread down with your feet the rest of your pasture; and to drink of
clear water, that you must foul the rest with your feet?" George Per-
kins Marsh, the great nineteenth-century naturalist, lawyer, and or-
chardist, reminded his contemporaries of the same message: "Man
has forgotten that the earth was given to him for usufruct alone, not
for consumption, still less for profligate waste." Damaging or using
resources unnecessarily, even if they are plentiful, seems wrong to
most people.

Concern about the careful use of resources applies readily to
water. Water is a renewable but limited resource. It serves many uses
and many users. The wasteful use of water—as by consuming large
quantities of water unnecessarily, by taking water but not using it, by
polluting water—affects its availability for others. The careful husbandry of water—water conservation—is a value shared by most
westerners.

Our theme of rediscovery is illustrated well by the evolving meaning of water conservation in the West. The conservationist philosophy articulated around the end of the nineteenth century stressed
the importance of development and use of resources for human
benefit and considered non-use as waste. Many equated conservation with development, water conservation with water storage.

Not everyone, even in the early 1900s, though, believed that resources were only for development and use. For example, national
parks advocate Stephen Mather argued that some resources should
remain indefinitely in their pristine state. The national parks and

monuments provided a battleground for the competing views of resource conservation, and water was often at the center of those battles. The fight over the construction of Hetch Hetchy Reservoir in
Yosemite National Park in the early 1900s is an example.

Today, conservation comprehends a wider view of resources. The
focus is no longer exclusively on fulfilling immediate human wants.
There is a deeper recognition that humans are part of a larger system and are obliged to conserve natural resources for their own
good as well as the good of future generations and other species.

The principle of conservation calls for meaningful consideration
of consequences of proposed water uses. It demands that the advantages and disadvantages of every water use be carefully weighed. It
asks that a proposed use be considered in relation to the whole community, that the use be no more than necessary, that its harmful effects on others be minimized or avoided. It seeks to find a balance
among the competing interests in water while adhering to the principles of equity and ecology.

In an important way, existing water law already reflects this principle. The prior appropriation doctrine allows water users to establish private rights only to the extent of "beneficial use." Beneficial
use expresses the fundamentally public character of water and in
that sense incorporates the full range of values that society holds for
water. Individuals can establish and maintain water rights to the extent that society benefits from private property in water use. Water
rights that use water in a manner contrary to societal values cannot
be regarded as beneficial and should be subject to revision and possibly even revocation.

In practice, however, the beneficial use doctrine has meant much
less. Court decision after court decision rails against wasteful uses of
water; yet only the most extravagantly profligate uses (in one case,
for example, using water to flood fields to drown gophers) has ever
been found to be nonbeneficial. Today, a firmer acceptance of the
principle of conservation is leading to the development of both incentives and requirements for greater efficiency of water use. Still,
the doctrine has not yet approached its potential.

The principle of conservation is also causing a wholesale recon-
sideration of the subsidies that have fostered much of the existing

water development and use. The policy of free water has caused a serious misallocation of resources in favor of consumption, diversion, and contamination of water. It has distorted the economic and social value of water, leading to both misuse and overuse of this resource. As the principle of conservation invokes sound economics to tame the policy of free water, society will no longer accept wasteful uses of water and will require water users to pay the marginal costs— the full additional cost of developing water for their uses. The beneficial use doctrine will begin to clarify the limited property interest in a water right and will exclude aspects of use that fail to serve both the private and the public interests. Users will pay for the use of this public resource, with the funds then used to improve, protect, and restore the resource for all of the relevant public values.

THE PRINCIPLE OF EQUITY: THE WHOLE COMMUNITY SHOULD BE TREATED FAIRLY

> Water . . . symbolizes such values as opportunity, security, and self-determination. . . . Strong communities are able to hold on to their water and put it to work. Communities that lose control over water probably will fail in trying to control much else of importance.
>
> HELEN INGRAM : *Water Politics: Continuity and Change*

The principle of equity arises out of the shared, public nature of water. Water is fundamental to life and to all living systems. The essential importance of water places a special value on the manner in which decisions are made respecting its use and availability. The whole community must be considered in those decisions, and all interests must have a meaningful opportunity to participate. There is a deeply felt sense today that water decisions, many made years ago, reflect only a narrow range of interests and concerns. People are frustrated with a policy that allows one user to flood-irrigate alfalfa in a time of drought, while others are forced to curtail their uses or even go without any water at all. Decisions based on political or economic strength alone offend a sense of fairness. So too does the hoarding or monopolizing of a fundamental resource like water, as does profiteering beyond the normal economic return necessary to justify an investment. The principle of equity expresses the need for community participation in charting a vision for western water.

In a democracy, fairness demands that people with a stake in a public decision have the opportunity to participate in it. This is the basis of the guarantee of "due process" found in the U.S. Constitution. Fairness does not mean that everyone must agree with the decision. Rather it means that there must be a balanced process: people's opportunity to influence a decision should be appropriate to their stake in the outcome. Water decision making now simply fails to meet this standard.

Disregarding the principle of fairness can lead to dissension, destructive competition, and a deterioration of social institutions. The tragic results of bad decisions made in a political system insensitive to affected communities of interest led to the demise of governments in Eastern Europe and the Soviet Union. Closer to home, people are outraged when western cities buy out and dry up distant farmlands as a source of water for growth without answering the concerns of farmers and local businesses harmed by those transfers. Organized societies are threatened when decisions insult their values, like justice, aesthetics, and community integrity. Yet, under present water policies, those widely held ideals are often overwhelmed by interests with greater, or at least more concentrated, political or economic power. Because present water institutions were organized to spur economic activity and sustain the economic security of the earliest users, the political system focuses on preserving the status quo and respecting private property. Protecting those economic values has tended to eclipse other values, to the detriment of the interests of the whole community.

What is wrong with this? A drive to acquire and control resources is fundamental to human nature. Wealth—individual dominion over resources—at the most basic level ensures individual survival. Taken to its logical extreme, wealth gives some humans power over others. Most societies accept the legitimacy of power relationships based on wealth, up to a point. But society's balance is threatened when control of wealth becomes so absolute or extensive that one or a few individuals monopolize resources crucial to survival or to satisfying basic needs of society.

Elwood Mead explained the prior appropriation doctrine as a response to the fear of giving landowners along streams an effective monopoly over water. For a time early in our history, a system of attaching water rights to land ownership—the riparian rights doctrine—worked in the East. In the West, however, the government was giving land away to settlers, states, and railroads as incentives to economic development. It made more sense to distribute water rights to those who first put the water to productive use—essentially severing it from the land—rather than allowing a relatively small number of fortunate recipients of waterfront land to monopolize water rights. Indian tribes were dealt out entirely, and Hispanic communities could retain their traditional use of water only if they could fit within the rigid requirements of prior appropriation.

Private rights to use water were recognized first, as we have described elsewhere, by community custom among California miners concerned primarily with putting water to work extracting minerals with a minimum of conflict among themselves. State law, with federal acquiescence, later embodied these customs. Water rights became a form of property. The key to acquiring and keeping them was simply to put water to use. In theory, this meant that private individuals could acquire rights only to quantities of water that could be used productively for society.

Much of the public doubt and questioning about western water policy today has arisen because some water users appear to be using too much water, while others do not have enough. This apparent unfairness has arisen because the prior appropriation doctrine's use-based rights are ranked according to when water was first put to use. This means that if there is insufficient water for all users, only the earliest ones can take the full amount of their water. In a drought, farmers with old irrigation rights may pour large amounts of water on fields to produce crops worth relatively little, though this may deny water to a city with a burgeoning population. The law may or may not let the city buy some of the farmers' water; if it does, it may or may not allow the interests of the farm community or others to be considered along with those of the city and the farmer. The water law that fit the simple needs of small communities of nineteenth-century miners must be refined to meet the complex needs of twentieth-century communities.

Most societies give special respect to universal water needs like drinking, washing, and cooking. Beyond these basic needs there are other uses of broadly public value—refreshment, recreation, spiritual renewal, and aesthetic satisfaction. Public values derived from water include the community identity and cultural integrity that is drawn from, say, a river that runs through the heart of a town. Taken together, these add up to a substantial public stake in water decisions.

The value and importance of some uses only became apparent after most water in the West was spoken for. Today, one of the largest and fastest-growing water uses is for outdoor recreation. Yet the availability of unspoiled rivers for boating, fishing, and other forms of enjoyment is limited and actually declining because of increased diversions for agricultural, municipal, and industrial uses. Even where water can be bought and sold, recreational users are rarely well enough organized or rich enough to pay for the water they need.

The bedrock value underlying beneficial use is that resources should be used wisely, in the words of nineteenth-century conservationist Gifford Pinchot, to produce "the greatest good for the greatest number in the long run." Though Pinchot advocated full economic use of resources, he recognized that the whole community should be served and that long-range perspective was needed. Thus, water uses that promote only individual wealth and disregard broader interests of the public may not be truly beneficial. Accordingly, prior appropriation only allowed private uses because it presumed they benefitted the community. A hard look at water policy should seek distributional fairness. At a minimum, these should be opportunities to hear people who do not have sufficient water for the uses they care about and for their views should be taken seriously by decision makers.

What does this mean in practice? The public, through some acceptable process, must first decide which waters are for public use and which are available for private use within a market system. The waters that will be subject to private control and markets are, in the parlance of state constitutions, "subject to appropriation." This appropriation ought to be limited to the amount that is not needed by the whole community for the satisfaction of public values. If reasonably secure private rights are established in appropriated waters, they can be transferred and used according to market forces. The use of waters appropriated for private use is subject to regulation like any other activity. For instance, regulation can limit pollution and define how markets operate. In many states and for the huge quantities of water that are controlled by federal water projects, it will take further legal changes to free up the water to marketing.

State and federal agencies can further the principle of fairness in water decision making by creating new processes for comprehensive, integrated decisions; public interest is an inclusive concept and should not be left to fragmented consideration. This means that water quality should be considered together with the allocation of water, not separated for decision in a different agency. It means that water planning and management should be considered in land-use planning and regulation. For example, groundwater recharge areas should be protected from incompatible development. It means that effects on water resources should be considered in establishing agricultural policy. Farm land development has been the primary cause of wetlands loss in the United States since the 1950s.

This principle firmly supports the need for broader community participation. Water decisions will be fairer if decision makers must answer to those affected by their decisions. Laws should require governments to account for impacts of their water decisions at all levels. Now, water districts, cities, state engineers, tribes, and agencies of all kinds have only fragmented responsibilities. A district board appointed by a judge and charged with supplying enough water for irrigation in several counties can do its narrowly defined job very well and still disregard the interests of wildlife, city dwellers, Indians, boaters, and others. A state engineer may administer water rights strictly according to priorities but dry up a stream, kill all the fish, favor production of worthless crops while letting valuable crops die, and serve irrigators who follow unconscionably wasteful or polluting practices. Simply enforcing old rights and laws can be downright unfair to interests throughout the community.

The only way significant changes in water policy will come about is through new awareness and inclusion in the process of people who are not the traditional water experts. Public education about the importance of water and its linkages to so many of society's values can help develop an awareness of consequences and of the unfairness of excluding affected people and communities from the process of finding solutions.

THE PRINCIPLE OF ECOLOGY:
NATURE SHOULD BE RESPECTED

> All ethics so far evolved rest upon a single premise: that the individual is a member of a community of interdependent parts. His instincts prompt him to compete for his place in that community, but his ethics prompt him also to cooperate (perhaps in order that there may be a place to compete for). The land ethic simply enlarges the boundaries of the community to include soils, waters, plants, and animals, or collectively: the land.
>
> ALDO LEOPOLD : "The Land Ethic," in *A Sand County Almanac*

The significance of human behavior toward natural resources has been dramatized by solid evidence that people are changing nature, largely for the worse. While there were plenty of environmental disasters in ancient irrigation societies, major conflicts between human water demands and nature only recently became obvious in North America. Furthermore, we now know that other resource uses have altered weather patterns, accelerated the extinction of species to hundreds of times the natural rate, depleted stocks of resources it took millions of years to create, and produced poisons that will remain potent for a thousand generations.

The principle of ecology emerges when beliefs and values come face to face with a growing awareness of the awesome consequences of human activity on natural systems. It means recognizing humankind's position in the larger context of the natural environment: acknowledging that ultimately there is no such thing as an environmental impact that is not also a human impact.

Sometimes other parts of the environment benefit when manipulated to serve human desires. Consider the incidental positive effects that coincide with self-interest: anglers insist on stream conditions that produce fish, the insects that nourish fish, the vegetation that gives them cover, and so on; birdwatchers and hunters defend the preservation of biologically important wetlands; boaters demand protection of rivers and canyons that provide the flows and scenery that give them pleasure; or a downstream farmer asserts an old water right against upstream users, keeping water flowing and the stream natural at least as far as the farm. Dams retain and release water primarily to fill human needs, yet sometimes their operation can provide water flows and temperatures beneficial to fish and other natural features.

These incidental benefits are dwarfed by the harms that human water uses have imposed on nature. The fact is that today's water decisions and water policy generally do not take into account the links between human uses and their broader environmental effects.

The trade-offs required by multiple demands for water, of which nature protection is one, call for tough choices in water policy— choices that may require people to act against their immediate self-interest: curtailing decorative landscape planting, limiting suburban growth, funding expensive pollution controls, reducing use of electricity and its products. It is hard enough to forgo a green lawn as the hypothetical price of preserving a favorite fishing stream; it is even harder to do so for the sake of a brine shrimp population that supports migrating seabirds hundreds of miles away. It becomes increasingly difficult for people to appreciate the consequences of their actions when the consequences seem remote and attenuated from an innocent individual action.

Of the three components of our water ethic, the principle of ecology is perhaps most difficult to explain as a guidepost for how people ought to live their lives. It argues that people are obliged to protect natural systems, even beyond whatever "payoff" there may be for humans as a part of nature. This brings the ethical dimension into focus: people are expected to do something because it is right even when it conflicts with their immediate self-interest. What is the argument for a duty to engage in such apparently unselfish behavior?

Philosophers have struggled to articulate why humans should respect nature. Many of their suggestions are appealing to a point, but then fail. One view grounds the ethical value of nature in aesthetics. The literary work of Romantics like Wordsworth, Byron, and Coleridge instills a moving reverence for nature as a source of beauty and spiritual satisfaction. Much of the preservation movement in the United States today traces to this aesthetic appreciation of natural places and things. Even places and things people cannot actually visit or personally view—the Arctic Plain of Alaska, for example, or Amazon rainforests—are considered worthy of respect. It is satisfying to know that a waterfall seen only in photographs will be protected in its natural state or that the pristine habitat of otters, the likes of which most people see only in the zoo, will not be molested. Yet this view maintains a critical separation between humans and their environment. Natural places, birds, and plants are all viewed as instruments of human enjoyment. Thus, although an aesthetic motive is not inconsistent with the principle of ecology, it does not fully support it.

Taking a different tack, some philosophers have grounded a sense of duty toward nature by assigning rights to nonhuman beings. This goes beyond the idea that humans have reciprocal duties to respect one another's welfare, found in the writings of John Locke and, much later, John Rawls in *A Theory of Justice*. But an approach based on notions of reciprocal rights and duties does not translate well to nonhuman creatures that are incapable of moral judgment or conduct. Expressing obligations to the natural world in terms of rights may seem attractive to lawyers accustomed to ledgers of duties and rights, but law professor Christopher Stone has urged that the issue of environmental ethics not be bogged down in rights-duties analysis. He wrote, "In deciding what we ought to do . . . [t]he challenge is to devise a coherent moral viewpoint" that enables us to "account for a Thing [like a river and] serve[s] to revaluate decisions reached on the basis of ordinary Person-dominated welfare consideration alone."

Both the aesthetics and the rights-based theories, then, are inadequate. We believe, however, that the science of ecology provides information and understanding that will strike a responsive chord in most people and justify their taking on moral responsibility toward the natural world. By teaching the essential interdependence of everything, ecology furnishes the "coherent moral viewpoint" that Stone called for. Ecology relates the effects of what we do to an animal or a place to consequences people can comprehend and perhaps feel, and make intelligent choices about. An ecologist can explain how the destruction of the Mono Lake brine shrimp population by Los Angeles' diversions of water topples a line of biological dominoes, through the food chains of birds, predators, and so on, and affects natural systems continents away. So it is when a canyon is dammed—blocking fish migration, extinguishing some species, changing conditions for wildlife feeding, altering estuarine life, killing natural vegetation, and introducing exotic plants. Pull one thread of the intricate fabric of life, and you affect the whole tapestry.

Appreciation of the interconnectedness of all things is not a new idea. John Muir wrote in 1869: "When we try to pick out anything by itself, we find it bound fast by a thousand invisible cords that cannot be broke to everything in the universe." This understanding was also inherent in the lifestyle and mores of the Native peoples, who learned it and internalized it in their cultural norms after millennia of trial and error experience on the American continents.

The most famous and original articulation of the principle of ecology is Aldo Leopold's classic collection of essays, *A Sand County Almanac*. His "land ethic" places humans in a larger ecological community; membership in this community obligates people to act in ways that perpetuate the ecosystem. The land ethic is captured in Leopold's oft-quoted maxim: "A thing is right when it tends to preserve the integrity, stability, and beauty of the biotic community. It is wrong when it tends otherwise." Once the truth of ecology—the interconnectedness of all things—is understood, the ethical dimension, the link to the fate of all things and beings, becomes obvious.

Rules for human conduct that may affect other humans arise from an understanding of the consequences that one person's actions have on another. Similarly, rules for human conduct that may affect any part of the world (human or nonhuman) flow from an understanding of the consequences of a human action for all other things. An ecological perspective places regard for other people in a more complete context. People can understand that membership in a *human* community carries with it moral obligations to their fellow members. At this level, ethics differentiate "social from anti-social conduct." Leopold explained that any ethic people adopt in any realm can be viewed "ecologically, [as] a limitation on freedom of action in the struggle for existence." Likewise, evolution theorist Charles Darwin saw ethics and other social restraints as the product of natural selection. At first, we learn "modes of cooperation" as survival skills for members of the community of humankind. Humans long ago moved beyond the simple logic of "If I take your spear, you will try to take mine, and the community then won't work; therefore, it is not right to steal."

By Leopold's reckoning, "The land ethic simply enlarges the boundaries of the community" to include "soils, waters, plants, and animals, or collectively, the land." It follows that, "accordingly, we should evolve or assume actual limitations upon our conduct" for the benefit of the community. Armed with the knowledge of ecological science, and constantly striving to unravel its complexities and mysteries, people can try to make the life-or-death survival decisions for the ecological community on an ethical basis. Limits on immediate self-interest can promote the well-being of the ecological community just as self-restraint is needed for the benefit of the social, or human, community included within it. Understanding this and acting in accord with it surely is an evolutionary step.

Evolution favors the individuals and species that behave in ways leading to survival. Unlike other species, humans have a chance consciously to influence their own survival (along with that of the host environment and companion species) by using their genetic equipment well. Humans are distinguished from other creatures by their power of reason. Indeed, that power is what implicates ethics, because of the choices humans can make. Moreover, powers of intellect and reason may be able to train human behavior to a path of survival and successful interdependence. Other (nonhuman) members of the community have embedded survival behavior as instinct after evolution has weeded out misbehaving individuals during millions of generations of random experimentation.

Leopold saw the quest for ethical footholds as progress along an evolutionary trail. He saw ethics generally as "possibly a kind of community instinct in-the-making." The human species has the basic information about ecology and specifically about water's importance. Thus, we are able to take an evolutionary step now, not based on the scars of instinct, but upon reasoned and principled judgment. The alternative is for humans to be culled through natural selection, perhaps leaving only a vestige of the species.

The principle of ecology expresses Leopold's land ethic. (For him, of course, "land" encompassed water.) The principle of ecology stands on its own as a basis for making sound decisions, but it also informs how the other two principles—oriented as they are primarily to adjusting conduct among humans for the benefit of humans—are applied. Conserving water, using what is necessary but avoiding excessive consumption and preventing pollution, is right not only because of its regard for other people, but also because it protects the biotic community of which people are a part. Similarly, fair decision making processes provide a forum to discuss and act on ecological concerns, and thus the fairness principle also complements the ecological principle. For instance, equity demands that water decisions be made at an appropriate level, one that reflects the communities affected by those decisions. That often means that decisions will be more local and watershed-oriented. Elevating the importance of the watershed reflects an ecological reality: that a river system ties together everything in the watershed. This approach leads to a new emphasis on basin planning, river basin organizations, and redirecting agency decisions and problem solving to match the dimensions of the problems that are common to or create a community of interest.

A BALANCED APPROACH TO WATER USE: REALIZING THE WATER ETHIC

> We have been fighting about water for 20 years now. I don't understand what all this fighting is about.
>
> The Great Spirit put us here and put the fish and birds and animals here. He put the grass and trees here. The Great Spirit put the water here so everything could live. Everything must have water.
>
> Why are we fighting about this? Everyone must know this. Does the law not know this?"

STAR WEED, SHOSHONE TRIBE OF THE WIND RIVER INDIAN RESERVATION :
speaking at a meeting on Indian water rights, December 12, 1988

Following the principles that make up our water ethic is not ultimately at odds with satisfying human needs and comforts. Though it sometimes requires that human self-interest be tempered in the short-run, it favors survival, in the fullest sense. This requires keeping the system in balance; natural processes that complement one another have to be understood and respected. Choices of action should lead to a path that reflects a natural and equitable balance, that allows humans and other species to thrive.

As soon as conflicts between human uses and protection of natural systems arise, people must choose which will get the water. Is it right to make concessions in ethical judgments to favor humans? To risk or sacrifice consciously other things and beings for the sake of humans? Thinking of humans as one species within a vast, interdependent complex of natural things carries not only obligations to other species, but also the expectation that humans can rely on a system that is kept in balance to support their needs and activities. People bear the heady responsibility of trying to perceive where the balance lies. If an irrigation diversion will produce food for several families but reduce fish populations, is it fair? The answer may depend on the extent of the impact. Fewer fish may be tolerable; extinction is another matter. If a family were starving, however, and the situation was so extreme that they had no alternative for sustenance, risking extinction of the fish might even be considered an acceptable option.

Thus, our water ethic cannot be taken as a set of absolute commands. The biblical commandment "Thou shalt not kill" sounds absolute, but every society and almost every individual who embraces it admit exceptions—self-defense, defense of others, defense of the state, and so on. And the commandment generally is not considered to prohibit killing nonhumans.

All ethics require constant evaluation of opportunities and conscientious striving to strike the right balance. In Aldo Leopold's terms, an "ecological conscience" that "reflects a conviction of individual responsibility for the health of the land" can guide decisions. Still, Leopold accepted the realities of politics and economics. He conceded that "economic feasibility limits the tether of what can or cannot be done for land. It always has and it always will." But he emphatically rejected the idea that all land use and land relations (meaning all those things that make up "the land") are determined by economics. He pointed out that "human dedication of time, forethought, skill, and faith," not abstract movements of cash, are behind natural resources decisions. Thus, attitudes and actions based on ethical precepts can have a strong influence. Concessions that favor humans are inevitable; they should be made with consciousness of the trade-offs.

The ideal of balance is well expressed in the work of philosopher Holmes Rolston. He suggested "optimizing values carried by water," including the "just distribution to persons, so that each gets what is due" and "letting water take its course naturally in ecosystems."

This begins to explain how to apply the three principles of water use: The principle of ecology should be seen as an overarching or integrating value that informs how the others are to be applied in the search for a balanced and fair result for the whole community. A use of water that satisfies the three principles that make up the water ethic is balanced. The ideal of balance is what some writers mean by the popular term *sustainable use*. Striving for balanced—sustainable or optimal—uses of water requires difficult decisions about whether a particular water use or, more broadly, a particular policy, plan, law, or method of allocating water is consistent with the three principles of water use. The test of the principle of ecology should be applied, along with the principles of conservation and fair distribution, in looking at existing water policy or proposals for new water policy. It is, in other words, a standard by which society should evaluate its options with regard to water.

Individuals and Balanced Water Use

> There once were men capable of inhabiting a river without disrupting the harmony of its life.
>
> ALDO LEOPOLD : "Song of the Gavilan," in *A Sand County Almanac*

People are not accustomed to thinking about water in an ethical framework. The consequences of water use are rarely clear to the person using it, and the balancing issues remain subtle if not invisible. The big decisions—a new dam, diversion of water away from a farming community to a city, drying up an ancient lake, wiping out a species of fish—do occasionally seem consequential enough to be "right" or "wrong." Individuals can be outraged by these acts, but feel insulated from blame for their part in causing them. It is hard to see the effects of a particular decision about water, because each use often seems infinitesimally small compared to the problem, and because the rightness or wrongness of causing the effect is ambiguous. No one has to look into the eyes of a famine-ridden family and say: "I have decided to fill my hot tub with the water you need to sustain life."

The trade-offs inherent in water decisions can be calculated in broad equivalents: a car wash in Los Angeles consumes the water of a family farm in the Owens Valley; a farm in La Paz County is worth two golf courses in Tucson; a subdivision in the Denver suburbs with Kentucky bluegrass lawns uses the amount of water needed to keep a pristine western Colorado mountain stream full of fish; turning down the air-conditioning temperature by two degrees in Phoenix requires releases of water from hydroelectric dams that destroy a season's boating in the Grand Canyon. What does all this mean to the L.A. car wash customer, the Denver lawn waterer, the cattle rancher, the golfer, or the Phoenix resident? It's tough to appreciate the difference one more clean car, green lawn, golf course or cool Phoenician will make.

People do seem capable of appreciating the significance of their individual actions during a drought. Several years into a dry spell, reluctant city officials in Los Angeles finally mustered the courage to tell people in Southern California that there was not enough water for all; they installed rather weak conservation requirements, mostly voluntary. To the surprise of the politicians, people conserved more water than the targeted goals. They responded to a serious situation once they knew the problem and what could be done about it. When people in the Denver area learned that the proposed Two Forks Dam would destroy a beautiful canyon and fishing river near the city and dewater streams in western Colorado, they opposed it even though they were told that Denver needed new water to meet its growth projections.

With the benefit of knowledge and understanding of the consequences, it appears that people are willing to modify their own actions to do what is better for the larger community, even if it causes them some discomfort, expense, or problems. Under the right circumstances, people will act against their immediate self-interest and tolerate—even demand—government action that helps them curb free exercise of their self-interest. This suggests that we possess at least an essential ingredient of a fully realized water ethic: a fundamental sense of fairness and justice.

The Community's Role in Fulfilling a Water Ethic

> Places have a way of claiming people. When they claim very diverse kinds of people, then those people must eventually learn to live with each other; they must learn to inhabit their place together, which they can only do through the development of certain practices of inhabitation which both rely upon and nurture the old-fashioned civic virtues of trust, honesty, justice, toleration, cooperation, hope, and remembrance. It is through the nurturing of such values (and in no other way) that we might begin to reclaim that competency upon which democratic citizenship depends.
>
> DANIEL KEMMIS : *Community and the Politics of Place*

Governments can integrate society's values into policy and take collective action on behalf of people to achieve policy goals. Institutions and laws also should complement and support individual actions. In this capacity governments must develop and disseminate information about the consequences of water use. As the experiences of Southern California in drought show, full information can lead individuals to more balanced decisions. Water policy—plans, decisions, laws—ought to be designed to achieve clearly identified community goals. Alternative strategies for reaching them should be laid out and debated.

The guiding principles in all water plans, policies, and laws should be conservation, equity, and ecology. These are basic values shared by most people in our society, though they are rarely articulated as the guiding principles of water decisions. Conservation recognizes that waste is harmful, that diverse uses are not possible without care, that limits must be imposed on some uses, and that some reasonable charge must be imposed on developers who now use public water for free. Ecology requires that watercourses, as living ecosystems, be given specific and meaningful protection. The principles of conservation and ecology merge into the overarching idea of sustainability: water policies should include hard-edged guarantees so that water use will allow both living watersheds and economies to be sustainable indefinitely for the good of future members of the community.

Fairness dictates that the whole community be involved in a meaningful way in water decisions that affect it. Everyone who is touched by the effects of water use—even those separated by distance and time—are part of a community. Indeed, ecological understanding leads inescapably to the conclusion that water and people be seen among the interdependent elements in complex natural systems. Such a wide community of interests goes far beyond the usual concept of human concerns.

Government intervention is surely warranted when collective ethical judgments are overwhelmed by powerful and independent individuals or institutions. In the case of the proposed Two Forks Dam near Denver, the community judgment—at the national, state, and local levels—ran against building the dam. Colorado's governor opined that the project would be environmentally destructive and was not necessary, at least at that time. Yet neither he nor any state agency had authority under traditional Colorado water law to stop the water developers from building it. The developers' single interest in supplying water did not admit full enough consideration of the other values implicated by building a dam at that time and place. Citizens' groups appealed to federal agencies charged with issuing a permit to fill in wetlands, asking them to halt the project; finally, the federal Environmental Protection Agency did so. The governor and most people in the region decried the lack of adequate institutions to incorporate the considerations necessary for a balanced decision and the awkward recourse to a distant federal agency under provisions of a peripheral law.

Because government has been so deeply involved in shaping the way water is used in the West, it is obliged to support the kind of balanced water use people want: conservation, fairness, ecological protection. Since the beginning of western expansion, the federal government has championed program after program, law after law to promote the extensive development of water resources. Westerners now know that many of those efforts led to unbalanced, unethical uses of water.

Consider the effect of some reclamation projects. Earlier we described the water rights held by the Pyramid Lake Band of Paiutes in Nevada. The nearby Newlands Reclamation Project, built early in the century, aids a small group of hay farmers but wastes enormous quantities of water in old, leaky ditches and irrigation systems. The project diverted most of the flow of the Truckee River, depriving Pyramid Lake of water, driving Lahontan cutthroat trout and cui-ui to the brink of extinction and destroying the traditional economy and culture of the tribe. When growing cities upstream of the Newlands Project needed water, they could not take it from the river, because the Project had an earlier right. All three components of the water ethic were violated by the Newlands Project.

Though it took years of battle, a way was found to undo some of the waste, to correct some of the unfair distribution, and to remedy some of the harm to natural systems. People went outside the usual systems and institutions for water decisions and negotiated their own solutions. It required reallocating rights, changing some of the conditions on which some people have grown to depend, and spending new federal money. The Fallon Paiute–Shoshone and Truckee–Carson–Pyramid Lake Water Rights Settlement Act of 1990 provides for changes in operations of Truckee River reservoirs, for voluntary acquisition of Newlands Project irrigation rights, and for enhanced water-use efficiency measures in both Reno-Sparks water use and Newlands Project water use. Water made available through these measures will be used to enhance the Lahontan Valley wetlands and Pyramid Lake.

The West is full of examples of public policy decisions—water laws and projects—designed many years ago for the sake of narrow interests and without comprehensive consideration of the principles underlying our water ethic. When it became obvious that policies and laws were at odds with public sentiment, additional laws and programs were layered on to protect water quality, endangered species, wetlands, and the like. Yet there has not been a serious reappraisal of water programs or policies at the federal or state level, asking whether they should be reshaped to conform with an emerging understanding of fundamental values in water—to return to the headwaters of western water policy. Now is the time for the whole community to step back, take stock, and infuse water decision making with an ethic—at once new and deeply traditional—that looks ultimately to individual consciences and the long-term good of our communities, economies, and waters.

Epilogue

History Need Not Repeat Itself

From its beginning the fate of civilization has been tied to water
and the management of water resources.

HELEN M. INGRAM, LAWRENCE A. SCAFF, AND LESLIE SILKO:
"Replacing Confusion with Equity," in *New Courses for the Colorado River*

S PECULATION ABOUNDS over
why ancient societies in arid regions from Mesopotamia to the
southwestern United States abandoned their homelands. The Anasazi had sophisticated societies in deserts in the heart of the Southwest with irrigation systems and agricultural developments, but they
failed, at least partly because of excessive dependence on water in an
arid environment. Many early civilizations throughout the world
appear to have met their demise when they tried to defy aridity.

Intensive agriculture in arid regions throughout the world and
across history has enabled and incited rapid population growth.
This would have been impossible without irrigation. For millions of
years people had lived in widely dispersed small bands that followed
game and growing seasons from place to place. The development of
"civilization"—permanent societies concentrated in a single place—
began about ten thousand years ago with the birth of agriculture. Efficient food production made it no longer necessary for everyone to
participate in hunting, gathering, and growing. Farmers could produce far more than their own needs. Trade developed, and there
were time and provisions enough to support merchants, bureau-
crats, and armies. Sophisticated cultures with literature, art, and
music began to flourish.

Eventually, the growth of population created demands that over-

199

took the ability of the land to produce. Farmers pressed marginal lands into service as the better lands declined in productivity. By stretching resources to the limits of their capacity to provide for an ever-increasing population, societies became vulnerable to drought, pestilence, and war. They became vivid illustrations of "unsustainable" societies. Virtually every early civilization repeated irrigation practices that led to soil erosion, desertification, salinization, and waterlogging.

For example, in the "cradle of civilization," Mesopotamia, water storage and irrigation allowed cultivation of the region's rich soils. Yet, in the hot climate water evaporated quickly and salts built up on the soil's surface, destroying productivity. To solve the problem and wash away the salts, farmers spread even more irrigation water on the land. However, the area's high water table meant that irrigation water would not drain, and the soils became so saturated with increasingly saline water that plants could not grow. Farmers cultivated new lands when they were unable to grow grains on the old ones, but the same patterns were repeated. As the land and food ran out, the military society that they supported waned. A series of conquests followed. The Sumerian city-states that had flourished in 3000 B.C. were essentially extinct by 2000 B.C.

A similar story unfolded in the Americas, where the Mayan Indians established large cities and made remarkable cultural and intellectual achievements centuries before the birth of Christ. They relied on a system of agriculture that used terraced hillsides and the raised fields of filled-in swamps that were drained by systems of ditches. Growing urban populations provided soldiers and workers to build pyramids and other ceremonial buildings. Feeding this labor force put more pressure on the soils, which eroded and lost their nutrients, and drainage efforts became more difficult. Rather suddenly, people died from lack of sufficient food to eat and in battles over scarce food.

Among these ancient civilizations there was a remarkably similar pattern of straining the limits of water. Populations grew to a point that too many people depended on a fickle water supply, or inequitable distribution led to conflict and violence, or excessive water use ruined the land. The consequences of overuse, misuse, and denial of use to some for the benefit of others were hard-learned. Without widespread communications, it may not be surprising that trial-and-error lessons had to be repeated again and again, from place to place.

The modern world should be able to build on these and many other lessons. Yet, instead of avoiding past mistakes in water use, countries throughout the world are repeating them, often on even grander scales. The costs are counted in thousands of lives lost to disease and poverty, in millions of acres of farmlands ruined, in species gone extinct, and in constant feuding over waters that are becoming too depleted or too polluted to use. This seems inexcusable, given the information available for centuries.

The worst of the modern disasters perhaps can be explained by political exigencies and the distress of poverty and growing population. Future generations may forgive a country like Pakistan its extreme misuse of the Indus River. And the excesses that led to the Aral Sea disaster in Central Asia can be blamed on a Soviet system of central decision making that was preoccupied with relieving a desperate economic condition. The excesses and problems caused so far by misguided water policy in the United States pale next to these examples. But someone born fifty years from now will find it harder to understand and to excuse the blunders and excesses of a society that could have done better and knew that it should.

The people of the American West have a better understanding than ever of the consequences of ignoring the social and ecological realities of water management. A willingness to make water use sensitive to the limits of natural and human communities, with an ethical concern rooted in the principles of conservation, fairness, and ecology, is central to determining the long-term success of communities in the American West.

Never before have people understood better the social and ecological consequences of water policies and decisions. A commitment to make water use sensitive to the realities of natural and human communities can be rooted in this knowledge and ethically driven by the principles of conservation, fairness, and ecology. The long-term

vitality of communities across the American West, like the sustainability of societies throughout the world, depends on such commitments. This frames a momentous challenge to the vision and responsibility of all who have an opportunity to influence the process
of reshaping water policy. And so the challenge reaches everyone
who cares about water in the West.

Appendix

The Language
of Water

THROUGHOUT this book we have included voices of people concerned about water. Sometimes people speak as judges in water cases; sometimes they are naturalists whose perception of the world is shaped by water; and occasionally government officials express the importance of water through statements of policy. Chapter 3 sets forth longer excerpts from literature, poetry, and song, each expressing a personal connection to water. Water is a regular subject in the West, and westerners are comfortable talking and reading about water. In that sense, the language of water is as familiar as any other important part of people's lives, and a good deal more understandable than complex issues related to human health and safety. Who, for example, can comprehend the implications of disposing of radioactive waste that will remain dangerous for thousands of years? Compared with such difficult concepts, it appears relatively easy to discuss the merits of one water use compared with another; anyone with a serious interest in the issue can grasp the implications of moving water from a farm to a city.

Yet, despite this seeming familiarity, the language of water approaches the realm of the incomprehensible in the hands of water "experts," who freely use a specialized vocabulary out of their own narrow fields of expertise, intentionally or unintentionally excluding others without this background from participating in the discussion. Water lawyers, for example, throw around terms like "prior appropriation," "reserved rights," and "general stream adjudications."

Scientists speak of "perched aquifers" and "watersheds." People familiar with the Clean Water Act speak knowingly about "point" and "nonpoint" source pollution. Environmentalists promote "instream" uses of water and complain about overemphasis on "consumptive" or "extractive" uses of water. Little wonder that many people feel that water policy is simply too complex and must be left to the experts.

We reject this barrier to public participation in water decisions. Water touches and concerns every living thing. Everyone is an expert about water, and no one is *the* expert. We try in this book to illustrate the breadth of interests in water and argue that policies governing water uses in the West during the past 150 years have excluded many of these interests. Evidence of exclusion is embedded in the language of western water law. Inevitably, we have to use this language, but it is essential that these terms not interfere with the larger purpose of the book. To help address this problem, we present here an explanation of some of the more technical terms used in the book that might not be familiar to some of our readers.

Ecosystem: the interacting components of air, land, water, and living organisms essential to life within a defined area; the area may be as small as a drop of water or as large as the whole planet.

Extractive water uses: uses that require "diversion," or removal of water from a stream through a ditch or pipeline.

Instream flow: water flowing in a natural waterway, as compared with water that is removed for use elsewhere; "in-river" or "instream" values refers to the needs of fish, recreationists, and others whose use of water requires it to remain in the stream. Increasingly these values are protected through "instream flow programs," a relatively new kind of water right that protects in-river values, recognizing them as beneficial water uses.

Nonpoint source pollution: water pollution derived from diffuse sources (for example, pesticides and salts in irrigation return flows), as compared with water pollution entering a river from a specific "point" source (such as a pipeline or ditch returning processing water from a factory).

Prior appropriation: the dominant law of water allocation in the western United States, premised on the rule that the first person to put water to a beneficial use is entitled to continue that use without interference from those making subsequent uses; the prior appropriation doctrine is thus based on use rather than land ownership. A person holding an earlier water right is called the "senior appropriator" in relation to one claiming a water right later (the "junior appropriator").

Public trust doctrine: a historical doctrine that imposes a duty on public officials to supervise the private use of public resources to ensure protection of the public's interest.

Reserved water rights: a judicial interpretation saying that when Congress established reservations (Indian reservations, national forests, and military reservations, for example), it intended to reserve sufficient water to satisfy the purposes of each reservation.

Riparian vegetation: plants that grow along a stream, especially those plants whose roots reach down to saturated soil.

Riparian water law: the law of water allocation prevalent in the eastern United States, providing that landowners abutting a stream are the only ones entitled to water rights; the riparian doctrine permits those landowners to make reasonable use of the water on their land, so long as the use does not interfere with the needs of other riparian landowners.

Watersheds: the land area through which water drains to reach a stream; on a larger scale, we refer to "river basins."

References

ONE

Getches, David, Lawrence MacDonnell, and Teresa Rice. *Controlling Water Use: The Unfinished Business of Water Quality Protection*. Boulder, Colo.: Natural Resources Law Center, 1991.

In re The General Adjudication of all rights to use water in the Big Horn River System and all other sources. Wyoming Supreme Court decision (June 5, 1992).

Lawrence, D. H. "The Third Thing," in Katherine Scott Sturdevant, ed. *Sundays in Tutt Library with Frank Waters*. Colorado Springs: Hulbert Center for Southwestern Studies, 1988.

Miller, Taylor O., Gary D. Weatherford, and John E. Thorson. *The Salty Colorado*. Washington, D.C.: The Conservation Foundation, 1986.

Nehlsen, Willa, Jack E. Williams, and James A. Lichatowich. "Pacific Salmon at the Crossroads: Stocks at Risk from California, Oregon, Idaho, and Washington." *Fisheries* 16, no. 2 (1991):4–21.

Yardas, David. *Restoring Endangered Ecosystems: The Truckee-Carson Water Rights Settlement*. Boulder, Colo.: Natural Resources Law Center, Occasional Paper, 1992.

TWO

Abbey, Edward. *Desert Solitaire*. New York: Simon and Schuster, 1968.

American Indian Training Program. *Indian Water Policy in a Changing Environment*. Oakland: AITP, 1982.

Austin, Mary. *Stories from the Country of Lost Borders*. New Brunswick, N.J.: Rutgers University Press, 1987.

Brown, F. Lee, and Helen M. Ingram. *Water and Poverty in the Southwest*. Tucson: University of Arizona Press, 1987.

Canfield, Chauncey L., ed. *The Diary of a Forty-Niner*. Boston: Houghton Mifflin, 1920.

Carson, Rachel Louise. *Silent Spring*. Boston: Houghton Mifflin, 1962.

Chaney, Ed, Wayne Elmore, and William S. Platts. *Livestock Grazing on Western Riparian Areas*. Washington, D.C.: Environmental Protection Agency, 1990.

Conkin, Paul. "The Vision of Elwood Mead." *Agricultural History* 34 (1960):88–97.

Crawford, Stanley G. *Mayordomo: Chronicle of an Acequia in Northern New Mexico*. Albuquerque: University of New Mexico Press, 1988.

DeVoto, Bernard, ed. *The Journals of Lewis and Clark*. Boston: Houghton Mifflin, 1953.

Driver, Harold E. *Indians of North America*. Chicago: University of Chicago Press, 2d ed. rev., 1969.

DuMars, Charles T., Marilyn O'Leary, and Albert E. Utton. *Pueblo Indian Water Rights: Struggle for a Precious Resource*. Tucson: University of Arizona Press, 1984.

Ehrlich, Gretel. *The Solace of Open Spaces*. New York: Viking Penguin, 1985.

Eiseley, Loren C. *The Immense Journey*. New York: Random House, 1957.

Folk-Williams, John. *Water for the Energy Market: A Sourcebook*. Santa Fe: Western Network, 1983.

Folk-Williams, John. *Water and the Cities of the Southwest*. Boulder, Colo.: Natural Resources Law Center, Western Water Policy Project Discussion Series Paper No. 3, 1990.

Folk-Williams, John, Susan Fry, and Lucy Hilgendorf. *Western Water Flows to the Cities: A Sourcebook*. Santa Fe: Western Network, 1985.

Getches, David, Lawrence MacDonnell, and Teresa Rice. *Controlling Water Use: The Unfinished Business of Water Quality Protection*. Boulder, Colo.: Natural Resources Law Center, 1991.

Gregg, Josiah. *Commerce on the Prairies*. New York: H. G. Langley, 1844.

Houghton, Samuel G. *A Trace of Desert Waters: The Great Basin Story.* Glendale, Calif.: A. H. Clark, 1976.

Hughes, J. Donald. *American Indian Ecology.* El Paso: Texas Western Press, 1983.

Hultkrantz, Ake. *The Religions of the American Indians.* Berkeley: University of California Press, 1979.

Illich, Ivan. "H$_2$O and the Waters of Forgetfulness." *The Dallas Institute Newsletter* (Fall 1984):20.

Ingram, Helen M., and Cy R. Oggins. *Water, the Community, and Markets in the West.* Boulder, Colo.: Natural Resources Law Center, Western Water Policy Project Discussion Series Paper No. 6, 1990.

Kittredge, William. *Owning It All.* Saint Paul, Minn.: Graywolf Press, 1987.

Kittredge, William, and Annick Smith, eds. *The Last Best Place: A Montana Anthology.* Helena: Montana Historical Society Press, 1988.

Knack, Martha C., and Omer C. Stewart. *As Long As the River Shall Run: An Ethnohistory of Pyramid Lake Indian Reservation.* Berkeley: University of California Press, 1984.

Knappen, Theodore M. "The West at Washington." *Sunset* 55 (1925):41.

Leopold, Aldo. *A Sand County Almanac.* New York: Oxford University Press, 1949.

Leopold, Aldo. "The Round River." Luna B. Leopold, ed. *Round River: From the Journals of Aldo Leopold.* Minocqua, WI: Northword Press, 1991.

Limerick, Patricia Nelson. *The Legacy of Conquest: The Unbroken Past of the American West.* New York: W. W. Norton, 1987.

Maass, Arthur. *Water Law and Institutions in the Western United States: Comparison with Early Developments in California and Australia, Contemporary Developments in Australia, and Recent Legislation Worldwide.* Boulder, Colo.: Natural Resources Law Center, Western Water Policy Project Discussion Series Paper No. 7, 1990.

Maass, Arthur, and Raymond L. Anderson. . . . *and the Desert Shall Rejoice: Conflict, Growth and Justice in Arid Environments.* Malabar, Fla.: Robert E. Krieger, 1986.

Maclean, Norman. *A River Runs through It.* Chicago: University of Chicago Press, 1976.

Matthiessen, Peter. *Indian Country.* New York: Viking Press, 1984.

McClintock, James H. *Mormon Settlement in Arizona.* Tucson: University of Arizona Press, 1985 (first copyright 1921 by Jas. H. McClintock).

Mead, Elwood. *The Ownership of Water.* Denver: Times Printing Works, 1887.

Mead, Elwood. *Irrigation Institutions.* New York: Harper and Brothers, 1900.

References 209

Meyer, Michael C. *Water in the Hispanic Southwest: A Social and Legal History, 1550–1850*. Tucson: University of Arizona Press, 1984.

Meyers, Charles J., et al. *Water Resource Management: A Casebook in Law and Public Policy*. Mineola, N.Y.: Foundation Press, 1988.

Morgan, Dale. *The West of William H. Ashley*. Denver: Old West Publishing Co., 1964.

Nabhan, Gary Paul. *The Desert Smells Like Rain: A Naturalist in Papago Indian Country*. San Francisco: North Point Press, 1982.

Nash, Roderick. *Wilderness and the American Mind*. New Haven: Yale University Press, 3rd ed., 1982.

Nehlsen, Willa, Jack E. Williams, and James A. Lichatowich. "Pacific Salmon at the Crossroads: Stocks at Risk from California, Oregon, Idaho, and Washington." *Fisheries* 16, no. 2 (1991):4–21.

Ostrom, Vincent. *Water and Politics: A Study of Water Policies and Administration in the Development of Los Angeles*. Los Angeles: The Haynes Foundation, 1953.

Pascua, Maria Parker. "Ozette." *National Geographic* 180, no. 4 (Oct. 1991):38–53.

Paul, Rodman W. *California Gold: The Beginning of Mining in the Far West*. Cambridge: Harvard University Press, 1947.

Powell, John Wesley. *The Exploration of the Colorado River and its Canyons*. New York: Viking Penguin, 1987 (originally published by the Government Printing Office in 1875).

Powell, John Wesley. *Report on the Lands of the Arid Region of the United States*. Washington, D.C.: Executive Document No. 73, vol. 13, 45th Congress, 2d Session, 1878. (Reprinted in 1983 by the Harvard Common Press, Massachusetts.)

Reisner, Marc. *Cadillac Desert: The American West and Its Disappearing Water*. New York: Viking Press, 1986.

Robbins, John. *Realities 1990*. Santa Cruz, Calif.: EarthSave, 1990.

Schad, Theodore M. *The Changing Scene in the American West: Water Policy Implications*. Boulder, Colo.: Natural Resources Law Center, Western Water Policy Project Discussion Series No. 8, 1991.

Smythe, William E. *The Conquest of Arid America*. New York: Macmillan, 1905.

Stegner, Wallace E. *Beyond the Hundredth Meridian: John Wesley Powell and the Second Opening of the West*. Boston: Houghton Mifflin, 1954.

Stegner, Wallace E. *The Sound of Mountain Water*. New York: E. P. Dutton, 1980.

Taylor, Paul S. "California Water Project: Law and Politics." *Ecology Law Quarterly* 5 (1975):1.

Twain, Mark. *Life on the Mississippi*. New York: Harper and Brothers, 1896.

United States Department of the Interior, National Park Service. *Federal Recreation Fee Report to Congress 1990*.

Walton, John. *Western Times and Water Wars: State, Culture, and Rebellion in California*. Berkeley: University of California Press, 1992.

Waters, Frank. *The Man Who Killed the Deer*. New York: Farrar & Rinehart, 1942.

Weatherford, Gary D. *From Basin to "Hydrocommons": Integrated Water Management without Regional Governance*. Boulder, Colo.: Natural Resources Law Center, Western Water Policy Project Discussion Series Paper No. 5, 1990.

Wilkinson, Charles F. *The American West: A Narrative Bibliography and a Study in Regionalism*. Niwot, Colo.: University Press of Colorado, 1989.

Wilkinson, Charles F. *Crossing the Next Meridian: Land, Water, and the Future ᴄ the West*. Washington, D.C.: Island Press, 1992.

Williams, Chuck. "The First Salmon Ceremony Still Honors the Spring Chinook." *High Country News* 23, no. 7 (April 22, 1991):6–7.

Wood, Nancy C. *Taos Pueblo*. New York: Alfred A. Knopf, 1989.

Worster, Donald. *Rivers of Empire: Water, Aridity, and the Growth of the American West*. New York: Pantheon Books, 1986.

Wyoming State Engineer. *26th Biennial Report, 1941–42*. Cheyenne: Wyoming State Engineer's Office, 1942.

THREE

Abbey, Edward. *Desert Solitaire*. New York: Random House, 1968.

Austin, Mary. *Stories from the Country of Lost Borders*. New Brunswick, N.J.: Rutgers University Press, 1987.

Bass, Rick. "Valley of the Crows." *Witness* 3, no. 4 (Winter 1989):151.

Brown, Bruce. *Mountain in the Clouds: A Search for the Wild Salmon*. New York: Simon and Schuster, 1982.

Crawford, Stanley G. *Mayordomo: Chronicle of an Acequia in Northern New Mexico*. Albuquerque: University of New Mexico Press, 1988.

deBuys, William, and Alex Harris. *River of Traps*. Albuquerque: University of New Mexico Press, 1990.

Guthrie, Woody. "Roll, Columbia, Roll." New York: Ludlow Music Inc., 1958.

Holthaus, Gary, et al., eds. *A Society to Match the Scenery: Personal Visions of the Future of the American West*. Niwot, Colo.: University Press of Colorado, 1991.

Kittredge, William. *Owning It All*. Saint Paul, Minn.: Graywolf Press, 1987.

Leopold, Aldo. *A Sand County Almanac*. New York: Oxford University Press, 1949.

Palmer, Tim. *The Snake River: Window to the West*. Washington, D.C.: Island Press, 1991.

Rennicke, Jeff, cont. ed. *River Days: Travels on Western Rivers*. Golden, Colo.: Fulcrum, 1988.

Schad, Theodore M. *The Changing Scene in the American West: Water Policy Implications*. Boulder, Colo.: Natural Resources Law Center, Western Water Policy Project Discussion Series Paper No. 8, 1990.

Stegner, Wallace E. *The Sound of Mountain Water*. New York: E. P. Dutton, 1980.

Waters, Frank. *People of the Valley*. Chicago: Swallow Press, 1941.

FOUR

Association of California Water Agencies. *California's Continuing Water Crisis*. Sacramento: ACWA, June 1991.

Bajwa, Rajinder S., et al. *Agricultural Irrigation and Water Use*. Washington, D.C.: U.S. Department of Agriculture, Information Bulletin Number 638, 1992.

Berke, Richard L. "Oratory of Environmentalism Becomes the Sound of Politics." *New York Times* (April 17, 1990):1.

Brickson, Betty. "Sea Water Desalination." *Western Water* (July/August 1991):4–11.

California Department of Water Resources. *California's Continuing Drought 1987–1991*. Sacramento: California Department of Water Resources, 1991.

Field Institute. *Californians' Views on Water: A Survey of Californians' Opinions About Issues of Water Supply, Development, Quality, and Policy*. San Francisco: Field Institute, 1990.

Fetterman, Mindy. "Homing in on Housing Help: More Firms Help Workers Buy Homes." *USA Today* (February 7, 1990):1B.

Foster, Charles H. W., and Peter Rogers. *Federal Water Policy: Toward an Agenda for Action: A Report of the Harvard Water Policy Project*. Cambridge: Harvard University Press, 1988.

Hamilton, Denise. "Wilderness Outfitter Patagonia Offers Different Kind of Corporate Climbing." *Los Angeles Times* (October 15, 1987):1.

Holthaus, Gary, et al., eds. *A Society to Match the Scenery: Personal Visions of the*

Future of the American West. Niwot, Colo.: University Press of Colorado, 1991.

In re The General Adjudication of all Rights to Use Water in the Big Horn River System and all Other Sources, State of Wyoming. Wyoming Supreme Court decision (June 5, 1992).

MacDonnell, Lawrence J. *The Water Transfer Process As a Management Option for Meeting Changing Water Demands.* Boulder, Colo.: Natural Resources Law Center, research report submitted to the U.S. Geological Survey, 1990.

Marston, Ed. Keynote speech at the Grand Canyon Trust's Colorado Plateau Community Initiatives Symposium, Cedar City, Utah, September 18–20, 1991.

Membrino, Joseph R. "Indian Reserved Water Rights, Federalism and the Trust Responsibility." *Land and Water Law Review* 27, no. 1 (1992):1–31.

Obmascik, Mark, and Patrick O'Driscoll. "Water: From Growing Crops to Growing Cities." *Denver Post* (July 19, 1992):1, 12–13.

O'Gara, Geoffrey. "Waterless in Wind River?" *High Country News* 22, no. 6 (August 27, 1990):1, 10–11.

Rasker, Ray, Norma Tirrell, and Deanne Kloepfer. *The Wealth of Nature: New Economic Realities in the Yellowstone Region.* Washington, D.C.: The Wilderness Society, 1992.

Reid, T. R. "From Spuds to Scenery: West Shifts Economic Focus." *The Washington Post* (February 12, 1987):A1.

Reisner, Marc. "The Big Thirst." *New York Times Magazine* (October 28, 1990):36–37, 54–60.

Rudzitis, Gundars, and Harley E. Johansen. "How Important Is Wilderness? Results from a United States Survey." *Environmental Management* 15, no. 2 (1991):227.

Sharp, Kathleen. "Firms Move As Housing Costs Rise." *New York Times* (July 31, 1988): Sec. 8, p. 1.

Stegner, Wallace. *Where the Bluebird Sings to the Lemonade Springs.* New York: Random House, 1992.

U.S. Department of Commerce. *1990 Census of Population and Housing.* Washington, D.C.: Bureau of Census, 1992.

U.S. Geological Survey. *National Water Summary 1987.* Washington, D.C.: U.S. Geological Survey, Water-Supply Paper 2350, 1987.

Wald, Matthew L. "Earth Day at 20: How Green the Globe?" *New York Times* (April 22, 1990):1.

Weinstein, Bernard L., and Harold T. Gross. *The Western Economy in Transi-*

tion: Nature, Causes and Implications. Denver: Report prepared for the Western Governors' Association, May 1986.

Winters v. United States, 207 U.S. 564 (1908).

FIVE

Abbey, Edward. *Desert Solitaire.* New York: Random House, 1968.

Arizona v. California, 373 U.S. 546 (1963), decreed entered 376 U.S. 340 (1964).

Austin, Mary. *The American Rhythm.* Boston: Houghton Mifflin, 1930.

Baumhoff, Richard G. *The Dammed Missouri Valley, One Sixth of Our Nation.* New York: Alfred A. Knopf, 1951.

Bodi, F. Lorraine. "Protecting Columbia River Salmon Under the Endangered Species Act." *Environmental Law* 10, no. 2 (1980):332–387.

Brown, Bruce. *Mountain in the Clouds.* New York: Simon & Schuster, 1982.

Carrels, Peter. "Missouri River Feud Could Dry Up Navigation." *Chicago Tribune* (August 15, 1991):1.

Carrels, Peter, and Lawrence Mosher. "Missouri: A River Basin at War." *High Country News* 23, no. 4 (March 11, 1991):1, 10–12.

Clark, Ira G. *Water in New Mexico: A History of Its Management and Use.* Albuquerque: University of New Mexico Press, 1987.

Dana, Julian. *The Sacramento: River of Gold.* New York: Farrar & Rinehart, 1939.

deBuys, William E. *Enchantment and Exploitation: The Life and Hard Times of a New Mexico Mountain Range.* Albuquerque: University of New Mexico Press, 1985.

Designwrights Collaborative, Inc. *People and Water in New Mexico.* Santa Fe: Designwrights Collaborative, 1984.

DuMars, Charles T., Marilyn O'Leary, and Albert E. Utton. *Pueblo Indian Water Rights: Struggle for a Precious Resource.* Tucson: University of Arizona Press, 1984.

Engelbert, Ernest A., and Ann Foley Scheuring, eds. *Competition for California Water.* Berkeley: University of California Press, 1982.

Fergusson, Harvey. *Rio Grande.* New York: Tudor, 1933.

Ford, Pat. "The Snake's Imperiled Salmon." *High Country News* 23, no. 12 (July 1, 1991):1, 10–12.

Fox, J. P., T. R. Morgan, and William J. Miller. "Trends in Freshwater Inflow to San Francisco Bay from the Sacramento–San Joaquin Delta." *Water Resources Bulletin* 26, no. 1 (February 1990):101–116.

Fradkin, Philip L. *A River No More*. New York: Alfred A. Knopf, 1981.

Getches, David H. *Water Allocation During Drought in Arizona and Southern California: Legal and Institutional Responses*. Boulder, Colo.: Natural Resources Law Center, Research Report, 1991.

Guhin, John P. "The Law of the Missouri." *South Dakota Law Review* 30 (Spring 1985):346–487.

Guthrie, A. B., Jr. *The Big Sky*. New York: William Sloane Associates, 1947.

High Country News 23, no. 7 (April 22, 1991); entire issue devoted to "Northwest Salmon at the Crossroads."

High Country News. *Western Water Made Simple*. Washington, D.C.: Island Press, 1987.

Horgan, Paul. *Great River: The Rio Grande in North American History*. New York: Holt, Rinehart and Winston, 1954.

Huffman, James L. "Agriculture and the Columbia River: A Legal and Policy Perspective." *Environmental Law* 10, no. 2 (1980):281–314.

Huser, Verne, ed. *River Reflections*. Chester, Conn.: Globe Pequot Press, 1988.

Kemmis, Daniel. "How the River Taught People to Talk." *Mending a River*, undated tabloid published by the Northern Lights Institute, Missoula, Montana.

Landau, Jack L. "Empty Victories: Indian Treaty Fishing Rights in the Pacific Northwest." *Environmental Law* 10, no. 2 (1980):413–456.

Leathers, Kenneth L., and Robert A. Young. *Evaluating Economic Impacts of Programs for Control of Saline Irrigation Return Flows: A Case Study of the Grand Valley, Colorado*. Denver: U.S. Environmental Protection Agency Region VIII, Project 68-01-2660, June 1976.

Lee, Kai N. "The Columbia River Basin: Experimenting with Sustainability." *Environment* 31, no. 6 (July/August 1989):6–11, 30–33.

Leopold, Aldo. *A Sand County Almanac*. New York: Oxford University Press, 1949.

Mensik, J. Gregory, and Patrick O'Halloran. "Monitoring Marsh Management on the Sacramento National Wildlife Refuge." *1990 Transactions of the Western Section of the Wildlife Society* 26 (1990):24–28.

Miller, Joaquin. *Unwritten History: Life Amongst the Modocs*. Eugene, Oregon: Orion Press, 1972 (originally published in 1873).

Muckleston, Keith W. "Salmon vs. Hydropower: Striking a Balance in the Pacific Northwest." *Environment* 32, no. 1 (January/February 1990):10–15, 32–36.

Mueller, Jerry E. *Restless River: International Law and Behavior of the Rio Grande*. El Paso: Texas Western Press, 1975.

National Audubon Society. *Audubon Wildlife Report 1986*. New York: National Audubon Society, 1986.

Nehlsen, Willa, Jack E. Williams, and James A. Lichatowich. "Pacific Salmon at the Crossroads: Stocks at Risk from California, Oregon, Idaho, and Washington." *Fisheries* 16, no. 2 (1991):4–21.

O'Keefe, Mark D., et al. *Boundaries Carved in Water: An Analysis of River and Water Management in the Upper Missouri Basin*. Missoula, Mont.: Northern Lights Institute, n.d.

Phinney, Lloyd A. "Chinook Salmon of the Columbia River Basin." In National Audubon Society. *Audubon Wildlife Report 1986*. New York: National Audubon Society, 1986.

Powell, John Wesley. *The Exploration of the Colorado River and Its Canyons*. New York: Viking-Penguin, 1987 (originally published by the Government Printing Office, in 1875).

Reisner, Marc. *Cadillac Desert: The American West and Its Disappearing Water*. New York: Viking Press, 1986.

Seiser, H. E. "Dam Symbol of Broken Promises." *United Press International Newswire* (March 14, 1986).

Stuebner, Steve. "Can a New Plan Save the Fish?" *High Country News* 24, no. 4 (March 9, 1992):1, 10.

Thorson, John Eric. *River of Promise/River of Peril? Building Missouri River Management Institutions in a Federal Setting*. University of Southern California Doctoral Dissertation, May 1991.

Tondre v. Garcia, 45 N.M. 433, 116 P.2d 584 (1941).

U.S. Bureau of Reclamation. *Plan for Development: Middle Rio Grande Project, Rio Grande Basin, New Mexico*. Washington, D.C.: U.S. Department of the Interior, 1947.

U.S. President's Water Resources Policy Commission. *Ten Rivers in America's Future*. Washington, D.C.: U.S. Government Printing Office, 1950.

Volkman, John M. "Making Room in the Ark." *Environment* 34, no. 4 (May 1992):18–20, 37–43.

Waters, Frank. *The Colorado*. New York: Rinehart & Co., 1946.

Weatherford, Gary D., and F. Lee Brown, eds. *New Courses for the Colorado River: Major Issues for the Next Century*. Albuquerque: University of New Mexico Press, 1986.

Wells, Andrew J. *The Sacramento Valley of California*. San Francisco: Southern Pacific, 1906.

Wilkinson, Charles F. *Crossing the Next Meridian: Land, Water, and the Future of the West*. Covelo, Calif.: Island Press, 1992.

Williams, Albert N. *The Water and the Power: Development of the Five Great Rivers of the West*. New York: Duell, Sloan and Pearce, 1951.

Williams, Florence. "Government Tames Its Wild, Destructive Dam." *High Country News* 23, no. 15 (August 26, 1991):1, 10–12.

SIX

American Water Works Association. *Water Industry Data Base* (an unpublished, regularly updated information source).

Beck, Robert E., ed. *Waters and Water Rights*. Charlottesville, Va.: Michie, 1991.

Anderson, Terry L., ed. *Water Rights: Scarce Resource Allocation, Bureaucracy, and the Environment*. San Francisco: Pacific Research Institute for Public Policy, 1983.

Coffin v. Left Hand Ditch Company, 6 Colo. 443 (1882).

Colorado Water Conservation Board and Colorado Agricultural and Mechanical College. *A Hundred Years of Irrigation in Colorado*. 1952.

Conkin, Paul K. "The Vision of Elwood Mead." *Agricultural History* 34 (1960):88–97.

Cox, James L. *Metropolitan Water Supply: The Denver Experience*. Boulder, Colo.: Bureau of Governmental Research and Service, 1967.

Cox, William E., and Leonard A. Shabman. "Virginia's Water Law: Resolving the Interjurisdictional Transfer Issue." *Virginia Journal of Natural Resources Law* 3 (1984):181–234.

Eggertsson, Prainn. *Economic Behavior and Institutions*. New York: Cambridge University Press, 1990.

Enterprise Irrigation District v. Willis, 284 N. W. Rep. 326 (1939).

Folk-Williams, John A. *Water and the Cities of the Southwest*. Boulder, Colo.: Natural Resources Law Center, Western Water Policy Project Discussion Series Paper No. 3.

Foster, Dick. "Water Shortage Sucks Colorado Farming Town Dry." *Rocky Mountain News* (July 23, 1990).

Geer v. Connecticut, 161 U.S. 519 (1896).

Gibbons, Diana. *The Economic Value of Water*. Washington, D.C.: Resources for the Future, 1986.

Goldsmith, Edward, and Nicholas Hildyard. *The Social and Environmental Effects of Large Dams*. San Francisco: Sierra Club Books, 1984.

Hobbs, Gregory J., Jr., and Bennett W. Raley. "Water Rights Protection in Water Quality Law." *University of Colorado Law Review* 60, no. 4 (1989):841–900.

Holmes, Oliver W. *The Common Law*. Boston: Little, Brown & Co., 1881.

Howe, Charles W., and K. William Easter. *Interbasin Transfers of Water*. Baltimore: Johns Hopkins Press, 1971.

Hughes v. Oklahoma, 441 U.S. 322 (1979).

Hurst, James Willard. *Law and Economic Growth—The Legal History of the Lumber Industry in Wisconsin, 1836–1915*. Cambridge: Belknap Press of Harvard University Press, 1964.

Hutchins, Wells A. *Water Rights Laws in the Nineteen Western States*. Washington, D.C.: U.S. Department of Agriculture, Economic Research Service, 1971.

Hutchins, Wells A., H. E. Selby, and Stanley W. Voelker. *Irrigation-Enterprise Organizations*. Washington, D.C.: U.S. Department of Agriculture, Circular No. 934, October 1953.

Kahrl, William L. *Water and Power: The Conflict Over Los Angeles' Water Supply in the Owens Valley*. Berkeley: University of California Press, 1982.

Lasky, Moses. "From Prior Appropriation to Economic Distribution of Water by the State—Via Irrigation Administration." *Rocky Mountain Law Review* 1 (1929):161–216, 248–270.

Leopold, Aldo. "The Virgin Southwest." In Susan L. Flader and J. Baird Callicott, eds., *The River of the Mother of God and Other Essays by Aldo Leopold*. Madison: University of Wisconsin Press, 1991.

Leshy, John D. *The Mining Law: A Study in Perpetual Motion*. Washington, D.C.: Resources for the Future, 1987.

MacDonnell, Lawrence J. "Transferring Water Uses in the West." *Oklahoma Law Review* 43 (1990):119–130.

MacDonnell, Lawrence J., and Charles W. Howe. "Area-of-Origin Protection in Transbasin Water Diversions: An Evaluation of Alternative Approaches." *University of Colorado Law Review* 57 (1986):527–548.

Matthews, William B. *Matthews' Guide for Settlers Upon the Public Lands*. Washington, D.C.: W. H. Lowdermilk, 1889.

Mead, Elwood. *The Use of Water in Irrigation*. Washington, D.C.: U.S. Department of Agriculture, Office of Experiment Stations, Bulletin 86, 1900.

Mead, Elwood. *Irrigation Institutions*. New York: MacMillan Company, 1903.

Missouri v. Holland, 252 U.S. 416 (1920).

Palmer, Tim. *The Snake River: Window to the West*. Washington, D.C.: Island Press, 1991.

Paul, Rodman W. *California Gold: The Beginning of Mining in the Far West*. Cambridge: Harvard University Press, 1947.

218   References

Pisani, Donald. *From the Family Farm to Agribusiness: The Irrigation Crusade in California and the West, 1850–1931*. Berkeley: University of California Press, 1984.

Pisani, Donald. "Enterprise and Equity: A Critique of Western Water Law in the Nineteenth Century." *The Western Historical Quarterly* (January 1987):15–37.

Pisani, Donald. *To Reclaim a Divided West*. Albuquerque: University of New Mexico Press, 1992.

Reisner, Marc, and Sarah Bates. *Overtapped Oasis: Reform or Revolution for Western Water*. Washington, D.C.: Island Press, 1990.

Sax, Joseph L. *The Constitution, Property Rights and the Future of Water Law*. Boulder, Colo.: Natural Resources Law Center, Western Water Policy Project Discussion Series Paper No. 2, 1990.

Schad, Theodore M. *The Changing Scene in the American West: Water Policy Implications*. Boulder, Colo.: Natural Resources Law Center, Western Water Policy Project Discussion Series Paper No. 8, 1990.

Sporhase v. Nebraska ex rel. Douglas, 458 U.S. 941 (1982).

Trade Dollar Consol. Mining Co. v. Fraser et al., 148 Fed. Rep. 585 (9th Cir. 1906).

United States General Accounting Office. *Federàl Charges for Irrigation Projects Reviewed Do Not Cover Costs*. Washington, D.C.: U.S. GAO Report No. PAD-81-07, March 13, 1981.

United States National Water Commission. *Water Policies for the Future: Final Report to the President and to the Congress of the United States*. Washington, D.C.: U.S. Government Printing Office, 1973.

Wahl, Richard W. *Markets for Federal Water: Subsidies, Property Rights, and the Bureau of Reclamation*. Washington, D.C.: Resources for the Future, 1989.

Weatherford, Gary D. *From Basin to "Hydrocommons": Integrated Water Management without Regional Governance*. Boulder, Colo.: Natural Resources Law Center, Western Water Policy Project Discussion Series Paper No. 5, 1990.

Wiel, Samuel C. *Water Rights in the Western States*. San Francisco: Bancroft Whitney, 3rd ed., 1911.

Williams, Stephen F. "The Law of Prior Appropriation: Possible Lessons for Hawaii." *Natural Resources Journal* 25, no. 1 (1985):911–934.

Wilson, David L., and Henry W. Ayer. *The Cost of Water in Western Agriculture*. Washington, D.C.: U.S. Department of Agriculture, Economic Research Service Staff Report No. AGE5820706, July 1982.

Worster, Donald. *Rivers of Empire: Water, Aridity, and the Growth of the American West*. New York: Pantheon Books, 1986.

Yunker v. Nichols, 1 Colo. 551 (1872).

SEVEN

Anderson, Terry L., ed. *Water Rights: Scarce Resource Allocation, Bureaucracy, and the Environment*. San Francisco: Pacific Institute for Public Policy Research, 1983.

Andrews v. Donnelly, 116 Pac. Rep. 569 (Ore. 1911).

Brown, F. Lee, and Helen M. Ingram. *Water and Poverty in the Southwest*. Tucson: University of Arizona Press, 1987.

Chambers, Reid Peyton, and John E. Echohawk. *Implementing Winters Doctrine Indian Reserved Water Rights: Producing Indian Water and Economic Development Without Injuring Non-Indian Water Users?* Boulder, Colo.: Natural Resources Law Center, Western Water Policy Project Discussion Series Paper No. 10, 1991.

Dunbar, Robert G. *Forging New Rights in Western Waters*. Lincoln: University of Nebraska Press, 1983.

El-Ashry, Mohamed, and Diana C. Gibbons, eds. *Water and Arid Lands of the Western United States*. Cambridge: Cambridge University Press, 1988.

Elias, Taslim O. *Nigerian Land Law*. London: Sweet and Maxwell, 4th ed., 1971.

House, Freeman. "To Learn the Things We Need to Know." *Whole Earth Review* 66 (Spring 1990):36–47.

Hudson County Water Company v. McCarter, 209 U.S. 349 (1908).

Ingram, Helen, and Cy R. Oggins. *Water, Community, and Markets in the West*. Boulder, Colo.: Natural Resources Law Center, Western Water Policy Project Discussion Series Paper No. 6, 1990.

Maass, Arthur. *Water Law and Institutions in the Western United States: Comparison with Early Developments in California and Australia, Contemporary Developments in Australia, and Recent Legislation Worldwide*. Boulder, Colo.: Natural Resources Law Center, Western Water Policy Project Discussion Series Paper No. 7, 1990.

Martin, William E., et al. *Saving Water in a Desert City*. Washington, D.C.: Resources for the Future; distributed by the Johns Hopkins University Press, 1984.

McClurg, Sue. "Changes in the Central Valley Project." *Western Water* (Jan./Feb. 1993):4–11.

Moore, Deborah, and Zach Willey. "Water in the American West: Institutional Evolution and Environmental Restoration in the 21st Century." *University of Colorado Law Review* 62 (1991):775–825.

National Research Council. *Water Transfers in the West: Efficiency, Equity, and the Environment*. Washington, D.C.: National Academy Press, 1992.

Pollock, Sarah. "Consciousness of Streams." *California* 15, no. 5 (May 1990):78–83, 151–152.

Reisner, Marc. *Cadillac Desert: The American West and Its Disappearing Water*. New York: Viking Press, 1986.

Roe, Charles B., Jr., and William J. Brooks. "Loss of Water Rights—Old Ways and New." *Rocky Mountain Mineral Law Institute* 35 (1989):23-1 to 23-30.

Sax, Joseph L. *The Constitution, Property Rights and the Future of Water Law*. Boulder, Colo.: Natural Resources Law Center, Western Water Policy Project Discussion Series Paper No. 2, 1990.

Schad, Theodore M. *The Changing Scene in the American West: Water Policy Implications*. Boulder, Colo.: Natural Resources Law Center, Western Water Policy Project Discussion Series Paper No. 8, 1990.

Shupe, Steven J. *Water Rights Decisions in the Western States: Upgrading the System for the 21st Century*. Boulder, Colo.: Natural Resources Law Center, Western Water Policy Project Discussion Series Paper No. 4, 1990.

Tarlock, A. Dan. "The Endangered Species Act and Western Water Rights." *Land and Water Law Review* 20 (1985):1–30.

Tennessee Valley Authority v. Hill, 437 U.S. 153 (1978).

Udall, Stewart L. "Pausing at the Pass: Reflections of a Native Son." In Stewart L. Udall et al., *Beyond the Mythic West*. Salt Lake City: Gibbs Smith, 1990.

U.N. Economic Commission for Asia and the Far East. *Water Legislation in Asia and the Far East*. New York: United Nations, Sales No. E.69.II. F.6, 1968.

U.S. National Water Commission. *Water Policies for the Future: Final Report to the President and to the Congress of the United States*. Washington, D.C.: U.S. Government Printing Office, 1973.

Wahl, Richard W. *Markets for Federal Water: Subsidies, Property Rights, and the Bureau of Reclamation*. Washington, D.C.: Resources for the Future, 1989.

Wahl, Richard W. *New Roles for the Bureau of Reclamation*. Boulder, Colo.: Natural Resources Law Center, Occasional Paper, 1989.

Weatherford, Gary D. *From Basin to "Hydrocommons": Integrated Water Management without Regional Governance*. Boulder, Colo.: Natural Resources Law Center, Western Water Policy Project Discussion Series Paper No. 5, 1990.

Wilkinson, Charles F. "The Headwaters of the Public Trust: Some Thoughts on the Source and Scope of the Doctrine." *Environmental Law* 19 (1989):425–472.

Winters v. United States, 207 U.S. 564 (1908).

EIGHT

Blackstone, William T. "Ethics and Ecology." In William Blackstone, ed., *Philosophy and Environmental Crisis*. Athens: University of Georgia Press, 1974.

Brajer, Victor, and W. E. Martin. "Allocating a 'Scarce' Resource: Water in the West." *American Journal of Economics and Sociology* 48 (July 1989):259.

Brajer, Victor, and Wade E. Martin. "Water Rights Markets: Social and Legal Considerations." *American Journal of Economics and Sociology* 49 (January 1990):35.

Butler, Lynda L. "Defining a Water Ethic Through Comprehensive Reform: A Suggested Framework for Analysis." *University of Illinois Law Review* 1986:439–480.

Callicott, J. Baird. *Companion to A Sand Country Almanac*. Madison: University of Wisconsin Press, 1987.

Callicott, J. Baird. *In Defense of the Land Ethic: Essays in Environmental Philosophy*. Albany: State University of New York Press, 1989.

Coyle, Kevin J. "President's Message: An Emerging Ethic for Rivers." *American Rivers Newsletter* 18 (Fall 1990):2.

Crawford, Stanley G. *Mayordomo: Chronicle of an Acequia in Northern New Mexico*. Albuquerque: University of New Mexico Press, 1988.

Fox, Stephen. *The American Conservation Movement: John Muir and His Legacy*. Boston: Little, Brown & Co., 1981.

Freyfogle, Eric T. "Water Justice." *University of Illinois Law Review* 1986:481–519.

Hargrove, Eugene C. "Anglo-American Land Use Attitudes." In Donald Scherer and Thomas Attig, eds., *Ethics and the Environment*. Englewood Cliffs, N.J.: Prentice-Hall, 1983.

Hays, Samuel P. *Conservation and the Gospel of Efficiency: The Progressive Conservation Movement, 1890–1920*. Cambridge: Harvard University Press, 1959.

Ingram, Helen. *Water Politics: Continuity and Change*. Albuquerque: University of New Mexico Press, first rev. ed., 1990 (first published in 1967).

Kemmis, Daniel. *Community and the Politics of Place*. Norman: University of Oklahoma Press, 1990.

Leopold, Aldo. *A Sand County Almanac*. New York: Oxford University Press, 1949.

Leopold, Luna B. "Ethos, Equity and the Water Resource: An Abiding Regard for the Integrity of the Hydrologic Continuum Is Strangely Lacking Among the Nation's Resource Agencies." *Geotimes* 36, no. 12 (December 1991):6.

McKibben, Bill. *The End of Nature*. New York: Random House, 1989.

Nash, Roderick. *The Rights of Nature: A History of Environmental Ethics*. Madison: University of Wisconsin Press, 1989.

Odum, Eugene. "Environmental Ethic and the Attitude Revolution." In William Blackstone, ed., *Philosophy and Environmental Crisis*. Athens: University of Georgia Press, 1974.

Ponting, Clive. *A Green History of the World: The Environment and the Collapse of Great Civilizations*. London: Sinclair-Stevenson, 1992.

Rawls, John. *A Theory of Justice*. Cambridge: Belknap Press of Harvard University Press, 1971.

Regan, Tom, ed. *Matters of Life and Death: New Introductory Essays in Moral Philosophy*. New York: Random House, 2d ed., 1986.

Rolston, Holmes, III. "Is There an Environmental Ethic?" In Donald Scherer and Thomas Attig, eds., *Ethics and the Environment*. Englewood Cliffs, N. J.: Prentice-Hall, 1983.

Rolston, Holmes, III. "Philosophy Gone Wild." Buffalo: Prometheus Books, 1989.

Rolston, Holmes, III. *Using Water Naturally*. Boulder, Colo.: Natural Resources Law Center, Western Water Policy Project Discussion Series Paper No. 9, 1991.

Sagoff, Mark. "Ethics, Ecology, and the Environment: Integrating Science and Law." *Tennessee Law Review* 56 (1989):77–229.

Sax, Joseph L. *The Constitution, Property Rights and the Future of Water Law*. Boulder, Colo.: Natural Resources Law Center, Western Water Policy Project Discussion Series Paper No. 2, 1990.

Scherer, Donald. "The Game of Games." In Donald Scherer and Thomas Attig, eds., *Ethics and the Environment*. Englewood Cliffs, N.J.: Prentice-Hall, 1983.

Stegner, Wallace E., and Page Stegner. *American Places*. New York: Dutton, 1981.

Stone, Christopher. *Earth and Other Ethics: The Case for Moral Pluralism*. New York: Harper & Row, 1987.

Tarlock, A. Dan. "Earth and Other Ethics: The Institutional Issues." *Tennessee Law Review* 56 (1988):43–76.

Yardas, David. *Restoring Endangered Ecosystems: The Truckee-Carson Water Rights Settlement*. Boulder, Colo.: Natural Resources Law Center, Occasional Paper, 1992.

Weatherford, Gary D., and F. Lee Brown, eds. *New Courses for the Colorado River: Major Issues for the Next Century*. Albuquerque: University of New Mexico Press, 1986.

Worster, Donald. *Rivers of Empire: Water, Aridity, and the Growth of the American West*. New York: Pantheon Books, 1985.

Western Water Policy
Working Group

F. Lee Brown, University of New Mexico, Albuquerque, New Mexico
James E. Butcher, Mill Valley, California
Michael J. Clinton, Bookman-Edmonston Engineering, Glendale,
   California
Harrison C. Dunning, University of California, Davis, California
John E. Echohawk, Native American Rights Fund, Boulder, Colorado
Kenneth D. Frederick, Resources for the Future, Washington, D.C.
Helen M. Ingram, University of Arizona, Tucson, Arizona
Edwin H. Marston, *High Country News*, Paonia, Colorado
Steven J. Shupe, Crestone, Colorado
John E. Thorson, Arizona General Stream Adjudication, Phoenix,
   Arizona
Gilbert F. White, University of Colorado, Boulder, Colorado
Zach Willey, Environmental Defense Fund, Oakland, California

Western Water Policy
Workshop Participants

Walt Coward, The Ford Foundation, Washington, D.C.
Dan Decker, Confederated Salish & Kootenai Tribe, Pablo, Montana
Bruce Driver, Denver, Colorado
Joe Ely, Pyramid Lake Paiute Tribe, Nevada
John Folk-Williams, Western Network, Santa Fe, New Mexico
Tom Fredericks, Fredericks, Pelcyger, Hester & White, Boulder, Colorado
Professor Frank Gregg, University of Arizona, Tucson, Arizona
Professor Charles Howe, University of Colorado, Boulder, Colorado
Professor Dale Jamieson, University of Colorado, Boulder, Colorado
Professor Patricia Nelson Limerick, University of Colorado, Boulder,
    Colorado
Dan Luecke, Environmental Defense Fund, Boulder, Colorado
Professor Arthur Maass, Harvard University, Cambridge, Massachusetts
Professor Dan McCool, University of Utah, Salt Lake City, Utah
John F. Munro, Roy F. Weston, Inc., Washington, D.C.
Professor James Nickel, University of Colorado, Boulder, Colorado
Professor Susan Christopher Nunn, University of New Mexico,
    Albuquerque, New Mexico
Professor Cy Oggins, University of Arizona, Tucson, Arizona

Monte Pascoe, Ireland, Stapleton, Pryor & Pascoe, Denver, Colorado
Bob Pelcyger, Fredericks, Pelcyger, Hester & White, Boulder, Colorado
Marc Reisner, San Francisco, California
Teresa Rice, Natural Resources Law Center, Boulder, Colorado
Professor Holmes Rolston III, Colorado State University, Fort Collins, Colorado
Professor Joseph Sax, University of California School of Law, Berkeley, California
Theodore M. Schad, Arlington, Virginia
Dick Trudell, American Indian Resources Institute, Oakland, California
Richard Wahl, U.S. Department of the Interior, Washington, D.C.
Gary D. Weatherford, Payne, Thompson, Walker & Taaffee, San Francisco, California
Jeanne Whiteing, Whiteing & Thompson, Boulder, Colorado
Duane Woodard, former Colorado attorney general, Denver, Colorado
Professor Robert Young, Colorado State University, Fort Collins, Colorado
Patricia Zell, Senate Select Committee on Indian Affairs, Washington, D.C.

Discussion Papers Prepared for the Western Water Policy Project

(1) Charles F. Wilkinson. *Values and Western Water: A History of the Dominant Ideas.* 1990.

(2) Joseph L. Sax. *The Constitution, Property Rights and the Future of Water Law.* 1990.

(3) John A. Folk-Williams. *Water and the Cities of the Southwest.* 1990.

(4) Steven J. Shupe. *Water Rights Decisions in the Western States: Upgrading the System for the 21st Century.* 1990.

(5) Gary D. Weatherford. *From Basin to "Hydrocommons": Integrated Water Management without Regional Governance.* 1990.

(6) Helen M. Ingram and Cy R. Oggins. *Water, the Community, and Markets in the West.* 1990.

(7) Arthur Maass. *Water Law and Institutions in the Western United States: Comparisons with Early Developments in California and Australia, Contemporary Developments in Australia, and Recent Legislation Worldwide.* 1990.

227

(8)   Theodore M. Schad. *The Changing Scene in the American West: Water Policy Implications*. 1990.

(9)   Holmes Rolston III. *Using Water Naturally*. 1991.

(10) Reid Peyton Chambers and John E. Echohawk. *Implementing Winters Doctrine Indian Reserved Water Rights: Producing Indian Water and Economic Development Without Injuring Non-Indian Water Users?* 1991.

About the Authors

Sarah F. Bates is assistant director of the Natural Resources Law Center at the University of Colorado School of Law. She was the coauthor, with Marc Reisner, of the book *Overtapped Oasis: Reform or Revolution for Western Water* (Island Press, 1990). Prior to joining the Natural Resources Law Center, she practiced law with the Sierra Club Legal Defense Fund in San Francisco.

David H. Getches, professor of law at the University of Colorado School of Law, is a nationally recognized water resources and Indian law expert. He formerly served as executive director of the Colorado Department of Natural Resources under Governor Richard D. Lamm, and as the founding executive director of the Native American Rights Fund. His many publications include *Controlling Water Use: The Unfinished Business of Water Quality Control* (Natural Resources Law Center, 1991), *Water Law in a Nutshell* (West, 1990), and legal texts on water and Indian law.

Lawrence J. MacDonnell, director of the Natural Resources Law Center and adjoint professor at the University of Colorado School of Law, has written widely on subjects of water resources law and policy. Much of his work has focused on issues related to reallocation of water uses.

Charles F. Wilkinson, the Moses Lasky Professor of Law at the University of
Colorado School of Law, is one of the nation's leading scholars and
lecturers on issues relating to natural resources law and policy in the
American West. His most recent books include *Crossing the Next
Meridian: Land, Water, and the Future of the West* (Island Press, 1992) and
The Eagle Bird (Pantheon, 1991). He has also published legal texts on
federal public lands and Indian law.

The authors gratefully acknowledge permission to quote from the
following previously copyrighted material:

Excerpt from *Desert Solitaire* by Edward Abbey. Copyright © 1968 by
Edward Abbey. Reprinted by permission of Don Congdon Associates,
Inc.

Excerpt from *Stories from the Country of Lost Borders* by Mary Austin, edited
by Majorie Pryse. Copyright © 1987 by Rutgers, The State University.
Reprinted with permission of Rutgers University Press.

Excerpt from "Rain Songs from the Rio Grande Pueblos" from *The
American Rhythm* by Mary Austin. Copyright © 1923, 1930 by Mary
Austin. Copyright renewed 1950 by Harry P. Mera, Kenneth M.
Chapman, and Mary C. Wheelwright. Reprinted by permission of
Houghton Mifflin Co. All rights reserved.

Excerpt from "Valley of the Crows" by Rick Bass. First published in
Witness, vol. 3, no. 4, 1989; subsequently published in *On Nature's Terms*,
edited by Tom Lyon and Peter Stine, Texas A&M University Press,
1992. Reprinted with permission of Rick Bass.

Excerpt from *Mountain in the Clouds* by Bruce Brown. Copyright © 1982 by
Bruce Brown. Reprinted with permission of Bruce Brown.

Excerpt from *Mayordomo* by Stanley Crawford. Copyright © 1988 by
University of New Mexico Press, Inc. Reprinted with permission of
University of New Mexico Press.

Excerpt from *River of Traps* by William deBuys and Alex Harris. Copyright
© 1990 by University of New Mexico Press, Inc. Reprinted with
permission of University of New Mexico Press.

"Roll, Columbia, Roll" (The Grand Coulee Dam). Words and music by
Woody Guthrie. TRO–Copyright © 1958 (renewed), 1963 (renewed),
and 1984, Ludlow Music, Inc., New York, NY. Used by permission.

Excerpt from "Owning It All" by William Kittredge. Copyright © 1987 by
William Kittredge. Reprinted from *Owning It All* with the permission of
Graywolf Press, St. Paul, Minn.

Excerpt from *A Sand County Almanac: And Sketches Here and There* by Aldo
Leopold. Copyright © 1949, 1977 by Oxford University Press, Inc.
Reprinted by permission.

Excerpt from *The Snake River: Window to the West* by Tim Palmer. Copyright
© 1991 by Tim Palmer. Reprinted with permission from Tim Palmer.
Published by Island Press, Washington, D.C.

231

232

Excerpt from "The Dolores River" by Jeff Rennicke, from *River Days: Travel on Western Rivers*, Jeff Rennicke, contributing editor. Fulcrum Publishing, 350 Indiana #350, Golden, Colo. 80401.

Excerpt from *The Changing Scene in the American West: Water Policy Implications* by Theodore M. Schad. Copyright © 1990 by the Natural Resources Law Center, University of Colorado School of Law, University of Colorado at Boulder. Reprinted with permission of the Natural Resources Law Center.

Excerpt from "A Geography of Hope" by Wallace Stegner. Reprinted by permission of the University Press of Colorado from *A Society to Match the Scenery* (1991), edited by Gary Holthaus, Patricia Nelson Limerick, Charles F. Wilkinson, and Eve Stryker Munson.

Excerpt from *The Sound of Mountain Water* by Wallace Stegner. Copyright © 1969 by Wallace Stegner. Used by permission of Doubleday, a division of Bantam Doubleday Dell Publishing Group, Inc.

Excerpt from *People of the Valley* by Frank Waters. Copyright © 1941, 1969, by Frank Waters. Reprinted with permission of the Ohio University Press/Swallow Press, Athens, Ohio.

Index

Abiquiu Dam, 105
Abbey, Edward, 52, 115
Acequias, 15, 21–22, 24–25, 30, 104
Agricultural use of water. *See also*
    Irrigation
  conservation, 89, 148, 158–159
  irrigation practices:
    Hispanic, 15, 21–22, 30, 102
    Mormon, 15, 30, 31
    Native American, 15, 18–20,
      100, 123, 200
  statistics, 32, 81, 103, 110
Ak-Chin Indians, 169
Alaska, 8, 93, 189
Alaska Purchase, 131
Albuquerque, New Mexico, 103–
    105
American Fisheries Society, 5, 98–
    99, 112
American Water Works Associa-
    tion, 134
Anasazi water use, 18, 199

Andrews v. Donnelly, 163
Appropriative rights. *See* Prior
    appropriation
Arapaho Indians, 85
Arapahoe County, Colorado, 83
Area of origin protection, 140
Arikara Indians, 124–125
Arizona, 5, 9, 18, 19, 39, 44, 75, 78,
    116–117, 163, 169
Arizona v. California, 117
Arkansas Valley, 85
Army Corps of Engineers, U.S., 28,
    98, 103–104, 110, 124
Ashley, William Henry, 28
Assiniboine Indians, 169
Association of California Water
    Agencies, 87
Austin, Mary, 49

Bandelier National Monument,
    106
Bannock Indians, 169

Island Press
Board of Directors

SUSAN E. SECHLER, CHAIR, Director, Rural Economic Policy Program, Aspen Institute for Humanistic Studies

HENRY REATH, VICE-CHAIR, President, Collector's Reprints, Inc.

DRUMMOND PIKE, SECRETARY, President, The Tides Foundation

ROBERT E. BAENSCH, Senior Vice President/Marketing, Rizzoli International Publications, Inc.

PETER R. BORRELLI, Executive Vice President, Open Space Institute

CATHERINE M. CONOVER

PAUL HAWKEN, Chief Executive Officer, Smith & Hawken

CHARLES C. SAVITT, President, Center for Resource Economics/ Island Press

PETER R. STEIN, Managing Partner, Lyme Timber Company

RICHARD TRUDELL, Executive Director, American Indian Resources Institute